A Contemplative Study of the Mind, Emotions, and Body

Studies in Critical Social Sciences Book Series

Haymarket Books is proud to be working with Brill Academic Publishers (www.brill.nl) to republish the *Studies in Critical Social Sciences* book series in paperback editions. This peer-reviewed book series offers insights into our current reality by exploring the content and consequences of power relationships under capitalism, and by considering the spaces of opposition and resistance to these changes that have been defining our new age. Our full catalog of *SCSS* volumes can be viewed at https://www.haymarketbooks.org/series_collections/4-studies-in-critical-social-sciences.

A Contemplative Study of the Mind, Emotions, and Body

Krzysztof T. Konecki

Haymarket Books
Chicago, IL

First published in 2025 by Brill Academic Publishers, The Netherlands

Published in paperback in 2026 by
Haymarket Books
P.O. Box 180165
Chicago, IL 60618
773-583-7884
www.haymarketbooks.org

ISBN: 979-8-88890-934-8

Distributed to the trade in the US through Consortium Book Sales and Distribution (www.cbsd.com) and internationally through Ingram Publisher Services International (www.ingramcontent.com).

This book was published with the generous support of Lannan Foundation, Wallace Action Fund, and the Marguerite Casey Foundation.

Cover design by Jamie Kerry and Ragina Johnson.

Printed in the United States.

Library of Congress Cataloging-in-Publication data is available.

Contents

PART 3
Applying Contemplation to Understand Suffering

Acknowledgments

Chapter 1 is a revised version of the lecture presented at the laudation of a prize of Stefan Nowak that the author received in 2021 at Warsaw University and which was published in the Polish language: Konecki, Krzysztof K. 2021. *Przekraczanie granic, zamykanie granic. Perspektywa pierwszoowobowa w badaniach socjologicznych.* Warszawa: Wydawnictwo IFiS PAN. ISBN 978-83-7683-200-5

Chapter 2 was published in the paper: Konecki, K.T. 2024. "Phenomenological and Interactional Interpretations of Corporality and Intersubjectivity in Hatha Yoga," Denzin, N.K. and Chen, S.-L.S. (Ed.) Essential Issues in Symbolic Interaction (*Studies in Symbolic Interaction*, Vol. 59), Emerald Publishing Limited, Leeds, pp. 105–124.

Chapter 3 is a revised version of the published paper: Konecki, Krzysztof T. 2022. "Who Am I When I Am Teaching? Self in Yoga Practice." *The Qualitative Report*, 27(11), 2623–2658.

Chapter 4 is a revised version of the published paper: Konecki, Krzysztof T. 2024. "Can you stop your mind and your daily activities? An analysis of meditation in yoga practice." *Kultura i Społeczeństwo*, 68(3), 169–203.

Chapter 5 is a revised version of the published paper: Konecki, K.T. 2022. "Empathy! So What?" *Przegląd Socjologii Jakościowej*, 18(4), 194–233.

Chapter 6 first published in *Polish Sociological Review* no 4 (228)2024, https://doi.org/10.26412/psr228.05.

Figures

Introduction

Studying the mind is common practice in social sciences, though it is not often referred to explicitly as such. It is generally assumed that the mind produces thoughts, opinions, attitudes, motives, and emotions because these are expressed through language, which has grammar and internal logic and is rooted in cultural memory. This cultural memory provides the clichés and categories through which we perceive social reality in more or less coherent ways. However, this assumption is rarely examined in depth.

Thinking is not solely a mental process; it is also embodied and situated within specific material and social contexts. The mind interacts with others and with itself, maintaining an internal dialogue that helps us perceive, categorize, and initiate actions within the lifeworld, often from the perspective of others (Mead 1934; Blumer 1969; Bakker 2005).

The body plays a significant role in this interaction, even if we are unaware of it (Konecki 2005). The body is already engaged in the situation before we consciously realize it. It defines space through its physical proximity to other people and material objects. This proximity is perceived through various senses, including sight, smell, and touch. We also experience emotions that are connected to the bodily sensations we feel. However, when we are in a situation, we are already in a particular mood – we might feel sad, happy, or frightened (Heidegger 1996). Mood is not necessarily linked to specific emotions. Emotions are intentional and directed toward particular objects, whereas mood is more general; we might be happy about life or feel a pervasive sadness that seems to color the entire world. Certain places have an associated mood; for example, cemeteries are often linked with grief and sorrow (Konecki 2021), parks with relaxation (see Chapter 3), and meditation rooms with calmness and mental clarity (Chapter 4). Mood provides proof of our existence in the world and shapes our experience of it. However, we exist not only with our bodies but also with emotions that often arise from mood, directing our attention toward certain objects.

It is difficult to stop thinking – I have drawn this simple yet essential thesis for functioning in daily life from observing beginners in meditation practice (see Chapter 4). Even experienced yoga teachers find it hard to stop comparing their practice with other instructors (see Chapter 3). Yet, there are moments when this ceaseless thinking pauses spontaneously, and we find ourselves marveling at the beauty of yoga practice, meditation, landscapes, flowers, poetry, and more. In these moments, we stop thinking and exist, feeling our existence. Wonder arises. We engage with the world around us with care – not just for people, but for our concerns in our interactions with the social and material surroundings (Heidegger 1996: 197). In caring for the world, we use our bodies and are always in a certain mood – such as caring for something. To care, we use tools, which acquire meaning according to the aims of our activities. One of the main tools is the body, which we often use unconsciously, not necessarily linking it with the act of thinking. It is as if thinking were merely a tool for planning and executing the practical goals of our lives.

Turning our attention back to the body becomes possible when we stop engaging in constant mental activity. This shift often occurs during meditation and other similarly contemplative practices. In meditation, we can fully connect with our bodies, which are intertwined with our feelings and emotions. During this process, we may experience a distortion in our perception of time, self, and visions, leading us to realize that the mind creates many abstractions and constructs.

There is something beyond thinking – a realm where we can grasp the essence of being and understand who we are and our purpose in the world.

The body is often overlooked daily (Leder 1990; Merleau-Ponty 2005). We are generally unaware of what the body feels and what it means to inhabit a body. Body awareness helps us fully engage with the world and take responsibility for our existence. It also enables us to understand others better; we can build empathy by paying attention to our body's initial reactions to the suffering or happiness of others. Although social assumptions and prejudices can influence reflection, the body does not deceive. Suppose we physically sense signs of suffering, fear, or anxiety in response to another's plight. That suffering is real, regardless of the other person's background – from a different tribe, country, or continent. Empathy is an innate capacity that can be cultivated and strengthened (see Chapters 5 and 6 on the war in Ukraine). While empathy is socially constructed to some extent, something primal about it compels us to respond to the suffering of others. The body serves as a common foundation for empathy; humans often feel physical reactions to the suffering of others.

However, our ability to listen to our bodies is often impaired by our fast-paced lifestyles, the demands of work, and the general speed of life (Rosa 2020). Body awareness is closely linked to attentiveness to the workings of the mind. We can practice and enhance this skill, improving our capacity for empathy. Furthermore, reflecting on empathy and the consequences of its absence can help restore this faculty, as our research shows (Chapter 5).

How can we be more aware of our bodies if they are such a crucial tool in caring for the world? I am not advocating for any particular practice. The body is naturally given to us and the world, and it can spontaneously and naturally choose how to enhance our mindfulness. This could be through physical exercise, poetry, singing, dancing, meditation, or other activities (Konecki, Płaczek, Tarasiuk 2024). I have used contemplation of bodily sensations, yoga practice to train body awareness, and meditation to connect bodily feelings with the mind and emotions. However, I have also found that mindful walking, writing, reading poetry, painting, making collages, or engaging in any form of art or craftsmanship involving our hands and bodies can foster bodily mindfulness. This mindfulness connects our mind and emotions into a hybrid wholeness, enabling us to know and experience reality in a unified way (Konecki 2023).

Understanding the body and developing skills in observing bodily sensations and emotions are the first steps to existing in the world with full responsibility for life and concern for others. Our choices, concerns, and care for the world define our humanity. Social pressures often conflict with our bodies and intuitions. Initially, the body resists these pressures, but it may stop reacting over time. This happens because we become prisoners of the "iron cage" of obligations and norms, shaping us into social beings through socialization but not necessarily fully realized humans.

Sociology, social psychology, economics, and anthropology help us understand our limited and privileged societal positions. However, these fields often rely on deterministic thinking or explanations, allowing moral responsibility to be shifted entirely from the individual to society and its social and cultural institutions. While it is true that we are social beings, conditioned by our birth and upbringing, there exists a crack in social existence where we can distance ourselves from our social positions and roles, reflect on them, and act. This is why we need awareness of the connections between our body, mind, and emotions. This book shows the connection and also how to research it.

We can slip into that gap, reflecting on the initial bodily reactions and the emotional consequences of the conflicts between social expectations and individual experiences. The ever-present mood of fearing others' judgments and the pressure to choose between predetermined lines of action are both burdens and levers of our freedom. It would be exciting and liberating to undertake a contemplative experiment, suspend fear, and observe how it transforms our body and mind, revealing what we could achieve for ourselves, others, and the world. (Laing 2021)

This book reflects on the connections between the body, mind, and emotions from a contemplative perspective. The book aims to explore how we can investigate these connections through a first-person perspective inspired by contemplative studies and phenomenology, focusing on how to balance critical thinking with a deeper sense of responsibility. We want to go out of traditional qualitative inquiry to engage the researcher in social change for the suffering people. Not only to understand (Denzin 2017: 9) but also to ask, "When, where, and how am I?" Denzin 2017: 10), who understands this? Who is privileged in a given scientific study? (Hadley 2017: 53–58).

We need to envision a new sociology (and social sciences) focusing more on shaping and refining our thinking about social issues – wars, waste, destructive tourism, climate change, etc. We cannot access research participants' perspectives without involving the sociologist in self-analysis. Sociology should be more attuned to the world's pressing challenges, but if the sociologist isn't responsive, how can sociology, as a discipline, be responsive?

We live in a highly complex world that demands analysis on multiple scales, one of which is the mind. The minds of sociologists and research participants are shaped by the same forces in everyday life – media, consumption, consumerism, the educational system, and religious institutions all contribute to shaping our sense of relevance. Neglecting to analyze our engagement and embodiment in everyday interactions with others, objects, and ourselves overlooks how we collectively shape our world, how certain discourses dominate us, and how we are rendered silent (Laing 2021; Hadley 2017: 54), and how to oppose it (Grant and Young 2022; Grant 2023).

This is the critical and contemplative task of sociology.

We aim to continue drawing inspiration from C.W. Mills' concept of the *sociological imagination* (Mills 1959). We strive to expand this imagination to consider the historical and structural influences on the sociologist or social scientist and explore the primarily overlooked conditions that affect the social scientist's mind. These conditions include the body, emotions, and the material objects present in the context of research and analysis. Discourse is also essential here (Illouz 2010). Therefore, we want to add a first-person perspective to critical sociology and qualitative inquiry that includes these elements.

We cannot limit ourselves to merely analyzing connections, associations, and networks, as suggested by Science and Technology Studies (STS) (Pyyhtinen 2016). Instead, we must recognize that analysis is conducted by a concrete person with concrete research participants situated in an existential context, influenced by fate, mood, bodily sensations, and immediate horizons of perception and experience. When considering scalability, it is not only humans who create scales; non-human things also contribute, resulting in a multiplicity of scales (Pyyhtinen 2016: 59–60; Latour, Schultz 2022: 72). The global is connected to the local, but the local can sometimes disappear, rendering the global irrelevant. This disappearance occurs within the subject's consciousness, making it essential to gain insight into subjectivity. For instance, Nikolaj Schultz demonstrated this by contemplating climate change through his bodily reactions to the heat in Paris, linking the experience to distant elements of his socio-physical context (Schultz 2023).

Historical periods and contexts are crucial for social scientists' work (Mills 1959, chapter 8). However, we must also focus on the micro-level of experience, particularly the relationship between the mind, body, and emotions in a context. A sociologist or social scientist should critically examine their assumptions (Denzin 2017), intellectual history, and engagement with everyday life, including practical matters and political positions. Moreover, they should remain aware of how their mind operates. This is relevant to public sociology, though it may not seem so initially. The social scientist is a public figure, and public issues influence their work. Once shared through publications or the media, their conclusions feed into society and ultimately affect them. This creates a feedback loop that is hard to escape, as everything passes through the researcher's mind and emotions.

This thought process occurs in what Van Manen (2016) calls the "pathic dimension" and must be acknowledged by sensitive researchers. We call for researchers to be sensitive in their self-observation, paying attention to their empathy, emotions, and bodily sensations. Are researchers empathetic toward their being? If so, they can also empathize with societal issues and public problems. Public sociology is inherently tied to the individual efforts of the researcher (and research participants), who is also a participant in the everyday world and influenced by it. Researchers are not merely professionals but also individuals who use common assumptions to perceive and experience the world. They are homo duplexes, even when they deny it. This does not imply any moral superiority of the social scientist over ordinary people; they are also lay persons in two essential perspectives, scientific and lay perspective.

Contemplative studies add complexity to the researcher's connectivity on the individual level. The relationships they observe are mediated by intellectual interpretations and bodily experiences shaped by emotional contexts, which are crucial for seeing (or not seeing) the elements of the world. Our minds are filled with informational or intellectual "waste" due to technology and the constant flow of information. This flow must be analyzed, as it creates relationships between individuals, influencing the interplay between mind and body.

We accept the rhizomatic sociology proposed by some authors, emphasizing relationality and interconnectedness (Pyyhtinen 2016: 90). Understanding the web of interdependencies in which we are enmeshed is essential. However, we must know the researcher's mind, body, and emotions working in specific contexts with material objects and technology (as well as research participants). Humans in the material world are not merely an assemblage of forces but also beings endowed with consciousness.

The constant drive to develop new techniques for obtaining more reliable and credible results can lead to intellectual and physical fatigue (Byung-Chul Han 2015). Researchers may feel overwhelmed by the sheer number of new advancements, which can become a source of stress. Additionally, advanced technologies, including artificial intelligence, are increasingly integrated into social investigation and analysis. We need to contemplate what happens in the research situation when robots or intelligent algorithms do a significant part of research and analytical work instead of humans. What do the new language and narratives emerge with connections to the liberal capitalism that imposes the discourses of mind, emotions, and body meaning on us? (Illouz 2010).

What is contemplation? I define contemplation as follows: "Contemplation is a kind of activity that leads to a certain state of mind, and at the same time, it is a method of obtaining knowledge about some objects at the present time, and also about acquiring knowledge itself, here and now, through mindful insight into perceived (and also imagined) phenomena or objects, and into the self" (Konecki 2018: 21). Contemplation can be connected with activities such as reading, writing poetry or theory, philosophical reflection, meditation, and admiring nature. However, these activities are not the only way to contemplate. Contemplation involves conscious attention to the process of knowing through self-observation of the mind, bodily sensations, and emotions. By knowing yourself, you can also explore the world you are thrown into.

Self-observation is a first-person perspective method for researching situated and embodied social phenomena. It involves attentively observing and describing our conscious experiences, whether we are engaged in activity or inactivity. To gain insight from a first-person perspective, one must cultivate the ability to focus and monitor oneself. Self-observation requires concentrating on the workings of our minds, noticing the thoughts they generate, and observing how our bodies respond to external stimuli, including the emergence and sensation of emotions in various situations. We can reflect on and reconstruct key elements of phenomena, objects, or circumstances through self-observation. However, our perception of the world is influenced by language. Therefore, during self-observation, we should also monitor the words and labels we use for observed objects and how they align with our emotional responses (Konecki 2018: 229–230).

We should write *self-reports* after each self-observation. This method solidifies the phenomena we have encountered and provides a means to reflect upon them. Our description must be both thorough and holistic, encompassing the entire situation. The language should reflect our emotions; avoid limiting ourselves to factual statements and excluding feelings and evaluations.

Metaphorical language is acceptable. We can enhance our self-reports with visuals such as drawings, paintings, collages, photos, or videos and complement them with reflective written commentary (Konecki 2018: 231).

Writing contemplative notes (*memos*) during research is crucial to the research-analytic process. These notes serve as evidence of the thought paths and emotions the researcher experienced, for instance, while coding empirical material or drafting theoretical notes. They document how the researcher arrived at their conclusions, including moments of surprise, doubt, uneasiness, or euphoria over a new idea or concept. They also capture the origins of these ideas and the researcher's bodily reactions. Using epoché (a suspension of judgment) can help the researcher reflect on external influences, not to control the impact of other theories or research ideas but to be fully aware of how knowledge is produced while analyzing empirical data. This process is akin to self-observation while experiencing phenomena. Still, it focuses on self-observation during the analytical work of research, where the phenomenon being observed is Analysis and Explication.

When working in a group, reflections on mutual influences between researcher and analyst become evident. Observing oneself and others in interaction reveals how knowledge is simultaneously produced both collectively and situationally. Internal conversations, enriched by discussions with others, illuminate the uncertainties of knowledge generated at the moment – categories, hypotheses, theses, and interpretations – that may evolve during the lengthy process of negotiating meanings in the *analysis of data*.

There is also an important technique called the "*empathetic experiment*." In this method, we try to place ourselves in another person's perspective, fully aware of their viewpoint while observing our own emotions and bodily sensations. Imagining ourselves as someone else can aid in understanding and analyzing situations, social structures, and people's experiences, even from distant times or places. Experiencing and feeling a problem, even through imagination, engages our minds, emotions, and bodies in a way that goes beyond merely analyzing it cognitively and rationally through social filters and clichés (Konecki 2018: 234–235).

1 My Choice: Being Faithful to the Event

Now, a few words about the author motivation to write the book. I start from the concept of "event" by Alain Badiou (2001: 41). It is an occurrence "which compels us to decide a new way of being." (Badiou 2001: 41, see also 67–69). It is a turning point in some dimensions of life as they can happen in politics, science, art and love. The individual starts to think differently and act according to new concepts, style of life and change the ethics, way of thinking and acting. The new values are emerging. However, they are new, and their credibility is proved in the process of truth, the truth is not a priori category and it is not given. It is discovered in the process. "Such events are well and truly attested: the French revolution 1792, the meeting of Heloise and Abelard, Galileo's creation of physics, Hydn's invention of the classical musical style. But also: the Cultural Revolution in China (1965–67), a personal amorous passion, the creation of Topos theory by the mathematician Grothendieck, the invention twelve tone scale by Schoenberg" (Badiou 2001: 41). Such "event" happened also in sociology in the sixties of previous Century. The interpretative paradigm emerged and started invasion on the campuses and libraries (Willson 1971). Although it can be difficult to state what is the event and which one should be as such considered (it can be disputed here) but I have chosen the event of appearing of interpretative paradigm as the revolutionary change in the sociology and to prove it I am faithful to the event in all my dealings during my scientific career. I have started from symbolic interactionism that was the most influential theory and methodology on my work, later grounded theory, phenomenological sociology and ethnomethodology, and recently contemplative social studies. I think that the last one is still continuation of this radical change in sociology. So, I am faithful to the event, "fidelity to the event" compels me to invent new methods, new concepts to continue my walk on the road to the truth. I am all the time in the process, and this book is the prove of it. I am using concepts from phenomenology, contemplative studies, grounded theory and many others methods that are close to the break with the classical way of thinking and researching of the social reality. I try to be faithful to the event and in each situation I try to prove it reaching for the rich basket of concepts from the interpretative paradigm.

These concepts transcend the traditional boundaries of sociological thought. Crossing such boundaries is essential for unlocking the full potential of a given situation, particularly when a new way of understanding social reality emerges. This process involves dismantling established and widely accepted worldviews and perspectives on social reality. Achieving contemplative insights into a situation represents one of the few remaining possibilities for the theoretical and critical reconstruction of social situations from an individual's perspective.

However, pausing for contemplation is neither expected nor valued in a society defined by constant motion – focused on progress, the rat race (including in academia), and rational actions aimed at individual goals under the guise of serving collective interests. This difficulty in embracing contemplation stems not only from the need to radically redefine commonly accepted concepts but also from the challenge of overcoming emotional resistance and attitudes that bind us to the status quo.

Such a profound mental transformation is not without struggles; it also carries a pathic dimension (see Van Manen 2016). Yet, contemplation, as an intentional choice, represents an act of fidelity to the event itself. It can overcome emotional resistance – not only for the individual who initiates the contemplation but also for potential learners who engage with this practice and continue the way of truth in the interpretative paradigm.

2 Content of the Book

The book consists of six chapters, which serve as examples of a contemplative approach to investigating and understanding social phenomena and how research participants, including the researchers, experience them. It also offers insights into how to understand contemplation and how to conduct contemplative research.

The first chapter is a theoretical contemplation of the first-person approaches that describe socio-psychological phenomena to make them understandable more than explainable.

I want to present a contemplation of first-person perspectives and, at the same time, my contemplative approach to social research. I do it from a first-person perspective. I will present three approaches to first-person research: autoethnography, contemplative research, and transformational phenomenology. Finally, I will reconstruct first-person approaches (mainly autoethnography) from the position of Alfred Schütz's phenomenology and his concept of a finite province of meaning. I engage in theoretical contemplation regarding the reality of the first-person researcher and explore the dynamics of the relationship between the researcher and Others. Who exactly is the researcher? How do they navigate the boundary into the realm of the Other? In doing so, I delve into the specific domain of first-person research to understand how researchers perceive, feel, and articulate their experiences of the lifeworld.

In Chapter 2, I present my experiences of the body in hatha yoga practice using Maurice Merleau-Ponty's phenomenological concepts and perspective to understand the feelings about the body, thoughts, and emotions. I interpret the corporeality and intersubjectivity of hatha yoga practice in light of Merleau-Ponty's theory. Furthermore, I give some examples of embodied experiences from my practice. The examples I provide are based on my experience in yoga practice and self-observations that I have done during the research project on experiencing hatha yoga practice and knowledge transfer.

The third chapter examines the self-observation of practicing yoga led by a hatha yoga instructor, and it shows the transition between different identities: teacher, trainee, student, and researcher. It explains how the mind works on the various identities connected with the body's work. We can also see how important writing is in this process. Self-observation and self-description is a first-person presentation of the author's feelings about practicing and teaching hatha yoga, and the chapter presents extended narratives from self-observation. There will also be self-explication from the first-person, third-person, and impersonal perspectives. In a way, it will be an external look at the author's own experiences, although it must be remembered that this view is made by the person producing the records of lived experiences. The third-person and impersonal analysis makes it possible to be detached from assumptions, e.g., the conviction that direct and first-person relationships about situations and experiences are the only available truth about lived experiences because they come from immediately described incidents.

The fourth chapter investigates meditation as a state of consciousness that isolates an individual from the attitude of everyday life and the perspective of practical actions. It is a contemplative analysis of the process of minding during meditation. The paper analyzes self-reports from meditators' self-observations as part of hatha yoga practice and data from semi-structured interviews with hatha yoga teachers. Elements that disturb and help people to meditate are analyzed and interpreted. The features of the meditative state during sitting meditation are also reconstructed. Attention is paid to three essential aspects that are related to each other when beginners leave the working life and enter the meditative state: emerging thoughts, body sensations, and emotions. The analysis focuses on how practitioners deal with these obstacles to enter the meditation state of mind. What tactics do they employ to eliminate barriers or redirect attention and include them in the background of the concentration point? What is the role of teaching meditation? What are the effects of meditation from a practitioner's point of view? What are the essential features of meditation?

Empirical materials obtained from the first-person perspective of the researcher, the author of this text, and his collaborators in the study are also analyzed.

The fifth chapter deals with the concept of empathy applied in a contemplative experiment to understand the suffering of the victims of the war in Ukraine. I discuss the idea of empathy from a phenomenological perspective and symbolic interactionists' view. I needed this discussion to frame the conclusions from the contemplative experiment I did with my students. I used the contemplative methods of research. The students did self-observations and self-reports on their lived experiences while observing photos of the victims and refugees from Ukraine. Breathing exercises (pranayama) were practiced between different self-observations to clean the minds and release tensions. At the end of the experiment, the students were also asked about the empathy deficit in contemporary society and provided comments on it. Finally, I conclude how empathy is evoked and embodied, and I answer whether it is possible to be empathetic toward people in a different and traumatic situation. I end with the statement that empathy is a direct reaction to other people's suffering. However, it is also socially framed. I conclude that empathy could be socially developed to cope with the empathy deficit.

The sixth chapter aims to dereify the concept of war by presenting it through the first-person perspective of a direct participant in the war in Ukraine (Artem Chekh, a Ukrainian writer and journalist) and an external observer, the author of this book. The study will provide an explicit interpretation of the lived experiences of both participants and observers of the war, explored through the lived space, time, and body domains. The interpretative work will be approached from a contemplative perspective, drawing on phenomenological inspirations. Contemplation will be based on the explicitation of the narrations of the direct participants of the war, utilizing phenomenological understanding and artistic interpretations (poetry and visual art).

Bibliography

Badiou, Alain. 2001. *Ethics. An Essay on the Understanding of Evil.* London and New York: Verso.

Bakker, Johannes I. 2005. "The Self as an Internal Dialogue: Mead, Blumer, Peirce, and Wiley." *The American Sociologist* 36(1), 75–84. https://doi.org/10.1007/s12108-005-1013-3.

Balaska, Maria. 2024. *Anxiety and Wonder: On Being Human*. London: Bloomsbury.

Blumer, Herbert. 1969. *Symbolic Interactionism: Perspective and Method.* Berkeley: University of California Press.

Denzin, Norman K. 2017. "Critical Qualitative Inquiry." *Qualitative Inquiry*, 23(1), 8–16. https://doi.org/10.1177/1077800416681864.

Grant, Alec, and Susan Young. 2022. "Troubling Tolichism in Several Voices: Resisting Epistemic Violence in Creative Analytical and Critical Autoethnographic Practice." *Journal of Autoethnography* 3, no. 1: 103–117. https://doi.org/10.1525/joae.2022.3.1.103.

Hadley, Gregory. 2017. *Grounded Theory in Applied Linguistics Research: A Practical Guide*. New York: Routledge.

Han, Byung-Chul. 2015. *The Burnout Society*. Stanford: Stanford University Press.

Heidegger, Martin. 1996. *Being and Time*. New York: State University of New York Press.

Illouz, Eva. 2010. *Cold Intimacies: The Making of Emotional Capitalism* [translated into Polish as *Uczucia w dobie kapitalizmu*]. Warszawa: Oficyna Naukowa.

Konecki, Krzysztof T. 2005. "The Problem of Symbolic Interaction and of Constructing Self." *Qualitative Sociology Review* 1(1), 68–89.

Konecki, Krzysztof T. 2018. *Advances in Contemplative Social Research*. Lodz: Lodz University Press / Krakow: Jagiellonian University Press.

Konecki, Krzysztof T. 2021. "Experiencing the Space: Visiting Cemeteries on All Saints' Day and an Ordinary Day." *The Qualitative Report* 26(3), 832–860.

Konecki, Krzysztof T. 2023. "Walking in the City as an Experienced Practice." *Przegląd Socjologii Jakościowej* 19(4), 170–201.

Konecki, Krzysztof T., Aleksandra Płaczek, and Dagmara Tarasiuk. 2024. *Experiencing the Body in Yoga Practice: Meanings and Knowledge Transfer*. New York: Routledge.

Laing, Olivia. 2021. *Everybody: A Book about Freedom*. London: Canongate Books.

Latour, Bruno, and Nikolaj Schultz. 2022. *On the Emergence of an Ecological Class: A Memo*. Cambridge: Polity Press.

Mead, George H. 1934. *Mind, Self, and Society: From the Standpoint of a Social Behaviorist*. Edited by Charles W. Morris. Chicago: University of Chicago Press.

Merleau-Ponty, Maurice. 2005. *Phenomenology of Perception*. London: Routledge.

Mills, C. Wright. 1959. *The Sociological Imagination*. New York: Oxford University Press.

Moore, Robert. 1995. "Dereification in Zen Buddhism." *The Sociological Quarterly* 36(4), 699–723.

Rosa, Hartmut. 2020. *Beschleunigung und Entfremdung. Entwurf einer Kritischen Theorie spätmoderner Zeitlichkeit*. Polish translation by Jakub Duraj and Jacek Kołtun as *Przyspieszenie, wyobcowanie, rezonans. Projekt krytycznej teorii późnonowoczesnej czasowości*. Gdańsk: Europejskie Centrum Solidarności.

Schipper, Janine. 2012. "Toward a Buddhist Sociology: Its Theories, Methods, and Possibilities." *The American Sociologist* 43(3), 203–222.

Schultz, Nikolaj. 2023. *Land Sickness*. Cambridge: Polity Press.

Van Manen, Max. 2016. *Phenomenology of Practice: Meaning-Giving Methods in Phenomenological Research and Writing*. Abingdon and New York: Routledge.

PART 1

Self-Description with Reflection on Self and the World

∵

CHAPTER 1

Crossing Borders, Not Closing Them: the First-Person Perspective in Sociological Research

1 Introduction[1]

What will interest me in the chapter is the issue *of how and in what* context the researcher's mind works. I will analyze this context using Alfred Schütz's theory of multiple realities. At the beginning, I want to introduce you very briefly to the *first-person approaches* in which I have become interested in recent years. Then I want to make critical contemplation of first-person perspectives in social research, especially autoethnography and contemplative research, and partly transformational phenomenology. I do it not by accident because, as suggested by Stefan Nowak, "a sociologist should develop his axiological and ideological self-knowledge, deepening the awareness of one's criteria and social goals and define your hierarchy of values" (Nowak 1985/2010: 478). The following considerations are intended to show *the context of the thought and social processes* that accompany a particular form of the study. Some even mention a specific species of research (genre). "Deepening the awareness of your criteria" is a reconstruction of the assumptions on which we base our research. Moreover, sociological knowledge can be "[a] powerful tool to improve the world," as Stefan Nowak writes (Nowak 1985/2010: 478). So how can first-person research improve the world?

I will also use a particular metaphor of Antoni Sułek here. In the *Garden of Sociological Methodology* (Sułek 2002), you can find many interesting plants. Maybe they are not new, but when appropriately connected/crossed, old plants yield a unique genetic mix and a new plant. A gardener manages the garden, but he does not fully control the biological processes, which are based on the accidental mutation of evolution. The effects of deliberate genetic mixing can be different. The plant may not be resistant to external conditions. It may soon be lost; it may also be reborn in another place, country, or continent

1 The chapter is a revised version of the lecture presented at the laudation of a prize of Stefan Nowak that the author received in 2021 at Warsaw University and which was published in Polish language: Konecki, Krzysztof K. 2021. *Przekraczanie granic, zamykanie granic. Perspektywa pierwszoowobowa w badaniach socjologicznych*. Warszawa: Wydawnictwo IFiS PAN. ISBN 978-83-7683-200-5.

one day under favorable climatic conditions. Sometimes it may take the form of a monster that produces viruses that infect the healthy body of "the one and the right methodological tree." But maybe somewhere on the edge of the garden, it grows and blooms without dominating other plants as a new plant. And I would like to talk about such a plant today. It can create a particular enclave, a peculiar province of meaning with borders and a micro-ecosystem. The plant will survive and thrive, even as a medicinal herb. And here, it is necessary to indicate the role of the gardener – the plant may survive on condition that the caring gardener does not treat it as a weed; it will create *a boundary* to protect the enclave.

Therefore, in this chapter, I want to briefly analyze and critique first-person perspectives and my approach to social research. I will also do it from a first-person perspective.

I invite you to a thought experiment, to suspend your basic assumptions from the world of bureaucratic science and the attention generated by our socialization, which was shaped by our masters (Zerubavel 2015), and thus to suspend a set of assumptions about what the methodology of social sciences should look like. Using the theory of Alfred Schütz (Schütz 1962; Czyżewski 1984; Mokrzycki 1984; Manterys 2008), I invite you to jump into another reality. When I cross or, rather, jump over the boundary of a cognitive style (Alfred Schütz's term), a shock may appear (Czyżewski 1984: 31), anger, and even rage, but some people also understand another world or even find themselves in this new world. Be warned; it will not be easy emotionally because this procedure requires a great deal of openness and acceptance for the other and yourself in this relationship. Security guarantees disappear, doubts about one's own past identity arise. We are no longer supported by a scientific method; we are left to ourselves alone in a given situation, either in meeting with Other or with ourselves. The socialization and *significant others* do not help.

I will present three approaches to first-person research: autoethnography, contemplative research, and transformational phenomenology. But before I do that, I will begin with the concept of *sociological introspection* that preceded these first-person approaches and formed the basis of such research approaches in sociology. There are, of course, many other approaches in first-person studies, which are, in fact, studies of consciousness, including introspection. They use or often combine phenomenological and cognitive approaches, Buddhist and contemplative traditions, and hermeneutics (Varela, Shear 2002). They examine the functioning of the mind in various states of consciousness, such as during meditation or mindfulness practice, and how the self is produced and how it manifests itself (Varela, Thompson, Rosch 1993). Neurological studies of the brain sometimes support these analyzes as one of the elements of the functioning of the human brain/mind.

The concept of introspection in sociology is derived from the value-oriented method of sympathetic introspection, a term coined by Cooley. The easiest way to explain it is that it understands the other by making a person imagine him/herself in the situation and role of the other. It is an understanding of taking the role of others (Mead 1975; Piotrowski 1985; Bokszański 1986, 1989; Krzemiński 1986; Hałas 1987),[2] but with a focus on the emotions. Using this method had practical consequences on social reforms. There was also a specific theory of mind here, which involved idealizing when assigning mental states to others to cooperate with them (Gunderson 2017).

2 But the Other One I Want to Understand Might Be Me

Carolyn Ellis (1991) took a significant step in developing a contemplative style of research, although she did not use the term contemplation. She developed a concept of sociological introspection that deals with the study of emotions. This research technique gives access to the personal experiences of the social actor. For her, introspection is a sociological process that "can generate interpretive materials from self and others useful for understanding the lived experience of emotions" (Ellis 1991: 26). It also introduces interactive, introspective research *to reflect on the subjective part of cognition and experiencing emotions.*[3] In general, researchers do not want to admit that they are dealing with introspection in the field or analyzing empirical materials.[4] For Ellis, introspection is an important, albeit "covert communicative behavior"

2 See the entire thematic issue of "Symbolic Interactionism in Poland," *Qualitative Sociology Review*, 2020, 16 (4) (available online).

3 The researcher cooperates with the research participants, and a mutual dialogue about their interpretations is present.

4 Stefan Nowak used the term "introspective data" (Nowak 1965: 215–218), but they only introduced further causal explanations. Nowak is skeptical about the use of empathy in empirical research. As he writes: "The method of 'comprehensive empathy' has the disadvantage that it is not very suitable for standardization, and such complex wholes are usually unique, and thus cannot be introduced into the conceptual apparatus of the science of human behavior as empirical indicators of psychological theoretical constructs" (Nowak 1965: 230). And further: "The enormous number of psychological determinants of behavior cannot be described in introspective terms, as introspection is unavailable, or the system of relationships between these factors and action is quite different than what our introspection shows" (Nowak 1965: 239). However, part of our behavior is determined by conscious mental states and is correctly perceived by people (Nowak 1965). According to Nowak, a significant portion of our behavior is determined by patterns and values derived from socialization. People evaluate objects and events in the world in which they function. Therefore, for him, it is possible to use introspective data in social research, although they should be treated with a great deal of caution.

(Ellis 1991: 28). There is an internal dialogue with symbols, while an internal conversation takes place whenever we deal with others. Observing internal dialogue is essential for introspection (Ellis 1991: 28–29). What is significant in Ellis's approach is expressed in the following statement: "Sociologists, however, can generate interpretive materials about the lived experience of emotions by studying their own self-dialogue in process" (Ellis 1991: 28–29). The source of the data could therefore be an internal dialogue researcher. Introspection can be materialized, and we can thus obtain evidence of the existence of "internal conversations": "In summary, introspection can be accomplished in dialogue with self, and represented in the form of fieldnotes, or narratives: or it can be accomplished in dialogue with others, or by reading and analyzing their journals or free writing, where subjects write non-stop about what they are thinking and feeling and what it means to them" (Ellis 1991: 32). Techniques for producing materials based on introspective insight include keeping an "*introspective diary*," in which authors openly and honestly describe their inner thoughts and emotions. Introspection is represented as a narrative text (Ellis 1991: 34, 41); thus, this introspective journal can be seen as an introduction to writing autoethnography.

Therefore, for now, let us make the jump without theoretical contemplation, without putting the theoretical bit on what is going on in the first-person study.

3 A/ Autoethnography

First, I will try to answer the question: "What is autoethnography?" and describe it. I mainly rely on analyzing the book "Autoethnographic close-ups and distances. About autoethnography in Poland" (2020), edited by Marcin Kafar and Anna Kacperczyk, and which is already emblematic of Polish autoethnography. It follows from this work that autoethnography is our "own ethnography experience," where *I AM* is the zero point from which the subjects observes themselves and the outside world (see also Kacperczyk 2014; Ellis, Adams and Bochner 2010).

After reading this book, I have a simple, incomplete, fragmentary, yet essential answer. Autoethnography is writing about yourself. This is the first essential feature. The second feature: autoethnography is writing about your lifeworld (the lifeworld as defined by Alfred Schütz).[5] It is, in a way, the first

5 Schütz (2011: 170–174) shows that there are many realities (see also Schütz 1976: 135–136). Man lives in a world in a specific space and time and is open to the past and the future. It is open

step towards the objectification of experience. The signs present in language connect past knowledge with the current constitution of the meaning of one's own experiences (cf. Sebald 2011). There is no autoethnography without first-person writing. Though you can imagine it as a spoken story, it ends with a record; it was invented in and assigned to the culture of writing. You can also use images for first-person narratives but keep coming back to writing to communicate the story to the readers of the texts in scientific journals or readers of science books. The description of life situations, often detailed and dense,[6] and the contemplation of the meaning of important events and life derived from this description, takes place in action, graphs, and writing. A spoken story must always be written down to be called autoethnography (under different conditions, of course).

Printing and publishing self-narratives brings a new dimension of intersubjectivity to the constitution of meaning. There is no autoethnography without writing and without reading it. Writing enables the transfer of knowledge about oneself to others and facilitates communication, e.g., by printing a text and then others reading it. If this is the case, then the narrator's resources of reference knowledge, i.e., the language of the message, narrative styles, lexical resources, and the storyteller's linguistic imagination, are essential here. What is inherited from ancestors turns out to be crucial; the pre-constitution of meaning took place here. Autoethnography can be viewed as "linguistic facts" (Giza 1991) in which the institutionalization of language and power relations are essential. And they certainly are. However, the individual also plays a game with language, whether he realizes it or not. It can be struggling with the language, flowing together with ready-made culturally defined formulas, typifications, relevance systems, or with a routine supported by resources of

---

to many levels of reality; it can appear in the world of working, in a dream, in memories, fantasies, and thus in the so-called different provinces of meaning with specific intensities of attention awareness. It is also a world open to the individual concerning society, where it reveals itself concerning ancestors, successors, and contemporaries. It is this world that they experience. Although this world is structured differently according to the provinces of meaning and cognitive styles, the working world is our primary reality. This world, within our reach, can be shaped by us, but it also contains some repetitive routines. And here are some patterns of action, assumptions considered obvious, not subject to questioning and discussion. Having resources of reference knowledge, we can operate without problems, without resolving issues that have already been developed and settled in the past.

6 For example, in the autoethnography of C. Ellis, "With mother/with child. A true story" (2001) about her relationship with her mother while caring for her. The descriptions of everyday situations and the author's interactions with her mother are dense and very detailed; there is also an open description of her feelings, emotions, and ethical dilemmas related to caring for an elderly and partially physically disabled person, close to the narrator.

reference knowledge. He or she may use metaphors to cross certain boundaries, or write poems (Richardson 2018). The individual may also be strongly opposed to expressing his or her emotions conventionally, as in asking how you are feeling. Answer: I am fine. Even if the answer reflects our psychophysical feelings, what does it ultimately mean? The autoethnographer develops the understanding of the word "well," locating positive feelings in the context and about other lexical, synonymous, or metaphorical sets and the multidimensional context of the utterance. The lifeworld is open, as are different levels of reality, so the choice of questioning routines or basic assumptions here rests with the acting (writing) individual. As Aleksander Manterys states analyzing the concept of action and act according to Alfred Schütz, the design of the action may differ from the final result, and "the actor is a unique individual, not an objective evaluator of the situation, both his ego and motives are in a continuous process of becoming" (2008: XIII).

It is very tempting to enter into autoethnography fully, to experience life or fragments of it subjectively, e.g., significant events. It is a way of thinking and learning that is very close to me, allowing me to express myself in a situation here and now. Now, which can be described from a first-person perspective as my feeling and perception as I want to show them to the audience. On the other hand, I have a limitation here related to the socialization of grounded theory methodology or other research approaches and theories from academic education (compare also Kacperczyk 2020: 44).[7] I usually need to create patterns; I look for actions, processes, and central categories, integrating other categories and creating a coherent interpretation scheme. I feel an internal need to construct theses and hypotheses and their empirical grounding. Still, at the same time, I feel the need to fully express and describe myself concerning my cognitive, cultural, biographical, and class limitations because I believe that even in the formal analysis of empirical data, it may have a meaning. Anyway, what am I doing about the limitations that result from the adopted methodology of grounded theory and procedural thinking? The scientist thinks according to procedures, concludes according to procedures, interprets data according to certain patterns, and finally presents their analytical results. When the researcher can be themselves? When is they immersed in the world of science

7 "Methodologists from the Lodz center were convinced that the primary goal of their work is to improve the research technique of sociology by creating more and more appropriate and certain research techniques and procedures ... This approach resulted from the conviction that the value of sociological research is determined by reaching reliable and credible information ... Attempts to make the research process effective were to be based on the results of a unique study with methodological goals. For Lutyński and his students, the methodology had a practical and empirical dimension at the same time" (Kacperczyk 2020: 44).

that wants to completely enslave them and take over so that the lifeworld and experience would not have access to them?

There is an article on page 36 of Kafar and Kacperczyk (2020) entitled "Traces of autoethnographic identity". In it, Marcin Kafar refers to the American researcher Laurel Richardson, who writes that people always write about themselves even when they hide behind the wall of science. Zygmunt Bauman writes about this problem in a similar way. At one point in the interview, he says that he dialogues with a subjective experience (Bauman, Jacobsen, Tester 2014: 84, see also 131, 137). In Bauman, however, this subjective dialogue, the language used, camouflages many events. He does not talk directly. The author's "I" hides behind the authority of quasi-reporting sentences, generalizations, and sociological terms, pointing to trends described by sociological terms. He is distancing himself from past events through the strategy of scientific theorizing (see Bauman and Leoncini 2017a, where Bauman reflects on his bullying experience at school). The Bauman way of understanding experience is only an example of my thesis on two forms of introducing descriptions of experiencing the world into sociological texts. He also applies such a convention to scientific texts, presenting theses proven by examples, quotations from sociological dissertations and research reports, or quotations from newspapers, television, and other media. His writing is a reflection in the form of essay writing, usually theoretical, ultimately external to the direct experience of the world. I admire how Bauman dealt with adversity through his sociology or theoretical contemplation, as Schütz would say. What may be necessary here is the reading and reception of these essays. I feel comfortable with Bauman's texts, *Liquid Fear* (2006), *Retrotopia* (2017), and *Nati Liquidi* (2017a), because they resonate with my subjective experience of the contemporary lifeworld. Therefore, symbols, metaphors, and theoretical concepts that can be an apperception of Bauman's subjective world also reflect my way of experiencing this world, even if I operationalize it myself and concretize it differently based on my specific experience.[8]

The second strategy of describing and reflecting on experiencing the world is the approach whereby the researcher reveals his experiences and gives a full ethnographic description of this subjective experience of reality. This is what the authors of autoethnography do. However, what is needed here is courage or sensitivity and the ability to express oneself in a direct, revealing, even shameless way to gain the truth about oneself in a given historical and

8 In his reflection on well-being, I recognize myself, what has become a moral demand, a social norm (Bauman 2017). I also acknowledge my fluid fears, appearing in various contexts, the causes of which I cannot fully establish (Bauman 2006).

interactive social situation. I am not criticizing Bauman here; I am juxtaposing two types of sensitivity and ways of expressing oneself. One is hidden behind the still-scientistic scheme or a particular way it universalizes sentences. The other is autoethnographic, expressing our subjectivity and experiences directly in a given, precisely presented situation, and in interactions densely described (see, e.g., Carolyn Ellis 1993; 1995; 2001; Carol Rambo 1995; Grant 2018) and the suggested interpretations of the described situations, e.g., presenting toxic masculinity and silencing the voice of degraded women (Pruit, Pruit, Rambo 2021) or sexual harassment (Armitage 2021), or oppressive discourses (Grant and Young 2022).

Autoethnography is difficult to classify. Each classification impoverishes it. It is located on the border of different worlds and discourses, e.g., art and science, on the edge of ethnography and biographical research. It also resembles transformational phenomenology, where descriptions of lived experiences and phenomenological analysis of experiences, as well as the reconstruction of the structure of this experience, become a contribution to the internal transformation of oneself and attitude towards the lifeworld (Rehorick, Bentz 2008). Autoethnography, however, does not belong to these worlds and varieties of practicing science and the humanities. It seems to be a separate genre, crossing various boundaries, including its edges, when the researcher defines it, and it escapes them as a different genre (Anderson 2014; see Kacperczyk 2014).

Writing autoethnography becomes the subject's second life. They is in it writing as a researcher and a participant of everyday life. Without writing, they would not be both and conduct a dialogue with each other, initially hidden, and at some point, in the act of courage or desperation, reveal the internal dialogue in the form of a publication. Writing is their activity in this second life; they become themselves in writing about who they are. In writing, they arise, and their records may cross the boundaries of this separate world and enter the world of practical action. Without describing the subject's experience and the identities related to them, they would not exist in the lifeworld, only in their own and only imagined "finite province of meaning." (Schütz 1962: 229–234) Often, autoethnographies are interspersed with theoretical reflections and data from empirical research, including statistics. Therefore, in writing, the researcher transcends his/her subjective world by entering the world of theoretical contemplation.[9]

9 Here, too, there can be a mixture of genres, autoethnographic narrative, and theoretical reflection, and even pragmatic actions in the lifeworld (see Armitage 2021: 20–21).

4 B/ Contemplative Studies

We present the second example of first-person research in contemplative research. According to Valerie Janesick, what is most important for this type of research is holism, "the relationship in the context, body, and mind as instruments of knowing" and "the ethics of no harm and storytelling" (Janesick 2015: 34). "I use the term contemplative inquiry to refer to qualitative techniques that place a deep and serious emphasis on thought in every component of a study of the social world" (Janesick 2015: 34; see also Konecki 2021a; Konecki, Płaczek, Tarasiuk 2024). In projects of this type, we should be aware of ourselves and take care of the state of relationships with the research participants, such as achieving the state of "not-me" during a conversation/interview, to maintain respect for others. The researcher's attentiveness is very helpful when conducting field tasks and constructing descriptions of analyzed situations. The practice of meditation, breathing, or hatha yoga can be used to increase the researcher's attention during an interview or observation and focus on what the interaction partner is telling us. It can be seen that Janesick is not too radical in her approach; for her, contemplation is more a tool that supports classical research techniques.

Contemplation does not mean withdrawing from the world entirely, however. It is not related to Quietism or passivity in the lifeworld. Instead, it is about creating a new perspective and a new way to conduct research. Ultimately, contemplation may involve a commitment to worldly matters (Walsh 2016: 31–32). In general, contemplation is related to observing the work of the mind (Kabat-Zinn 1994, 2005). We act differently in contemplative research than in the lifeworld. There is a clear element of withdrawal here in the researcher's attitude. The researcher retreats into the state of contemplation to see more, to recognize how the mind works in a specific context of action, the mind of both the researcher and participants. If we study how the mind works in a particular context, when we observe the subjective "I," the "reflected self" of the individual (Cooley 1922), we assume that the mind exists, that the "I" exists, and that the "I" is strongly related to perceptions of us by others, even if they are only a vague image of a given situation (see Konecki 2017).

In my research, I assume that contemplation is a type of action that leads to a particular state of mind. At the same time, it is a method of gaining knowledge about objects here and now, about how knowledge is acquired through detailed insight into perceived (and also imagined) phenomena or objects, and insight into oneself and the work of one's mind. (Konecki 2018: 21; Konecki 2022) In this type of research, we employ diverse techniques including meditation, self-reporting, writing contemplative notes, and keeping a contemplative diary. These methods can serve as supporting techniques within the study, as demonstrated in Janesick's approach (2015), or as primary techniques for data generation, as discussed by Konecki (2018: 228; also see 2022).

An important technique based on previous meditation experience is self-observation: "Self-observation is a technique of concentrating on the work of the mind, to notice how it works and what kind of thoughts it produces at the moment, and how the body reacts to the incentives coming "from outside," i.e., what kinds of emotions appear and how they are felt by the individual in certain situations" (Konecki 2018: 229). Self-observation may relate to typical situations in everyday life that will be perceived. Self-observation ends with a self-description immediately after it occurs.

Zen experiments constitute another technique. They concern studying the following cognitive aspects of an individual: 1) mind/thoughts, 2) social situations in specific spaces, 3) experienced emotions, 4) body sensations. Thus, we can come up with many such experiments. For example, we may observe our feelings when we cross the boundaries of specific separate spaces, such as entering the university area (Konecki 2017a), correctional facilities, prisons, supermarkets, museums, churches, and yoga practice or meditation rooms. We can also observe the work of the mind while standing still in public places (Konecki 2017), for example.

In addition to natural Zen experiments, we can use another thought experiment, the experiment of empathetic perception: "Empathetic experiments are a part of the practice of contemplation. We put ourselves in the role of other, with the full awareness and observing our emotions and bodily feelings. We make an imaginative transfer of our body to the position of the other ... To experience (even imaginatively) and to feel the situation (in mind and emotions and body) is something different than just a cognitive and rational elaboration of it based on social stereotypes and pre-assumptions" (Konecki 2018: 234; Konecki 2022a). I describe these techniques in my book "Advances in Contemplative Social Research" (Konecki 2018; see also Konecki 2022).

However, when analyzing the data, we write contemplative memos/notes (see the research strategy "contemplative grounded theory," Konecki 2022, chapter 2) to see how our mind works and what it produces, what it duplicates, and what it connects. You can see your theoretical inspirations, thinking patterns, assumptions, and even prejudices (Woroniecka 1998/2003), which enter into an internal dialogue or are located in the background and do not allow you to see the complete picture of a given situation (see Konecki 2022, chapter 2 and 5). We de-theorize the world we observe (Zakrzewska-Manterys 1996) and reveal ourselves, just like in autoethnography. We also announce our relationships with research participants and colleagues. We show our emotions, how the body reacts, and our class and gender positioning in a given situation; we also do it in the historical dimension. The data analysis is overwritten with contemplative notes, which are then part of this analysis and research report because the research process takes place in a dialogue in the researcher's mind. Thus, these introspective data are essential for creating categories, hypotheses, and interpreting the processes involved in the subjects' interactions with researchers, who, in turn, also engage in internal dialogue and dialogue with other colleagues. It is essential to build a relationship based on trust with colleagues and reflect on what trust is in a given situation (Konecki 2019: 282–285).

Writing contemplative memos allows you to go beyond your cognitive limitations, better understand your hidden assumptions, and understand yourself in a given situation (Konecki 2022, chapters 2 and 5). You can answer the question of who you are as a Researcher, what your rights are to publish the obtained data, and what reality your publications create. Contemplative memos allow for ethical reflection, and often, they also allow you to change your moral perspective.

5 C/ Transformational Phenomenology Research

The last concept of first-person research discussed in this chapter is transformational phenomenology, created by Valery Malhotra Bentz and David Rehorick (Bentz 1995, Bentz, Rehorick 2008). In this concept, essential features of phenomena are sought, and an attempt is made to discover the meaning of the lived experience in everyday life (Rehorick, Bentz 2008: 3; Bentz, Marlatt 2021). A phenomenological inquiry into the experience of a phenomenon deepens awareness and leads to the transformation of individuals. We can finally look at ourselves and a particular phenomenon differently by conducting research. We can go deeper into the answers to the question "Who are we?" Phenomenology redirects us to the direct experience as the basis of our knowledge of the world. Direct experience is also encapsulated by a narrative derived from "I." From these positions, we can create dense descriptions of these experiences. In the final stage of explicating the phenomenon, we try to use phenomenological terms to describe these experiences as specific structures of consciousness. "The end points of phenomenological work are descriptions of essential structures of experience (following Husserl) and/or rich descriptions of lifeworlds (following Schütz)" (Rehorick, Bentz 2008: 6).

Studying phenomenology and conducting research simultaneously may lead to an internal transformation of the researcher (see Davidson, Decker, Tarasiuk 2021). And this inner transformation is the introduction to the transformation of the lifeworld. We start changes in the world from ourselves.

It can be said that this is not an approach typical of humanistic science. However, there is an attempt here to understand phenomena through the prism of experiences and then explicate them from the point of view of phenomenology. By finding the fundamental features of the studied phenomena, we can deepen our understanding of the lifeworld. Rehorick and Bentz offer basic phenomenological techniques concerning eidetic phenomenology: *bracketing, imaginative variations*, and *horizontalization*.

The first level of bracketing our knowledge is to suspend what we have learned about a phenomenon from scientific research, accepted theories, and other commonly credited sources of knowledge. Then, we should "bracket" terms and interpretations about the phenomenon derived from our cultural environment (Rehorick, Bentz 2008: 12). This knowledge is embedded in the language by typifications and cognitive constructs that we have internalized and use when naming people, objects and phenomena (Schütz [1932] 1962; 1976).

Imaginative variation, i.e., views on data from different points of view, is another phenomenological inquiry technique used to analyze research protocols that describe experiences. Here we look for other meanings, using our imaginations, different frames of reference, perspectives, positions, roles, and functions to fully describe the structures of our experience and its essential attributes. Using mental variations, we can distinguish between random features from those that are key and necessary for a given phenomenon to occur (Rehorick, Bentz 2008: 14–15; see also Bentz, Shapiro 1998: 99; Moustakas 1994; Van Manen 2003).

The third technique that applies to phenomenological reduction is horizontalization. It is essential to create a context for understanding the phenomenon within a particular here-and now experience. "Horizontalization involves making the elements in a situation equal and putting that situation at a distance to better view it without assumptions or bias. Normally, we think of some elements as much more important than others. Horizontalization gives each element equal value, opening up possibilities for seeing things differently and changing one's perspective. Let us say, for example, that in a given hour you tie your shoelaces, pet your dog, write a poem, and watch capsule news on CNN. If someone asked what you had done in that past hour, you might say, 'I wrote a poem and watched the news.' If your best friend, also a poet, telephoned, you might say, 'I wrote a poem.' If your spouse called, you might say that you played with the dog" (Rehorick & Bentz 2008: 16; see also Bentz, Shapiro 1998: 99; Hycner 1985; the description of the three techniques mentioned above comes from Konecki's monograph 2018: 20, 66, 149, 189).

The context of actions and statements decides the meaning of lived experiences. We are looking for typification here. We reconstruct systems of relevance, processes of changing points of view, etc. In the final phase of our research and narrative of experiences, we try to follow the path set by Alfred Schütz. The phenomenon arises in context; although it may have universal features, it is related to subjective experience in the here and now. Space and time are dimensions of experiencing phenomena. They create the necessary background for research participants and researchers to recall a phenomenon. And this is the moment when researchers get a more contemplative and careful insight into the research situation and finally reconstruct the way data is produced and interpreted. Ultimately, the phenomenological analysis leads to the researcher's transformation, self-esteem, awareness of themselves and attitudes. It may even have a therapeutic function.

6 Theoretical Contemplation of First-Person Research Approaches

We started with a different reality – the reality of autoethnography, contemplative research, and transformational phenomenology. Now it is time to return to the world of theoretical reflection and analyze this reality of first-person research. There will be a second leap. We are crossing the border again. It will reconstruct first-person approaches from the position of Alfred Schütz's phenomenology and his concept of a finite province of meaning.

The basis of our perception is the lifeworld, paramount reality. It is evident, unquestionable, intersubjective for the individual, and the subject is guided by pragmatic motives and a particular tension of consciousness (Schütz 1962). Our actions in this world stem from *the fundamental anxiety* of the gut feeling that each of us will inevitably die. However, as Ruth Ayass claims when analyzing Schütz's concept (2017: 540): "For Alfred Schutz, fundamental anxiety is of central relevance for the everyday world. It determines the basic experience of the natural attitude." First-person narratives often show this anxiety directly and clearly – they refer to meeting the death of loved ones, or one's own illness. Experiencing something life-threatening causes anxiety and often the need to deal with the anticipated problem, the disappearance of "I," my working ego. One can recall here the mental and emotional processes that take place in people during visits to a cemetery. In the presence of the symbols of the deathworld, observers, through the presentation procedure, trigger a feeling of death and the existence of the deathworld (Konecki 2021, 2022; cf. also Barber 2017 and his analysis of religion as a finite province of meaning).

In addition to this basic reality, we also have others, such as religion, humor, or the world of fantasy (ibid.). These different realities modify the underlying reality, each with a particular cognitive style. Schütz lists six features of the cognitive style: the tension of consciousness, specific epoché, a form of spontaneity, a form of self-experience, a form of sociality, and a particular time perspective.

In our lives, we constantly jump between realities: "… my mind may pass during one single day or even hour through the whole gamut of tensions of consciousness, now living in acts of working, now passing through a daydream, now plunging into the pictorial world of a painter, now indulging in theoretical contemplation" (Schütz 1962: 258, as cited in Barber 2017: 87). According to Schütz, there are "several, probably an infinite number of various orders of realities, each with its own special and separate style of existence" (Schütz 1962: 207; quoted in Ayass 2017: 520).

So, let us leap[10] from *the bureaucratic reality* in which we currently operate, and from the world of science, limited by rules, procedures, regulations, and instructions, but also a scientific, generally accepted assessment procedure, the norm of the need to evaluate the scientific achievements of others according to a priori assumed evaluation criteria ("everyone knows them"). The research methodology is included in the baggage of reference knowledge and is associated with the same bureaucratic logic, control, and rational action. Let us leave this baggage, a veil behind which there is a knowledge-producing *human scientist* (usually male, which also matters here), a cover through which we cannot see how knowledge is produced with our mind.

Let us fully enter this world, without assumptions, into the world as it is. The researcher communicates with the research participants here; they arranges meetings, where they plans what to ask about and what to learn by observing others. Let us make *a theoretical contemplation* of this reality. Two words come out: Researcher and Others. *Who is the Researcher?* Let us, therefore, enter

10 This leap can be treated as a particular epoché, one of the features of the "finite province of meaning" (Schütz 1962: 229–234, Czyżewski 1984: 30–31; Benta 2014) in everyday life. It is about suspending doubt and disbelief in certain facts, events, beliefs, basic assumptions of our actions, etc. We do not doubt in our everyday life; we suspend this doubt because then we would not act quickly and efficiently. It can be said that while evoking doubt, we would constantly stop at the here and now, and we would experience constant contemplation over the assumptions. The specific epoché allows us to doubt our everyday reality. But of course, we have the option of going back to the fundamental reality (Ayass 2017: 527).

this *finite province of meaning of first-person research* (Schütz 1962: 229–234; Benta 2014; Schütz 2011), leaving our world behind for a moment.

We do not usually ask ourselves this question during research or the analytical process. We take it for granted that the researcher is the one who asks research questions and tries to answer them. Questions are asked systematically, following the rules of logic, and the answers should be of the same nature. This is obvious to us. This assumption allows us to go further in our field and library peregrinations and apply the commonsense procedure "let it go," even if the questions arise: Who am I here and now in this situation? What am I doing here? What right do I have to ask questions and observe others, even if they agree?

After all, I will continue to do what I consider appropriate with this data, referring to the adopted research procedure. The respondents either do not know or have a vague idea about it. I do not ask myself the question of their location concerning the so-called object of the study. The word object is also used here on purpose (in the works of Jan Lutyński, it is the object of the study, 1994: 79, 100–102, and in the works of Stefan Nowak, it is the subject of the researcher's interest, 2010: 30). There is me and the object. The object is outside; I interact with it indirectly, and a research tool separates me from it, even if it is just my eyesight or the language I use.

Often, the concept of understanding in sociology or humanistic sociology pays attention to considering the actor's point of view, looking at the world from their point of view, and trying to understand their vision of the world. Or, as Stefan Nowak argued, one can use introspectively obtained data to build indicators of particular psycho-social phenomena (Nowak 1965). But then, my "I" is still outside the world of the respondents who provide me with knowledge about the object of the study; I do not cross the border of their world. Even immersion into their world, according to the procedures of ethnography, places me outside. Sometimes you can see difficulties with being outside, as was the case, for example, in an ethnography of Alice Goffman (2014) in her research on the life of an excluded community in an American city. And it is then that I reveal myself, I reveal myself feeling, accompanying another "I." This is the emotional, human "I".[11]

11 A similar situation – the presence of strong emotions and the building of trust and loyalty towards the participants of the research, along with the resolution of ethical issues – can be found in many contexts of ethnographic research, e.g., in the research of escort agencies (see Ślęzak 2015, 2018; Wojciechowska 2018) or in research on people with disabilities (Niedbalski 2016).

I keep answering the question, "Who is the Researcher?" It is difficult for me to leave this orderly world of scientific and technocratic procedures. This is a more profound question: Who am I, usurping the self-definition of a researcher? The word usurping indicates that I am appropriating something. I appropriate, so I can do it and put myself above the object because I am interested in it only as a carrier of information about the subject of my research – an elusive and abstract phenomenon that I took to the study.

So, I have the power. I appropriate the object of my research. The object of the study is mine, both when the data are obtained and afterward, when I have substantiated what happened during the interaction with the object, saving data and coding them. I WAS NEUTRAL when I analyzed them, not feeling anything, as in a surgical operation. *I am a data surgeon.* I can cut it, incorporate other data, discard unnecessary fragments, insert a foreign body in the form of quotations from the classics, create new indicators, insert or add statistical data that smooth *the dead body of the empirical data.* My mind is formatted by the convention of writing research reports and scientific articles; this format rarely allows me to see what is beyond.

There is the Other, which I will probably never understand, because he/she appears to me in terms of typification – "because" motives and "in-order-to" motives, systems of relevance often created not by me, but that have become part of my knowledge at hand. I can be open to new experiences, but I am immersed in the world of practical activities, and it has its rules. The Other is realized through my idea of how the lifeworld, which is the only world for me, works to grasp it sufficiently and understand social processes and the individual perspective contained in these processes.

How hard it is for me to leave this world. The jump at this point seems impossible. But I try; I try to leave this world behind me and put brackets on the assumptions that guide the researcher. Do I already understand who I am? I think that I know, although I do not yet understand precisely on what basis it happened. Still, it has happened. I make decisions; I leap into reality without the procedural assumptions derived from the world of science. *I crossed the border.* I want to understand myself in a situation of meeting others. I start writing autoethnography, contemplative memos, contemplative diaries; I perform self-observation, which I write down in my memory, and then in electronic form. I reach experiences here and now (living experience), which in a moment become lived experiences. Getting to the primary experience becomes extremely difficult because the time variable is relentless; it does not allow me to stop in one place, even for a second, because the second includes milliseconds, and I am still in a linear time-experience flow. I am floating in my experience of the lifeworld. There is only here and now for me and what I am experiencing. What I perceive with my senses results from what I am experiencing and who I am entering this situation.

And who I am cannot be suspended because I cannot talk to someone else unless they know who I am. My self-definition is necessary so that they can locate me in their world and adjust, I emphasize, adapt their answers to my questions. This applies to the living person with whom I interact and the documents I analyze. They also conform to my questions; they are the "players," albeit *dead* partners of the interaction in my game which I call data analysis.

•••

But let us get out of this our primary world now and enter the world of theoretical contemplation. Let us see what happens in the *"finite province of meaning" of first-person research* and analyze it from the point of view of Alfred Schütz's theoretical concept.

The first feature of first-person research as a finite province of meaning (following Schütz's concept) is *the tension of consciousness.* In the world of everyday life, it is extended attention, focus on life, on everyday events, on implementing plans, on work, on achievements. The "motor memory" (Henri Bergson's concept) is activated, aimed at implementing often routine activities in the lifeworld. "Pure memory," which is directed at images of the past, requires pause, contemplation. This is what happens in writing autoethnography and contemplative notes or protocols in transformational phenomenology. Past experiences appear in our memory. The imagination starts to work, interpreting these events; images appear and/or sediments during the writing and allows us to see what others see (Sebald 2011). The tension of consciousness in first-person research is related to focusing on the description of one's own experiences, fragments of the biography, and, when describing incidents the narrator focus on a given moment, in a given space. The tension of consciousness is high, although not as high as in the lifeworld (or in the world of work). It is also due to the emotions experienced (shame, anger, fear, compassion) and the visibility of the experienced situation or memories that are of great importance to the individual, as well as the emotional load. In first-person contemplation, however, *this tension gradually diminishes, and emotions are released,* which pass after a while. After some time, there is a spontaneous calming down. We are no longer worried about the material side of life, at least when we are writing this auto-report. This reassurance is even necessary.[12] And

12 "Bergson ... cites Plotinus' comment, 'All action,' he said (and he even added 'all fabrication') 'weakens contemplation.' Similarly, the artist, in particular painters like Turner or

writing about the lived experience can be compared to a polonaise dance. The first movement is violent, and then there is a slow, gentle march, then a violent shudder again, calm, etc. Undoubtedly, it is not a mazurka or an *oberek* dance, which is so dynamic, and may end with the subject's complete exhaustion, or they may even faint. Autoethnography and self-observation require a contemplative attitude.

The second feature of a finite province of meaning is *the particular epoché* in everyday life. It is the suspension of doubt and disbelief in certain facts, events, beliefs, and the basic assumptions of our practical actions. We suspend our doubts about the observable and tangible world, the lifeworld as one of many, and perhaps not fundamental. On the other hand, the autoethnographer suspends the doubts in the narrator's memory, the inaccuracy of their memory, and describes what they thinks has happened. The narrator treats the described facts as a reality that is important to them, even if it is a fiction, a recovered memory, or a hazy reality, blurred by accumulated past events from the biography that may be mixed up with the situation being described. The case is worth describing, and once it is reported, it becomes a fact. The autoethnographer or contemplative researcher at the time of writing the autoethnography suspends their involvement in the lifeworld. At that moment, they enters the world where is the leading creator of reality and does not rely entirely on hard facts and limitations, i.e., the norms and rules that govern everyday life.

Then, the autoethnographer, contemplative researcher, or transformational phenomenologist can also make another *epoché*, in turn, suspending the faith in the cultural and social categories of perceptions of reality to subject them to critical reflection, thus achieving a deeper understanding of their existential situation. They gains an insight into the suggestions of their culture, typifications, and inherited systems of relevance.

The epoché, used by a first-person researcher, who lives his daily attention focused on the habitual perception of reality and himself, pushes these habits aside. The researcher begins the insight and penetration into the recesses of his consciousness, which, with all its complexity, makes it possible to see

---

Corot, is less preoccupied with the material side of life and the need to act and, as a consequence, better able than we are to see things that we had missed in our perceiving of reality" (Bergson 1968: 163, cited in Barber 2017: 85).

"By placing ourselves at this point of view, we shall perceive that the object of art is to put to sleep the active or rather resistant powers of our personality, and thus to bring us into a state of perfect responsiveness, in which we realize the idea that is suggested to us and sympathize with the feeling that is expressed" (Bergson 1910: 14, cited in Barber 2017: 8).

what they did not perceive or see before. Some aspects of memories become direct signs of specific processes; for example, states of embarrassment in a particular social situation can indicate the occurrence of the phenomenon of "public humiliation process" (Schoepfl in 2009; degradation ceremonies, see Garfinkel 1956).

Using the first-person *epoché* in qualitative research can be transformative, just as the phenomenological *epoché* allows the individual to overcome his cognitive limitations, prejudices, suppressions caused by trauma, low self-esteem, freeing from negative emotions, or accepting them. Returning to the lifeworld, the individual is already someone else, changed as it sometimes happens under the influence of mystical/religious experience.

The third feature of a finite province of meaning is *a form of spontaneity*, which in everyday life is based on the project and intention to implement this project in action (at work) in the outside world, not only in our thoughts but also using our own body.

The autoethnographer or transformational phenomenologist *has a lot of freedom* in expressing their feelings. Their spontaneity is not so limited by the rules of the lifeworld. They overcomes these barriers, bends the rules, e.g., regarding cultural taboos, the level of openness of beliefs and emotions, etc. This can happen thanks to the epoché I have just mentioned. The boundary of autoethnography protects the meanings expressed in the text: after all, this is autoethnography, so the performer/autoethnographer can say whatever they wants. The problem with the boundary of autoethnography and the world of practical action begins when subjects and objects from the lifeworld enter the world of autoethnography but still do not accept it and rummage through it as if in a protective uniform (bubbles) from another world, trying to violate the internal rules of this finite province of meaning.[13] It can be said that Sancho Panza comes into play with his rational view of reality (Schütz 1976).

Ultimately, however, spontaneity is not related to pragmatic activities. Even if we fail in the world of working, in the lifeworld, our commitment to our world of representation does not change. The body's involvement is minimal, similar to theoretical contemplation, and the body is associated only with the act of recording and formulating a message, thus communicating its reflections and self-descriptions to others. As in theoretical contemplation or religious practice, failures outside this province of meaning do not affect our involvement

13 The connections of the worlds are visible here, not only in terms of gaining resources in the lifeworld to enter the world of first-person narration but also in terms of the obstacles that can permeate from other worlds, penetrating the current world of cognitive immersion.

in this province in openly writing about ourselves and other companions (Barber 2017). The first-person world is not about controlling the surroundings but about focusing on yourself and your experiences and then getting a fresh perspective on the surroundings and the situation you find yourself in. The emerging self-experience is emotionally challenging at first, but we gradually release ourselves internally from the pressure of external forces. *There is a state of relaxation.* Even fundamental anxiety can be diminished for a moment. Of course, changes in the outside world can occur under the influence of writing about oneself. Still, they are consequences of these actions, not the primary goal. The focus is instead on internal transformation, which may also inspire others to look at themselves differently and act towards this change.

The way self is experienced is the fourth feature of the cognitive style. In everyday life, the working self is holistic, undivided, visible here and now, directed at realizing particular practical goals. We are often not aware of this in our actions because it is usually a habitual activity.

We feel differently when we write autoethnography; we are whole but emotional in a given fragment of the description of our reality. I AM immersed in an event or cycle of life events but living in memory, not completely real, and unrelated to implementing specific tasks, with the pragmatics of action. And yet we are here in a particular role, describing our own experiences and the role of an observer of these experiences. As in the theoretical province of meaning, this part of "I" engages in contemplation.[14] We experience ourselves as an emotional whole, e.g., when going through a turning point, experiencing trauma, or intense emotions that have already happened and which we recall through memory and reflection. Exposing yourself is part of experiencing yourself in writing a story. We express ourselves by focusing on ourselves as the zero point of all the described events. There is a rare third, passive perspective that emerges primarily due to the infiltration of the lifeworld into our transient enclave: "*Now I am at the center of the world.*" If another appears, it may be the alter-ego, an appresentation of the narrator himself. These accounts show that "I" is rooted in a world where it is difficult to separate the first-person, yourself, from others. But this world is a memory world. When it comes to the topicality of being the subject, they partially suspends the knowledge about their body. However, the body may also participate in recalling, e.g., traumatic events, and cooperate with the memory when emotions are intensely felt at the level of the body or physiology, for example. In the theoretical province of meaning,

14 "She becomes a 'scientist' with a special set of relevances and pursuits in contrast to her previous absorption in everyday working tasks …" (Barber 2017:119).

as in autoethnography, the subject suspends the knowledge and awareness of their body here and now, and the *ego agens* is invalidated.

The performativity of autoethnography is a consequence of writing and the next dimension of self-experience. After all, the autoethnographer creates facts that affect the recipients. Still, these written facts influence this province of meaning – both the narrator and the reader who identifies with it. Writing autoethnography, the narrator negotiates their own identity about who they was, is, and who they wants to be. Narrators explore their possibilities of being. Their I can be wholly transformed through public exposure to their thinking and feeling. This revealed I AM is/was different from the one with which the narrator works in the world of working. *There is a release from the limitations of the world of practice*, a reduction in the stress associated with these limitations, and the need for practical action; the released "I" gains self-confidence, and low self-esteem is questioned. Self-insight takes on a therapeutic meaning.

Individual experiences appear *unique*, allowing them to keep their self-esteem and avoid typifications or autotypifications from the lifeworld, which often degrade and lower their self-esteem.

The form of sociality (*the fifth feature of the cognitive style*) in everyday life is related to intersubjectivity, i.e., construction, maintenance, communication, and social activity in the lifeworld.

Building intersubjectivity takes place at the beginning of autoethnography. After all, it is intended for the reader whom it is supposed to touch or bind for that moment when they read it, and perhaps consequently trigger a social action. We are the point zero from which everything begins, but we also write for someone else, not only for ourselves. The future horizon is also considered here as in *modo futuri exacti*. Before the act of writing, we were also in a community where we had mastered our methods of writing and self-observation. I and you participated in a scientific discourse that may or may not accept my first-person research perspective, so others are with me, somewhat in the background of my immersion in memory. I can, of course, reject the scientific presuppositions of my colleagues. When contemplating my self and my mind, I am not with others in the here and now (the vivid present). *I do not meet their bodies in my presence* (Schütz 1962: 252).

The *we-relationship* also arises at the time of collaborating with other participants in the process of writing/dialogue of autoethnography and, for example, in collaborative autoethnography and or collaborative contemplative research. In addition, the Others with whom the writer designs and shapes a relationship at the time of writing may be potential reviewers, editors, colleagues, and colleagues who support the writer or other researchers that the writer communicates with and meets. Usually, it is a larger group, especially in collaborative autoethnography projects (Ellis and Rawicki 2020) and workshops. Communication is vital for the emergence of autoethnography and communication that is full of support, understanding, empathy, care for the dialogue partner, and openness to the other and in ways of presenting oneself. The *we-relationship* gives a sense of security to the autoethnographer, who often reveals painful and/or embarrassing facts from his life. The autoethnographer is never really alone; although the name of their identity begins with *auto*, this is the apparent individualistic benchmark for the activities of the autoethnographer. Their action is collective from the beginning, although in the course of writing, it may take place without the presence of other bodies in their *vivid present*; the writer is usually separated from them.

The sixth feature of the described cognitive style is the particular time perspective. It is the intersection of the subjective feeling of the duration of a durée and the standard time measured by a clock adopted in a given society; a measure of time.

We can wander in time; past events are available at our fingertips (the movement of awareness and the direction of attention). Time is evoked here by recalling a specific event from memory. Writing about this event, we immerse ourselves in it; we are absorbed by it. We are once again in the middle of the event. This is the time of our pure memory. It reminds us of events that we cannot change, but we immerse ourselves in them, including our body sensations and emotions. The intensity of this experience and its bodily availability may make us not want to return to past traumatic events because we can find ourselves in them as if in the real-time of their authentic experience. We do not want to relive the trauma of the Holocaust, genocide, earthquake, rape, public humiliation, etc. Recalling, recreating from memory, brings the past to life, and the event is brought back to the here and now. This time, however, in such a way as we want to integrate it, overcome difficult emotions and let the narrator live fully in the present and the future.

In the world of autoethnography, we do not necessarily relate to people who have experienced events with us. *We do not see the "same" flying bird*, as Schütz characterizes this situation (1962: 315–317); we are together with others only in the imagination. Unless we create a collaborative autoethnography, we participate in a specific event. Then my durée coincides with the time course of events in the outside world.

However, emotions recalled from the past or experienced are usually only an appresentation of specific phenomena that can be described by categories from the researcher's knowledge at hand. Experienced emotions can therefore be a stimulus to start narratives and descriptions of feelings, but also more general phenomena, e.g., the phenomenon of public humiliation, sexual violence, an academic conspiracy of silence or status-forced silence, and toxic masculinity (Pruit, Pruit, Rambo 2021).

At some point in the narrative, however, there is a reflective intersection of this duration with calendar time, when we locate a given event in time, just as we remember this moment in time (the season, month, or the exact date and time). *Time standardization*, the event as a point of time, appears; it is a spontaneous standardization of experience. And then, possibly, we can distance ourselves from a given described event.[15]

The individual is together here and now. He can then transform the interpretation of the event, transform himself through interpretive shifts, accept what happened, accept responsibility or indicate blame, and free himself from guilt (Rambo 1995). The emerging time structure becomes a transforming entity. You can transfer this transformation to the present and even imagine your own identity in the future as being different from that of a past experience, sometimes traumatic, but formative for a time other than the past. The individual abandons their restless self and leaves it in the past to move on to the pure present, cleansed of trauma and negative emotions. The writing becomes a demiurge that allows them to be liberated from past worries.

7 Summary and Conclusions

The end!

As a first-person researcher, I return to the primary reality, the reality of the lifeworld with its procedures, plus my role as a researcher. What does this return look like? The jump is not easy, just like coming back from different realities, e.g., dream realities, to the lifeworld. I am tired of the tension of consciousness, focusing on others, on their experiences and my own. I am returning to the world of procedures, evaluation criteria, and the compulsion to judge. How can I evaluate an article, doctorate thesis, or a habilitation thesis written in the form of autoethnography, a phenomenological or contemplative report?! A headache occurs! From a different point of view, I must (do I have to?) evaluate what someone has done and what I have done from the world of practical activities (working life)? And what do I perceive in the texts given to me to evaluate? A lack of objectivity is a severe problem of intersubjectivity in data production and control of this process. I go back to the culture of distance to the so-called object of the study. I experience the shock of jumping into

15 After all, it is always an event, an interaction, a situation described by someone and for someone.

my primary province of meaning, the world of practical action, the world of academia. Crossing boundaries is not emotionally easy. There is some invisible boundary between these worlds, the world of first-person visions of research and the world of intersubjectively corroborating objectivist research. *It is the border of the worlds*, which I hope will not be the place of the war of the worlds, but mutual penetration and dialogue in this beautiful garden of sociological methodology.

This shock and the emotions and predictable problems associated with it are the costs I incur for an authentic meeting with another. As in the lifeworld, I am adopting the perspective of the other as a condition of understanding and joint action. Although I am idealizing the adoption of another's point of view (idealization is the assumption that empathic understanding is possible), by adding the value of trust to it, I can live and communicate with another at least during the study.

The attitude of distance – as adopted by, for example, critical sociology – is based on a lack of trust (in oneself, in others, in the method); *The art of distrust acquires the status of a scientific value*, everything has to be checked and controlled. Trust is an obstacle, a barrier. It can even be treated as *an infantile methodological disorder*. Suppose we consider the question of trust in a finite province of meaning, from the first-person perspective, where it is necessary to obtain a narrative. In that case, the problem of cultivating the art of distrust may disappear. Everyone reveals as much as they trust themselves to say in a given situation.

So, we are dealing with different worlds here. The sense of the term "finite" in defining the province of meaning is significant; boundaries still exist.

Returning from certain finite provinces of meaning to fundamental reality may be a shock and have practical consequences for the wanderer. Suppose someone returns, for example, from a religious province of meaning and claims to have had apparitions. In that case, this may be a helpful indicator for assigning this type of experience to another province of meaning, *the "world of insanity"* (see the problem of Don Quixote described by Schütz, 1976). This, too, can be the experience of first-person narrators. Experiences of different realities often do not coincide with each other. The transition from first-person research to the world of science can be particularly shocking, and connecting these worlds can be a challenging task. Who should enable a painless transition? It seems that the interpreters and translators show the uniqueness of different worlds and the possibility of reconciling the criteria of science with subjective experiences confirmed by evidence found in both worlds (Varela, Shear 2002).

A sociologist should reflect on the consequences of his self-examination. As Stefan Nowak writes: "Avoiding this reflection is also a moral choice – a choice in favor of moral and social responsibility" (Nowak 2010: 478; see also Wyka 1993). *I tried to show the structure of the experience of the world by a first-person researcher.* Reconstructing this structure is very important for us to evaluate this type of research (if we must do so). I hope this chapter will contribute to a better understanding and crystallization of evaluation criteria for this research endeavor. In times of epistemological confusion and the resulting anxiety, it is essential to analyze cognition in other worlds and use, for example, theoretical contemplation, also from the first person perspective (Grant 2023). You can then see what is only narcissism,[16] self-presentation, and what is compassion or giving respect to others. What is a manipulation of the ego and potential recipients, and what is a plausible intersubjectively verifiable narrative? Does describing one's own experiences and relationships with others violate other people's welfare or mental well-being? The problem of ethical responsibility can be seen and considered here.

In autoethnographic discussion and collaboration, or the discussion of the contemplative report, it is possible to establish intersubjectivity. It is also joined by the reviewer, critic, and reader after the end of the self-narrative. Translators worldwide appear to negotiate between realities and agreement on interpretation patterns. The metaphors and general categories should create a community of understanding between the worlds. Metaphors and categories can be symbolic representations of many objects from given worlds. It is crucial to develop a "common language" that will be understandable in both universes of meaning. This is where the points of contact between the worlds and provinces of importance may appear. Suppose I agree to a particular emphasis on a given reality and understand its internal dialectics. In that case, I have no reason not to acknowledge the credibility and reliability of a given self-narrative. The evaluation criteria are relative and belong to specific worlds. As Alfred Schütz writes: "But does the meaning of wisdom and stupidity not depend on a given sub-universe in which only these measures are essential? What is stupidity, wisdom in the whole universe, the sum of all our sub-worlds?" (Schütz 1976: 157–158). If our world is the sum of other worlds, it is impossible to exclude the subjective reality from which their construction

16 When assessing the entirety of the presented narrative, the diagnosis of a narcissistic attitude is possible when it can be stated whether a given individual wants to live only for himself or whether he wants to direct his thoughts to improve the fate of others (see Lasch 1979).

begins. One only has to find linguistic structures that would translate the meanings of these two worlds to each other.

My considerations were "idealizing" the aforementioned features of the provinces of the meaning of first-person research. Of course, there may be studies whose primary goal is to lie to the audience, lie to oneself, make up, project one's feelings on others, narcissistic self-presentation, etc., the world of first-person social research. Finally, I want to say that this qualitative plant in the garden of sociological methodology (generally in humanistic and social sciences) can develop if there is cooperation and scientific and social activity of first-person researchers who will take care of communicating with the outside world and the intersubjectivity of their messages. Although the gardener may rest or fall asleep at times, the research and reporting to others must be continued.

Bibliography

Anderson, Leon. 2006. Analytic Autoethnography. *Journal of Contemporary Ethnography*, 35(4), 373–395. https://doi.org/10.1177/0891241605280449.

Armitage, Janet S. 2021. "When I Least Expected It: An Autoethnography of Reporting Workplace Sexual Harassment and Compassionate Bystanders". *Journal of Contemporary Ethnography*, June 2021, doi:10.1177/08912416211022817.

Ayass, Ruth. 2017. "Life-World, Sub-Worlds, After-Worlds: The Various 'Realnesses' of Multiple Realities." *Human Studies*, 40, 519–542.

Barber, Michael. 2017. *Religion and Humor as an Emancipating Provinces of Meaning*. Dordrecht: Springer.

Bauman, Zygmunt. 2006. *Liquid Fear*. Cambridge: Polity Press.

Bauman, Zygmunt (with Michael H. Jacobsen and Keith Tester). 2014. *What use is sociology?* Cambridge: Polity Press Ltd.

Bauman, Zygmunt. 2017. *Retrotopia*. Cambridge: Polity Press.

Bauman, Zygmunt. 2017a. (with Thomas Leoncini) *Nati Liquidi. Transformazioni nel terzo millennio*, Milano: Sperling & Kupfer.

Benţa, Marius Ion. 2014. *The Multiple Reality: A Critical Study on Alfred Schütz's Sociology of the Finite Provinces of Meaning*. Cork: University College.

Bentz, Valerie Malhotra. 1995. "Husserl, Schutz, 'Paul' and Me: Reflections on Writing Phenomenology". *Human Studies*,18, 41–62.

Bentz, Valerie M., Jeremy J. Shapiro. 1998. *Mindful Inquiry in Social Research*. London: Sage.

Bentz, Valerie and James Marlatt. 2021. *Deathworlds to Lifeworlds. Collaboration with Strangers for Personal, Social and Ecological Transformation*. Berlin, New York: de Gruyter.

Bergson, Henri. 1910. *Time and Free Will: An Essay on the Immediate Data of Consciousness*. Translated by F.L. Pogson. London/New York: George Allen and Unwin, Ltd./ The Macmillan Company.

Bergson, Henri.1968. *The Creative Mind.* Translated by M.L. Andison. Westport: Greenwood Press.

Bokszański, Zbigniew. 1986. "Koncepcja tożsamości jednostki w pracach Anselma L. Straussa". (The concept of individual identity in the works of Anselm Strauss) *Studia Socjologiczne*, 2, 89–110.

Bokszański, Zbigniew. 1989. *Tożsamość, interakcja, grupa.* (*Identity, interaction, group*) Łódź: Wydawnictwo Uniwersytetu Łódzkiego.

Cooley, Charles Horton. 1922. *Human Nature and the Social Order* (Revised edition). New York: Charles Scribner's Sons.

Czyżewski, Marek. 1984. *Socjolog i życie potoczne. Studium z etnometodologii i współczesnej socjologii interakcji.* (*A sociologist and everyday life. A study in ethnomethodology and contemporary sociology of interaction.*) Łódź: Wydawnictwo Uniwersytetu Łódzkiego.

Davidson, Lori, Jennifer Decker, Dagmara Tarasiuk. 2021. "Overcoming Deathworlds of Addiction, Self-Injury, And Stress", in *Deathworlds to Lifeworlds Collaboration with Strangers for Personal, Social and Ecological Transformation*, edited by V. Bentz, J. Marlatt. Berlin, New York: de Gruyter.

Ellis, Carolyne. 1991. "Sociological Introspection and Emotional Experience". *Symbolic Interaction*, 14(1), 23–50.

Ellis, Carolyne. 1993. "There Are Survivors": Telling a Story of Sudden Death. *The Sociological Quarterly*, 34(4), 711–730. http://www.jstor.org/stable/4121376.

Ellis, Carolyne. 1995. *Final Negotiations: A Story of Love, Loss, and Chronic Illness.* Philadelphia, PA: Temple University Press.

Ellis, Carolyn. 2001. "With Mother/With Child. A True Story". *Qualitative Inquiry*, 598–616.

Ellis, Carolyn, Tony E. Adams, and Arthur P. Bochner. 2010. "Autoethnography: An Overview." *Forum Qualitative Sozialforschung/Forum: Qualitative Social Research*, 12(1). http://nbn-resolving.de/urn:nbn:de:0114-fqs1101108.

Ellis, Carolyne and Jerry Rawicky. 2020. "A Researcher and Survivor of the Holocaust Connect and Make Meaning during the COVID-19 Pandemic." *Journal of Loss and Trauma. International Perspectives on Stress & Coping*, 25(8), 605–22.

Garfinkel, Harold. 1956. "Conditions of Successful Degradation Ceremonies." *American Journal of Sociology*, 61(5), 420–424.

Giza, Anna. 1991. *Życie jako opowieść: analiza materiałów autobiograficznych w perspektywie socjologii wiedzy.* (*Life as a Story: Analysis of Autobiographical Materials in the Perspective of the Sociology of Knowledge*) Wrocław: Ossolineum.

Goffman, Alice. 2014. *On the Run: Fugitive Life in an American City*. Chicago: University of Chicago Press.

Grant Alec. 2018. Drinking to Relax: An autoethnography of a highland family viewed through a New Materialist lens. In A. Sparkes. (Ed). *Auto/Biography Yearbook 2017*. pp 33–46. Nottingham: Russell Press.

Grant, Alec, and Susan Young. 2022. "Troubling Tolichism in Several Voices: Resisting Epistemic Violence in Creative Analytical and Critical Autoethnographic Practice." *Journal of Autoethnography* 3, 1, 103–117. https://doi.org/10.1525/joae.2022.3.1.103.

Grant, Alec. 2023. *Writing Philosophical Autoethnography*. New York: Routledge. https://doi.org/10.4324/9781032229126.

Gunderson, Ryen. 2017. "Sympathetic Introspection as Method and Practice: Cooley's Contributions to Critical Qualitative Inquiry and the Theory of Mind Debate". *Journal for Theory and Social Behaviour*, 47, 463–480.

Hałas, Elżbieta. 1987. *Społeczny kontekst znaczeń w teorii symbolicznego interakcjonizmu*. (*Social context of meanings in the theory of symbolic interactionism*) Lublin: Redakcja Wydawnictw Katolickiego Uniwersytetu Lubelskiego.

Hycner, Richard K. 1985. "Some Guidelines for the Phenomenological Analysis of Interview Data". *Human Studies*, 8(3), 279–303.

Janesick, Valerie J. 2015. *Contemplative Qualitative Inquiry: Practicing the Zen of Research*. Walnut Creek, CA: Left Coast Press.

Kabat-Zinn, Jon. 1994. *Wherever You Go, There You Are*. New York: Hyperion.

Kabat-Zinn, Jon. 2005. *Coming to Our Senses: Healing Ourselves and the World Through Mindfulness*. London: Piatkus.

Kacperczyk, Anna. 2014. "Autoetnografia – technika, metoda, nowy paradygmat? O metodologicznym statusie auto etnografii" (Autoethnography – technique, method, new paradigm? On the methodological status of autoethnography). *Przegląd Socjologii Jakościowej*, 10, 32–74.

Kacperczyk, Anna. 2020. "Autoetnograficzna inicjacja", w: Autoetnograficzne zbliżenia i oddalenia. O autoetnografi i w Polsce. ("Autoethnographic initiation", in *Autoethnographic close-ups and remoteness. On autoethnography in Poland.*) M. Kafar, A. Kacperczyk. (eds.) Łódź: Wydawnictwo Uniwersytetu Łódzkiego.

Kafar, Marcin, Anna Kacperczyk. (eds.) 2020. *Autoetnograficzne zbliżenia i oddalenia. O autoetnografii w Polsce*. (*Autoethnographic close-ups and remoteness. On autoethnography in Poland.*) Łódź: Wydawnictwo Uniwersytetu Łódzkiego.

Konecki, Krzysztof T., Anna Kacperczyk. 2020. "Symbolic Interactionism in Poland. Inspirations and Development". *Qualitative Sociology Review*, 16(4), 8–34.

Konecki, Krzysztof T. 2018. *Advances in Contemplative Social Research*. Łódź: Lodz University Press / Krakow: Jagiellonian University Press.

Konecki, Krzysztof T. 2017. "Standing in Public Places: An Ethno-Zenic Experiment Aimed at Developing the Sociological Imagination and More Besides …". *Czech Sociological Review*, 6, 881–901.

Konecki, Krzysztof T. 2017. "How the University Organizational Culture Is Being Experienced? Phenomenological Studies of Experiencing the Here and Now of the Organization". *Polish Sociological Review*, 4(200), 485–504.

Konecki, Krzysztof T. 2019. "Trust in Symbolic Interactionist Research and in Phenomenological Investigation". *Polish Sociological Review*, 3(207), 271–287.

Konecki, Krzysztof T. 2021. "Experiencing the Space: Visiting Cemeteries on All Saints' Day and on Ordinary Day". *The Qualitative Report*, 26(3), 832–860.

Konecki, Krzysztof T. 2021a. "Contemplative Grounded Theory: Possibilities and Limitations", in N.K. Denzin, J. Salvo, S.-L.S. Chen, eds. *Radical Interactionism and Critiques of Contemporary Culture* (*Studies in Symbolic Interaction*), Vol. 52. Bingley: Emerald Publishing Limited, 151–186.

Konecki, Krzysztof T. 2022. *The Meaning of Contemplation for Social Qualitative Research. Applications and Examples*. London, NY: Routledge.

Konecki, Krzysztof T. 2022a. "Empathy! So What?" *Przegląd Socjologii Jakościowej*, 18(4), 194–233.

Konecki, Krzysztof T., Aleksandra Płaczek, Dagmara Tarasiuk. 2024. *Experiencing The Body in Yoga Practice. Meanings and knowledge transfer*. New York: Routledge.

Krzemiński, Ireneusz. 1986. *Symboliczny interakcjonizm i socjologia*. (*Symbolic Interactionism and Sociology*) Warszawa: Państwowe Wydawnictwo Naukowe.

Lasch, Christopher. 1979. *The Culture of Narcissism: American Life in an Age of Diminishing Expectations*. New York: WW Norton & Co.

Lutyński, Jan. 1994. *Metody badań społecznych. Wybrane zagadnienia*. (*Social Research Methods. Selected Issues.*) Łódź: Łódzkie Towarzystwo Naukowe.

Manterys, Aleksander. 2008. "Działanie i sprawczość w socjologii Schütza" (Action and Agency in Schütz's Sociology), w: A. Schütz, *O wielości światów*. Kraków: Nomos.

Mead, George H. 1934. *Mind, Self, and Society from the Standpoint of a Social Behaviorist*. University of Chicago Press: Chicago.

Mokrzycki, Edmund. 1984. *Kryzys i schizma: antyscjentystyczne tendencje w socjologii współczesnej*. (*Crisis and Schism: Anti-Scientist Tendencies in Sociology contemporary.*) edited by Edmund Mokrzycki, Vol. 1–2. Warszawa: PIW.

Moustakas, Clark. 1994. *Phenomenological Research Methods*. London: Sage.

Niedbalski, Jakub. 2016. "Dylematy etyczne i problemy metodologiczne warsztatu badacza – rozważania na przykładzie badań prowadzonych w środowisku osób z niepełnosprawnością intelektualną oraz niepełnosprawnością fizyczną". (Ethical dilemmas and methodological problems of the researcher – considerations based on the example of research conducted in the environment of people with intellectual and physical disabilities) *Studia Humanistyczne* AGH, 15(4), 37–53.

Nowak Stefan. 1965. *Studia z metodologii nauk społecznych*. (*Studies in the methodology of social sciences*) Warszawa: PWN.

Nowak Stefan. 1985/2010. *Metodologia badań społecznych.* (*Methodology of Social Research*) Warszawa: PWN.

Piotrowski, Andrzej. 1985. "Pojęcie tożsamości w tradycji interakcjonizmu symbolicznego." (The concept of identity in the tradition of symbolic interactionism.) *Kultura i Społeczeństwo*, 29(3), 53–73.

Pruit, John C., Amanda G. Pruit, Carol Rambo. 2021. "'Suck it up, Buttercup': Status Silencing and the Maintenance of Toxic Masculinity in Academia", w: N.K. Denzin, J. Salvo, S.-L.S. Chen (eds.). *Radical Interactionism and Critiques of Contemporary Culture* (*Studies in Symbolic Interaction*). Vol. 52. Bingley: Emerald Publishing Limited, 95–114.

Rambo, Ronai C. 1995. "Multiple Reflections of Child Sex Abuse. An Argument for a Layered Account". *Journal of Contemporary Ethnography*, 23, 395–426.

Richardson, Laurel. 2018. "So, Why Poetry." *Qualitative Inquiry*, 24(9), 661–663.

Rehorick, David, Valerie Bentz, eds. 2008. *Transformative Phenomenology: Changing Ourselves, Lifeworlds, and Professional Practice.* Lanham: Lexington Press.

Schütz, Alfred. 1962. "On Multiple Realities." in M. Natanson, ed., *Collected Papers.* Vol. I: *The Problem of Social Reality*. The Hague: Nijhoff.

Schütz, Alfred. 1976. "Don Quixote and the Problem of Reality." in: A. Brodersen (ed.), *Collected Papers* II. *Phaenomenologica*, vol. 15. Dordrecht: Springer.

Schütz, Alfred. 2011. *Collected Papers* V. *Phenomenology and the Social Sciences.* Dordrecht, Heidelberg, London, New York: Springer.

Schoepflin, Todd A. 2009. "On Being Degraded in Public Space. An Autoethnography." *The Qualitative Report*, 14, 361–373.

Sebald, Gerd. 2011. "Crossing the Finite Provinces of Meaning. Experience and Metaphor." *Human Studies*, 34, 341–352.

Sułek, Antoni. 2002. *Ogród metodologii socjologicznej.* (*The garden of sociological methodology*) Warszawa: Scholar.

Ślęzak, Izabela. 2015. "Emocje badacza jako 'narzędzie' analizy i interpretacji danych. Doświadczenia z badań terenowych w agencjach towarzyskich". (Researcher's emotions as a "tool" for data analysis and interpretation. Experiences from field research in escort agencies) *Rocznik Lubuski*, 41(1), 183–196.

Ślęzak, Izabela. 2018. "Praca nad zaufaniem. Etyczne, praktyczne i metodologiczne wyzwania w relacjach badacz – badani na przykładzie etnografii i agencji towarzyskich". (Working on trust. Ethical, practical, and methodological challenges in the researcher-respondents relations on the example of ethnography and escort agencies) *Przegląd Socjologii Jakościowej*, 14(1), 138–162.

Van Manen, Max. 2003. *Researching Lived Experience: Human Science for an Action Sensitive Pedagogy.* London: The Althouse Press.

Varela, Francisco J., Evan Thompson, Eleanor Rosch. 1993. *The Embodied Mind.* Cambridge, Mass.: MIT Press.

Varela, Francisco, Jonathan Shear (eds.). 2002. *The View from Within. First-Person Approaches to the Study of Consciousness.* Thorverton: Imprint Academic.

Walsh, Zack. 2016. "The Social and Political Significance of Contemplation and Its Potential for Shaping Contemplative Studies." In: *Contemplative Social Research,* V.M. Bentz, V. Giorgino, eds. Santa Barbara: Fielding University Press.

Wojciechowska, Magdalena. 2018. Doing Research on Behind-the-Scenes Phenomena: Entering the Female Escort Industry. S.W. Kleinknecht, L.-J.K. van den Scott, C. Sanders, eds. *The Craft of Qualitative Research.* Toronto: Canadian Scholars' Press.

Woroniecka, Grażyna. [1998] 2003. *Interakcja symboliczna a hermeneutyczna kategoria przed-rozumienia.* (*Symbolic interaction and hermeneutic category pre-understanding*) Warszawa: Oficyna Naukowa.

Wyka, Anna. 1993. *Badacz społeczny wobec doświadczenia.* (*Social researcher and experience*) Warszawa: Wydawnictwo IFiS PAN.

Zakrzewska-Manterys, Elżbieta. 1996. "Odteoretycznienie świata społecznego. Podstawowe pojęcia teorii ugruntowanej". (De-theoreticalisation of the social world. Basic grounded theory concepts) *Studia Socjologiczne,* 1, 5–26.

Zerubavel, Eviatar. 2015. *The Elephant in the Room. Silence and Denial in Everyday Life.* Oxford: Oxford University Press.

PART 2

Working with the Mind and Body

∵

CHAPTER 2

Phenomenological and Interactional Interpretations of Corporality and Inter-subjectivity in Hatha Yoga

1 Introduction[1]

I will present Maurice Merleau-Ponty's possible interpretation of hatha yoga practice in this paper. I try to interpret the corporeality and intersubjectivity of hatha yoga practice in light of his theory. I had a lot of self-observations while practicing hatha yoga and experienced embodied perception. The examples given in the paper are based on my experience in yoga practice and self-observations.[2] According to Merleau-Ponty, it cannot be said that access to an individual's mind is only possible for the individual himself. In body-to-body interactions, a mind–body relationship is formed not only in the situation of the individual who initiates the interaction but also with the interaction partner. The mind is formed in the interaction between the "I" and the environment, which is reminiscent of George Herbert Mead's concept. The difference is that in Merleau-Ponty's case, it is mainly the body that is involved in this interaction. Relationships with the surrounding environment are also interactions with other entities that have a body, with objects, and with inanimate nature. Interactions with others are interbodily in nature, which suggests that meanings, definitions of situations, and self-definitions are formed in interactions between at least two bodies. One could summarize the symbolic–interactionist vision of intercorporality (Mead 1934; Blumer 1969; Strauss 1969) as consciously undertaken interactions and negotiations of meanings and definitions of situations and selves.

---

1 The chapter was previously published as the paper: Konecki, K.T. 2024. "Phenomenological and Interactional Interpretations of Corporality and Intersubjectivity in Hatha Yoga", Denzin, N.K. and Chen, S.-L.S. (Ed.) *Essential Issues in Symbolic Interaction* (*Studies in Symbolic Interaction, Vol. 59*), Emerald Publishing Limited, Leeds, pp. 105–124.

2 It is based on my research experience in an investigation conducted within the framework of the project sponsored by Narodowe Centrum Nauki (NCN; National Science Center) project Opus 15, number 2018/29/B/HS6/00513: "Experiencing the body and gestures in the social world of hatha yoga. Meanings and transmission of knowledge in bodily practice" (see further paragraphs: Intercorporeality in hatha yoga practice; Transformation of the body schema; Body as subject and object). Generally, I do not present the data from this project; they are extensively presented in other publications, where the transfer of knowledge and interactions with teachers are described in detail (Konecki 2022; Konecki et al. 2023; Tarasiuk, 2023).

However, in light of Merleau-Ponty's (2005) phenomenological theory, we experience the world through the body, often prereflectively, reacting with gestures without consciously recognizing their meaning; meaning is embodied in them prereflexively before linguistic naming and reflection occur. A sad face may be a reaction to the sad face of another, and a laugh expressing joy may be a direct reaction to the laughter of an interaction partner. Similarly, we can react to signals from our own body; pain can be felt before we name it, and we can even function with it in everyday life by unconsciously shifting it to the background of our perception. It then exists in the background of our daily activities.[3]

The sensation of the taste of food being eaten occurs immediately before we name what we are feeling, and often we don't even name it or reflect on it; the body keeps the sensation to itself. The touch of another living being evokes an immediate reaction in our body; the body knows whether the touch is friendly or hostile, authentic or artificial (Konecki 2005, 2008a, 2008b). These gestures can be "implicitly purposeful" (Churchill 2022: 57). The touch of companion animals is a way of communicating with them; we do not always subject what we feel then to reflection, and the sensation of friendship, for example, appears in the body and remains there. The consequence can be the production of psychological as well as social bonds (Konecki 2008). Although the context of our body's reaction to environmental signals is essential, it is not often subject to conscious reflection in the abovementioned situations.

In this article, I will discuss the practice of yoga, in which a practitioner interacts with his/her body, the body of the yoga teacher, and with the bodies of others in the same space. We will see how one can communicate with the body and how bodily intersubjectivity arises. The theme of prereflexive response to the movements of others' bodies and interbody communication in hatha yoga practice will also be addressed, i.e. how bodies are interpreted and what meanings are ascribed to them (the body as subject and object).

•••

3 "In an effort to elude the a priori tendencies of Husserl's concept of absolute consciousness, Merleau-Ponty took the notion of gestalt as his starting point, suggesting that man receives meaning from his world in addition to giving it. Meaning is both conferred upon the world and derived from it. The origin or genesis of meaning is to be sought by uncovering, as it were, the vertically constituted world – the world as experientially derived meaning. Meaning is not simply the product of a transcendental consciousness that maintains a distance between itself and its world of intended objects; it is a product of our experience, an experience that is prior to the idealistic dichotomization of subject and object" (Fontana & Van der Water 1977: 122; see also Moustakas 1994; Van Manen 2015).

According to Merleau-Ponty, it is possible to return to things in themselves through the body and the description of experience and, thus, what precedes our reflective knowledge:

> To return to things themselves is to return to that world which precedes knowledge, of which knowledge always speaks, and in relation to which every scientific schematization is an abstract and derivative sign-language, as is geography in relation to the country-side in which we have learnt beforehand what a forest, a prairie or a river is. (Merleau-Ponty 2005, pp. IX–X)

We do not consider causal explanations; we are interested in what is revealed to us, what "haunts" us, as it were, without psychological or scientific classification. Our primary relationship with the world is bodily and preconscious. We prereflectively know the world and others through bodily relations with them. Therefore, one can say after Merleau-Ponty, "We do not know what we see" (Van Manen 2016: 128). The perception of the world is prereflective; it has the character of the actual existence of us in the world, presence through the body thrown into the world, into the situation of the here and now. Thus, I can say that "I was already here before I thought of it." The distinction between the body and the outside world and the division of mind and body disappear (Morley 2001). Even though our speech has an embodied character, language and words are gestures. "The word is the body of thought" (Van Manen 2016: 129). Thought is the other side of the word. Things also speak to us, language is the expression of the meanings they convey to us, and this is especially true of the "pathic," or vocative, poetic, emotional language that is often expressed by artists in art (Van Manen 2016: 130).

2 I Practice Hatha Yoga in Yoga Session: Self-Report with Contemplative Reflection

I watch the yoga teacher, look at him, listen to his instructions, and repeat his movements; out of the corner of my eye, I watch others practicing beside me. I imitate the teacher, but sometimes I don't because I know what he will do in a moment, what the next move or position should be. My body knows I don't have time to reflect; I do what I should and can do. But he is there, and I, a professor of sociology at the University of Lodz, am his student. He is there himself, spatially isolated, showing me what to do. He has power over me, he is the teacher, and I am the student. I follow him.

I perform the bridge pose. Suddenly, I see him approaching me; he wants to correct something in my body positioning; I don't like it; I know well that my body knows what it can do and how it can perform the position! The body was frightened.

What does he want from me? He is a Hindu and probably doesn't understand our culture. Or I don't know who I am? Why is he going to teach me? He probably wants to show control of the situation here and now. How will it look to him that I can't and don't know how to? I have done so much to present myself well and what? And nothing?

I must abandon these assumptions; here, only the body works; I must concentrate; the rest are illusions, and I must reduce them. Only the body, mine and his. Oh, HE touches, corrects, grabs my hips, pulls my body up, and supports me momentarily! Shoulders straighten, a little pain, dizziness.

But in the end, I am grateful to him. He was right; I no longer feel discomfort in the position. I feel that I am fully here and now with him. My body and his body needed to merge momentarily; otherwise, how could I be here with him?

Thrown into the boundlessness of being, wanting to understand Other, I observed my own body and his during the practice and felt the space between our bodies; when we were close, we were close; when we were far, we were far away. Distance is measured with our bodies, but also with glances, hand gestures, gestures of greeting, or threatening. When body movements occurred, the length was measured by the meaning of those gestures. You are distant or close to me, hostile or friendly. You are watching me; you are curious. But I realized that later, not while those intermovements were happening.

I feel his body as it appears in my space. He is here, and I am here; we are together, and our relationship is narrowed down to a possible commonality. I am not fully aware of it; but he is, and I am here; it is evident we are together. Why wonder about motives? The intentionality of consciousness? What if I am unaware of his gestures but feel them repeating mechanically?

I am standing in the mountain position (*tadasana*). I concentrate on my feet, the hard floor, and the mat sticking precisely to it; out of the corner of my eye, I see that he (Other) next to me is wobbling; I am also swaying, and I can feel it. We are rocking, both of us. And at the same time, we regain our balance, here and now. I close my eyes, but he is next to me. Is he wobbling? I can't see. I'm rocking, so he's probably swaying, too; I don't need to know; I can feel it.

The muscles of my body drape over my bones, my muscles tense, and I feel the fascias even though I shouldn't feel them. And he probably feels them too; here, we are together in our bodies, not identical, but shared, in the same space. His feet and my feet touch the same surface, the same gravity, the same smell around and in him, and in me, the same light, the same touch of my own body, the same sounds, and the same breaths. We are together in this mood of unification and sameness of movement, smell and light, and the vastness of this space. It is my body that is in this all-encompassing mood.

Standing on my forearms (*salamba sirsasana*), I feel pain in my shoulders; he is standing next to me, but I don't know if he feels this pain, the same as I feel. There is a definite possibility that he feels identical; there is a potency of feeling identical pain. I sympathize with him if he is in pain, just as I sympathize with myself.

Muscles, bones, and tendons are similar, although they have a different history. We developed our bodies differently. We have different habits, limitations, and bodily habitus; hatha yoga enables us to recognize these barriers. I can recognize the world through my body and he through his, we recognize together through our bodies in the same space, together we identify ourselves, but at the same time, we recognize Other – a common perspective on the world, the same movement, the same position, and the same being. We stand on our forearms, legs up, head down, legs wobbling. I tense my thigh muscles, try to maintain balance, and not move. I sense stability and immobility of the inverted world. I cannot fall to the side because HIS space is there; I cannot violate it; my mat is my home; I can move and respect the home of another. My movement and my stability should express respect for Others.

He leaves the position, but I persist. Something makes us different; I exit the position identically after a while, and something connects us.

We both touch our foreheads to the mats. The touch with our foreheads is relaxing; there is satisfaction and the smell of mats and sweat. Silence all around. I do not observe others; I immerse myself in my self, and others do not observe me. I know they are next to me. I know what they are doing without looking. I know, they knows-we-know – a commonality, shared by a common space, connecting space and the bodies in it. There are bodies and something between them. What is it?

3 Interpretation

3.1 *There Is No Body without Space and No Space without a Body*

According to Merleau-Ponty, it cannot be said that access to an individual's mind is only possible for the individual himself. In body-to-body interactions, a mind–body relationship is formed not only in the situation of the individual initiating the interaction but also with the interaction partner. The mind is formed, as it were, in the interaction between the "I" and the environment, which is reminiscent of George Herbert Mead's concept, except that in

Merleau-Ponty's case; it is mainly the body that is involved in this interaction rather than the mind being separated explicitly from the body. Relationships with the surrounding environment are also interactions with other entities that have a body and with objects and inanimate nature. Interactions with others are interbody, suggesting that meanings, definitions of situations, and self-definitions are formed in interactions between at least two bodies.

By perceiving other bodies, we connect with them. They are part of our existential situation; we are no longer the same people we were alone seeing another person. Whatever the other does, and I see it, feel it, experience it here and now, in the same space; it affects the practitioner as in the session of yoga described in the example above.[4] And vice versa. We become a pair.[5] We can perceive the other's intentions prereflectively as soon as the gesture of the other appears. It is not necessary to cognitively adopt the other's perspective (reciprocity of perspectives); here, something happens beforehand that ensures mutual matching of actions in the interaction.[6]

Of course, reflection and categorization may come later. But the intention is shared intersubjectively earlier, such as when yawning or pretending to bite a child's finger, as in the example given by Merleau-Ponty. For Merleau-Ponty, intercorporeality is "carnal intersubjectivity" (Tanaka 2014: 268). Intersubjectivity here is understood as a communicative connection between two-minded bodies, not just minds. Understanding another is done through interaction related to one's actions and the actions of another. "Our basic ability to understand others is perceptual, sensorimotor, and nonconceptual" (Tanaka 2014: 269). To know the world is to act in the world:

4 "… the space experienced through the intermediary of my body is space 'lived through' (*éspace vécu*, as Merleau-Ponty calls it); that is, it is the open field of my possible locomotions" (Schütz 2011: 194).

5 "… the observations do not constitute the perception. A baby of 15 months opens its mouth if I playfully take one of its fingers between my teeth and pretend to bite it. And yet it has scarcely looked at its face in a glass, and its teeth are not in any case like mine. The fact is that its own mouth and teeth, as it feels them from the inside, are immediately, for it, an apparatus to bite with, and my jaw, as the baby sees it from the outside, is immediately, for it, capable of the same intentions. 'Biting' has immediately, for it, an intersubjective significance. It perceives its intentions in its body, and my body with its own, and thereby my intentions in its own body" (Merleau-Ponty 2005: 410).

6 Alfred Schütz assumed such a version of cognitive intersubjectivity: "In the first place, by the reciprocity of perspectives, one assumes that the other person and oneself see things with the same typicality and that differences in relevances are irrelevant for the purposes at hand" (Barber 2002:419). Schütz assumes collaboration in a common understanding of the situational aspects of the interaction. It is a clean type of reciprocity without any contextual disturbances.

"To perceive is first and foremost to act – perception is a reflection of the body's possible actions toward objects, and objects are the poles of this action" (Maciejczak 2001: 17).

Intercorporeality has two basic properties: behavior matching and interaction synchrony. Intercorporeality can be understood as behavior matching. We can observe this as early as infancy; hearing others cry, an infant usually starts crying itself. Another example is the imitation of facial expressions noticed in interaction partners, such as a grimace of pain or a smile. We can notice it in yoga practice when I see a grimace or smile on the face of Other (e.g., a teacher). I smile and feel the smile, not reflecting on it. ("I feel his body as it appears in my space").[7] Even if we don't mimic someone else exactly, there is the potency of matching our gestures to those of another (potential behavior matching, Tanaka 2014: 269–270). This is not emotional contagion because contagion implies a one-sided relationship, whereas what happens in behavior matching is about mutual adjustments and merging into a "we" relationship. This property of an inter-relationship is precisely the basis for the emergence of empathy.

Intercorporeality is also about interactional synchronicity. If someone is speaking quietly, I lean toward him to hear him better or try to focus on his mouth to reconstruct better-spoken words. If someone babbles, I also try to respond quickly. An infant also adapts its body movements to the speed of the caregiver speaking (Tanaka 2014: 273). In hatha yoga, we try to perform all actions at one pace. We are self-adjusting our rate to that of others, as it were ("I see that he (Other) next to me is wobbling; I am also swaying, and I can feel it. We are rocking, both of us.") Communication thus appears as an interaction between two or more bodies rather than two or more Cartesian minds. Minds are not private and hidden from interaction partners; they are available intersubjectively precisely in interbody interactions. Here we have a resonance between bodies; of course, this only happens when we are open enough to another person and, at the same time, closed enough to be ourselves constantly and distinct from another (Rosa 2020: 162).

Rhythmic synchronization in the form of behavior is especially possible in dance or an orchestra playing music but also in the practice of hatha yoga. The interaction of bodies can be synchronized but also transformative. Interaction is a distinct dimension in which we transform ourselves as a result of receiving specific signals from the other body and continuously responding to those signals (as to the signals from the master, see paragraph "I practice hatha yoga

7 Quotations in the bracket are the excerpt from my self-report presented earlier in the paper.

in yoga session. Self-report with contemplative reflection."). In hatha yoga, we transform ourselves by being with others in a given position; those others can be our predecessors, contemporaries, or future (imagined) interaction partners. Predecessors are all masters and their disciples who performed yoga postures similarly in the past; I unite with them as I do with contemporary practice partners in the here and now. In the future, there will be others who will perform yoga postures as I do it now. This property of intercorporeality is the basis for the emergence of a certain mood in a given interaction. Meetings with other interaction partners occur in a specific and often familiar environment. For example, when meeting others in the Yoga Practice Room, I associate this space with stretching the body, concentrating on performing certain postures and specific body movements, and ultimately relaxing the body and mind. A mood of calmness appears in this space. When I enter the room, I activate a specific body pattern. The space resonates with my body and mind ("The touch with our foreheads is relaxing; there is satisfaction and the smell of mats and sweat. Silence all around."). My mood of haste and practical matters from the lifeworld changes to slow and impractical physical actions, movements leading to the performance of hatha yoga postures. The mood changes are always connected with the feelings of the body, and the "body schema" matters: "[Body] schema is a system of sensory-motor capacities that function without awareness or the necessity of perceptual monitoring" (Gallagher 2005: 24; quoted in Tanaka 2018: 224). The body schema adapts itself to space and objects. Still, it has the same possibilities of modification depending on the environment, so the transformation comes together with the feelings and emotions, which also can change. The perception comes from body schema: "It also adjusts the whole bodily action in correspondence to the ongoing environmental changes (which implies that the body schema is also operating as a perceptual system). And thus, as a body-as-subject, "I" appears in the world with the mode of "I can" before "I think"" (Tanaka 2018a: 224).

In yoga exercises, my mat determines my movement space, I interact with it, and I do not go beyond the mat. The pattern of my body is such that to keep my balance, I can grab onto objects next to me, jump on one foot outside of my space (in this case, the mat), and stay standing. However, my "mat space" does not allow this; I have to manage inside this rectangle; I cannot violate this space because I can also enter the other's space. His mat space is not for me; his body is there; it fills his rectangle; it is not MY space. ("I cannot fall to the side because HIS space is there; I cannot violate it; my mat is my home.") My body pattern changes; I can do many movements and maintain stability in a small space. I do not have to prop myself up and appropriate the space of Other.

Interactions have an embodied character; we infer intentions from gestures. This happens even in interactions with animals. If my cat is looking in a specific direction and looks back at me, I notice it and will follow that direction. The movement of her body (head) indicates to me what to do. I often do this outside of consciousness. I know that I should go in the direction she suggests. She moves forward because she sees that I see what she is doing. We synchronize our movements and ultimately match our actions. Our intentions, based on intercorporeal interaction, become mutual. After a brief stroking ritual, the cat leads me to the bowl and gets food from me. The interactional context, the elements that were recognized in the distant past, delineates, together with our matching movements, the meanings of our actions. We understand the actions of others through our sensorimotority in a nonconceptual way, and thus mainly through the body rather than the mind.

The interaction between the two bodies becomes a separate entity. It becomes autonomous from the outside world and has unique characteristics. The goal is achieved by adjusting the body's movements. Intentionality arises between (in-between) bodies (Tanaka 2017: 342). In between bodies, the self is also formed. Tanaka cites Kimura (see also Tanaka 2018b: 277), who emphasizes the reality of the "in-between" (Japanese *aida*), which is not distance in the metric sense, but a space of interaction and adjustment between at least two people. This is the case in an orchestra, where there is a specific space between the playing of one musician and another and, further, the other musicians. Anticipation of the following sounds is created. There is an adjustment of body movements, both of the musicians and the audience (Tanaka 2017: 334–335). This space gains a certain autonomy; the subjectivity of one musician enters the realm of intersubjectivity. Eventually, a particular mood is created, and the individual self emerges in this ontological space. In the practice of yoga, knowing the sequence of movements in a particular pose or series of postures, like in the sun salutation, for example, I anticipate what the practice leader or my neighbor will do; I know what will happen to all of us, and he/she/they also know this and move as we all do.

However, the autonomy of this space of specific activities has rules. Certain behaviors are more expected and acceptable, considered natural to facilitate interactions, while others are the opposite (Tanaka 2017: 348). A painful corrective touch on the instructor's part in hatha yoga practice is not acceptable, while a gentle but explicit touch is accepted. An aching body is unlikely to be taken in yoga practice. Rules develop according to what we bring and agree on during practice, and agreements occur mainly in the interaction between bodies, e.g. corrective touching of another body, and the practitioner's reaction is precisely the interbody interaction regulated by norms.

3.2 *Intercorporeality in Hatha Yoga Practice*

Intercorporeality occurs in hatha yoga, based on bodywork and working with the body in an interactional context. We have already partially mentioned this in the previous paragraph. Practitioners' bodies match each other in movement, achieving a specific position (behavior matching). More specifically, interpersonal matching would refer to imitating and matching the body movements of a practitioner's subject to the body movements of Other, in this case, the hatha yoga instructor and other practitioners, and matching between practitioners.

On the other hand, synchronization, the second aspect of intercorporeality, would involve adjusting the practitioner's rate of executing positions after receiving instruction, verbal or bodily, from the yoga teacher. Anselm Strauss' term for matching ("articulation") could be used here (Strauss, 1988). Interactional sociological theory can also be helpful. We adjust our actions and schedules by arranging to go to a restaurant for dinner, scheduling business meetings with others, or arranging a date. But aligning ourselves with others also involves micro phenomena, such as coordinating our body movements with those of another. In hatha yoga, we coordinate the moves even when not looking at the teacher and close practitioners; we feel their pace of movement.

In the transmission of knowledge in the practice of yoga, we are not dealing with passive imitation of body movements (although the element of imitation exists). Instead, as the interaction develops, the practitioner adapts to the movements of the teacher's body, as well as the image of the yoga postures to be achieved, so performing movements similar to those presented by the interaction partner, in this case, mainly the hatha yoga instructor. The instructor often stops his movements while watching others to show his movements exactly, which are the model to follow at that moment. This momentary stop and the students' gaze directed at the teacher's body is that space in which intersubjectivity and understanding between bodies are created. Stopping in motion is a moment in the movement of the body. The student becomes aware of his limitations and the possibilities in his body by being in front of the teacher's body. Thus, his "I" can stand out; the student can be himself and be a student in this situation. However, without the teacher and other practitioners, this could not happen. Our subjective self is formed through the interdependence of being (in yoga practice) with others (Tanaka 2018b: 280). Focusing on the same object, the position (its shape) of hatha yoga allows us to be with others at the exact moment ("We are together in this mood of unification and sameness of movement, smell and light, and the vastness of this space.") And this happens regardless of the cultural conditioning of individual practitioners. The essence of forming the self in bodily interactions is universal.

In the practice of hatha yoga in pairs, it is essential to adjust the bodies of the two people (behavior matching; see Figure 2.1 from the mentioned research project, see footnote 1). The photo shows an example of performing a Warrior II pose. It is a matter of matching each other's arm and leg positions to look the same according to the teacher's instruction and how he demonstrates movements and positions. So, we have the matching of the teacher's body position and each other's body positions as a pair. In Figure 2.1, the left arms are synchronized perfectly, with no adjustment to the right arms. But there is such potency. The yoga teacher will make sure the alignment happens. The feet are aligned. We also see similar facial expressions; the couple smiles without seeing each other. All this is done gradually, with slight movement adjustments by both people when each person responds to the partner's movement so that both people are aligned with each other (articulation). The space between the partners is filled with intersubjective intention to articulate the body's position with body movements. In this space, the intersubjective agreement is created; there is mutual observation out of the corner of the eye and feeling the movements of the other (if we can't see the person). The final adjustment of the position evokes joy; what we can call positive emotional energy is created, derived from engaging in a given interaction ritual (Collins 2004).[8]

The performance of postures is just such a microritual within the broader pattern of hatha yoga practice sessions. In the session, the practitioners' body movements and postures are aligned and performed simultaneously and in the same space; the movements are repetitive, and sometimes the practice outwardly resembles a slow group ballet dance. From the faces in Figure 2.1, one can see that a joyful body appears; joy is visible in the body and is expressed with the body. It is the objectified body at the moment it is presented to

8 The practice of hatha yoga becomes a resonant sphere, as it were (in the sense of Hartmut Rosa 2020: 171), both horizontally (resonating with the yoga teacher and the values he presents) and vertically, when we resonate with our practice partner(s) in our exchange of gestures. And this is where the recharging of emotional energy takes place. Practicing hatha yoga during a retreat can be considered a "pure resonant oasis." According to Rosa, in this oasis there is a lack of self-effectiveness; there is a calming down, and there is no stirring that can lead to the transformation of the individual. However, one can't fully agree with this. Resonance oases can prepare someone for action; meditation retreat centers are precisely the place to transform the individual, which is the basis for transformative action in resonance with others outside these centers. It is not that these oases close down and isolate individuals from the world forever. The situation is similar to reading books, when I immerse myself in reading and am isolated from the lifeworld. However, after a while, I return to the reality of everyday life, not the one I was reading about, but the practical one, and I am still under the influence of the book I immersed myself in. I may already see the world differently, thanks to reading this book.

FIGURE 2.1 Matching positions (behavior matching) in hatha yoga practice in pairs, Warrior II Position
SOURCE: PHOTO BY THE AUTHOR

another body; the Other sees it, and the subject no longer influences how he or she perceives it. So, the body presented to others in the interaction, here to the photographer (the interaction with the camera and the photographer), is also relevant to the final interpretation of what intentions the body expresses (showing joy). I (the photographer) am the one who interprets them that way. My concentrated gazing and disciplined fascination (Churchill 2022: 54–55) allow me to arrive at the meanings contained in the movements, especially since I can empathize as an eyewitness to the event and as a yoga practitioner who can empathize with the position being performed. In Figure 2.2, we see body matching and concentrated faces – the students follow the teacher's instructions. They try to imitate his moves and the pose, and "concentrate on one point in front of them," which they can choose according to the instruction. The female student at the front of the group wants to check if she is matching the pose correctly; we see it from her glances. Generally, the bodies are still and focused; the eyes, faces, and poses show that, and then we can feel it.

FIGURE 2.2 Body matching
SOURCE: PHOTO BY KAMIL GLOWACKI

3.3 *Transformation of the Body Schema*

In hatha yoga, we experience body resistance when performing specific postures. This is especially the case at the beginning of the practice; sometimes, resistance to certain positions is due to the body schema developed during various life events. For example, this schema can refer to situations that we describe verbally, but their essence is contained in body movement habits. Here are descriptions of these habits: one does not stand on one's head, one stands on one's feet; bending the body backward is harmful, it can damage the spine, one cannot bend backward so much; one cannot stand still, one must act and move, the body is never stationary. These patterns are embodied, which is about perceiving the body as an entity that "can't" do something although we also have the perception of "I can" do it.

Body schema is a holistic and unconscious predisposition to perform particular movements and body positions in a specific physical space and environment: "Body schema is a system of sensory-motor capacities that function without awareness or the necessity of perceptual monitoring" (Gallagher 2005, p. 24; quoted in Tanaka 2018a: 224). "The body schema is also operating as a perceptual system. And thus, as a body-as-subject, 'I' appears in the world with the mode of 'I can' before 'I think'" (Tanaka 2018, p. 224). The body schema is subject to change. Additionally, it takes place in the prereflective mode, when we acquire certain habits:

> Since the body schema is a certain system open to the world, a correlate of the world, the acquisition of habits must be understood as its expansion, filling and concretization. The body schema is the scaffolding on which mastery, the world's inhabitation, is supported. The body's acquired knowledge of the world and itself, made possible by the body schema

> providing the general structures of all possible experiences, continuously expand it. This knowledge is available only through the body's efforts and cannot be reached through intellectual reflection. (Maciejczak, 2001, pp. 46–47)

Performing inverted postures, for example, is not usually part of the body schema for beginners in hatha yoga. In this case, the individual may feel resistance to performing specific movements and inverted postures when the head is down and the legs are up (See Figure 2.3). The body schema can explain a lot regarding so-called obstacles in the practice of hatha yoga. These obstacles mainly appear in beginner practitioners. However, it is not just resistance inherent in the mind that causes an individual not to want to perform specific postures; it is also the lack of a particular body schema to enable them to be performed that causes this resistance. Overcoming it involves transforming the body schema for different movements and positions. The lived body interacting with the physical body converts the physical body and brings out particular abilities that exist in the body to perform new movements. The lived-body experience changes as the body adjusts to being able to do something it didn't do before. Its range of motion expands.

FIGURE 2.3 Standing on the forearms (*salamba sirsasana*). An inverted position is not usually part of our body scheme
SOURCE: PHOTO BY KAMIL GLOWACKI

FIGURE 2.4
Mountain pose (*tadasana*). Standing still allows one to feel muscles and fascias and to notice the balance of the body and connect with the physical ground, interacting with the mat and the hardness and surface of the mat base
SOURCE: PHOTO BY KAMIL GLOWACKI

A similar transformation of the body schema can be accomplished by becoming aware of your feet touching the mat in a standing position, such as the mountain position (*tadasana*, see Figure 2.4). This may happen when the instructor says, "feel your feet, feel the touch of your skin to the mat, feel the connection to the floor, then the connection to the earth, then feel the connection to the whole world." The foot touching the mat allows me to connect with a physical object through the touch of the skin and the feeling of resistance in the toes; I feel the physical object, the mat, and the hard floor or ground beneath it. The mat is warm or cool, rough or smooth. It speaks to me. Then I feel that touch on my skin as I become aware of that place and what is happening there. This touch is inside me; I am the one who feels it and singles myself out as the subject of this touch. There is, after all, some space between my body and the mat; the mat is not me, I am not the mat, but I am not quite sure about that. And at the same time, I am connected to the materiality of this world. My body schema has been transformed; in this context, I feel my body wider outside, but my inside feeling of this connection is widened. I become "bigger" and "deeper." I reach farther because the body's sensations changed, followed only later by the reflective mind ("The muscles of my body drape over my bones, my muscles tense, and I feel the fascias even though I shouldn't feel them.")

Moreover, standing still, I can feel my body wobbling. I am standing still, stable, and struggling to maintain my balance. Paradox. I can feel this by concentrating on my feet and the ground of my feet. I feel the body wobble, and, therefore, some of my micromovement during the stability of the whole body. The body's schema of "moving-not-moving relationships" changes. The micromovement of my entire body provides the immobility of the standing position. Later, there is a reflection on what it means to be immobile. What does immobility mean in general? Reflective "I" is based on the pre-reflective movement of the body.

3.4 *The Body as Subject and Object*

There are interactional situations in which the body passes interchangeably from the subject role to the object role and vice versa; this happens, for example, in an erotic encounter. "The erotic experience is one that most poignantly reveals to human beings their ambiguous condition; they experience it as flesh and spirit, as the other and subject" (De Beauvoir 2010: 416). This interchangeability shows the referentiality of the body's roles and the ambivalence of subjectivity and objectivity. Moreover, we can gain acceptance for our own body and the body of the Other; this frees us from external definitions of roles, norms, and limitations. In such an encounter, "freedom" haunts us.

My body in yoga practice also appears interchangeably as subject and object (Tanaka 2018a; Tarasiuk 2023). There is a constant dynamic of subject–object interchangeability here. Ambivalence emerges. I feel it when, as the subject, I want to perform a difficult hatha yoga pose, and I can't do it. I want to, and by that, my body strives to perform the position, so the body appears here as an object. But on the other hand, the resisting body is a subject. I (the subject) act toward it (the object); I want to force it to perform the yoga position, but at a certain point, the subject does not express this desire:

> I entered the pose very quickly, and nothing distracted me. I was thinking only about my body, not about what others think about me. I followed the teacher's voice. My body obeyed me until I performed the side plank pose – *Vasisthasana*. When I leaned on my right hand, I kept my balance and wondered when others had a problem with it (then, for the first time, my attention was distracted, and despite focusing on the position, I watched what was happening around me). When we changed arm

> to the left and started to perform this position, I was terrified ... The left arm swayed in all possible directions. It behaved like a piece of rubber or a thin stick that bent under the influence of weight and could break at any moment. It did not cause me physical pain but fear. I didn't know what was happening because I had no control over it – my left hand was a foreign body. I felt angry with it; I wanted to tame my hand somehow, so I stopped the position and tried to do it again. However, the efforts did not bring results, and the "bending of the hand to all sides" continued. I found that it did not make sense, and I stopped trying again. I was surprised and scared. (self-report, woman exerciser, research collaborator)

In the description, we have an example of alternating perspectives of the body as subject and object. "My body obeyed me," i.e. it was an object, an obedient executor of the practitioner's commands although not precisely a practitioner because "I followed the teacher's voice," i.e. the teacher's voice materialized in her body and her movements. In addition, the practitioner observes others to see if other bodies have the same problem performing the pose. At a certain point, the body takes control of the mind; when it is not able to perform the pose, it gives a signal by rocking to all sides, fear appears, a feeling of lack of control; the body is Other, not me. "I" cannot handle it; eventually, "I" gives up. It has decided that I will not perform the pose at this moment. I feel the body's subjectivity, and "I" is its object, feeling surprised and fearful.

It can sometimes happen that the body directs our attention; when the body feels discomfort, our attention goes automatically there. To these points, the mind wants to check what is happening there. But the body decides about the work of the mind at that moment: "Please come to me, to this point, I feel discomfort here." We can paraphrase the signals from the body:

> In positions that did not involve discomfort, I directed my attention to the stretched body element – arms, legs, etc. Positions involving discomfort (e.g., those that demand significant effort, such as planks and later *chaturanga dandasana*, i.e., going down with hands on the mat and remaining horizontal 5 cm above the ground) absorbed my attention. They did it because of this discomfort. (man, exerciser, research participant)
>
> During the practice, I had a lot of control over my breathing, and I consciously used it to perform the postures better and hold them longer. Especially in the warrior sequence, I was always breathing deeply and thinking about my breath. The breath absorbed me so much that I could not think about anything else; I focused, and nothing distracted me.

> The greater the fatigue, the greater the focus. I was in a trance; I reacted instinctively to commands; I felt just like a warrior. (woman, exerciser, research collaborator)

In yoga, we experience intersubjectivity when, among other things, the teacher touches our body. Generally, I AM the owner of my body and the subject who can act. However, at the moment of the touch of the Other, I am only the owner of my own body, which can read the intention of the Other. But "I" does not know the intentions of the Other and cannot recognize them mentally. Touch can be interpreted as purely technical and instructional, but it can also be taken as an intrusion into my privacy and corporeality; it can threaten my integrity, the integrity of my body, and my self. The body as an object is vulnerable. One can even unconsciously violate its integrity and cross the privacy barrier. But the body knows what touch means before I give it an interpretation. Interpretations can change, just as touch can be perceived differently by the body, and the body can initially react differently to this touch. It reacts internally beforehand to what reaches it from the outside, for example, through explanations from the teacher. This is why yoga teachers prepare the recipient for possible touch; they pay a lot of attention to what they want their touch to look like or how it will be received. Before they touch, they ask permission to do it. Here they take up the perspective of another (interchangeability of viewpoints, Schütz 1970, 1972). One can differentiate how a touch is received due to body patterns shaped in the individual's past biography (memory is in the body, Samudra 2008). They can even be culturally shaped. For a traditional yoga teacher using the original Hindu school and practice, touch poses no problem. Touching seems normalized and natural, with no motives other than technically improving a pose or maximizing body stretch.

In contrast, a Western practitioner tends to have a body schema in which the boundaries of the body are delineated, and the privacy and even the degree of the delicacy of touch are very clearly defined (see my description of the response to touch in this article). A touch that is too delicate may not fulfill the technical purpose imagined in the student (the ascribed motive of the other) and may evoke associations from a different situational context in the recipient of the touch (e.g., an erotic touch or a touch that shows power or superiority). It is also the intention of the toucher not to violate the boundary of pain, but the recipient may read this intention differently. Therefore, there may be a clash of two body schemas here, incompatible intentionalities.

3.5 *Seen through Other*

Often, hatha yoga is an opportunity for self-presentation (Tarasiuk 2023). When I wish to present myself to others in hatha yoga, I become an object to them. But by seeing/knowing (realizing) how I am perceived, I am also an object to myself because of *ME*:

> External perception and the perception of one's own body vary in conjunction because they are the two facets of one and the same act. (Merleau-Ponty 2005: 237)

My being is corporeal, as Merleau-Ponty would say (Fontana & Van De Water 1977: 126). When I concentrate on performing a position perfectly, I want the teacher to notice this, and perhaps other practitioners and the audience to accept me as a competent practitioner. A silent negotiation of my self with the help of my body takes place here. My body is the subject of persuasion and image creation, but the moment I make it the object of others' perceptions, I contribute to its objectification. The perceptions of others clash with my perceptions of their interpretations, which is the basis of my self-definition, my "I," which at this moment is in yoga practice with others and becomes "me." Without juxtaposing my ideas about my bodily potentials expressed through my body with the gaze of others, I would not be able to be myself; I would not know who I am, here and now, for myself. ("He is a Hindu and probably doesn't understand our culture. Or I don't know who I am? Why is he going to teach me? He probably wants to show control of the situation here and now. How will it look to him that I can't and don't know how to?") Am, I a competent practitioner worthy of acceptance and even admiration? Or do I still need to practice a lot to reach acceptance in the eyes of the teacher and other practitioners? Others enable me to define myself and even separate myself from my own closed and seemingly inaccessible subjectivity to others.

3.6 *Connection with My Own Body*

Even when perceiving my body as an object, I perceive it reflectively, without introspection; it is mine, although as if external ("My body knows I don't have time to reflect; I do what I should and can do.") I constantly retain a sense of agency and a feeling that I am the one acting (mineness; Tanaka 2018c: 248). The body is mine, I do not experience depersonalization, but I ignore it as an object worthy of attention. The fact that I own my body does not evoke any feelings or emotions in me. Hatha yoga allows us to return to the body when we lose the connection. We are thinking here of the practice of yoga as an experimental situation, not therapeutic or in a religious context.

The body is absent from our daily lives (Van Manen 2015: 49). This is for two reasons: Firstly, the body is a given; it gives us the possession of a so-called minimal self, that is, it is in the background, but through it, we move and carry out daily projects. We do not focus on it, but we know it is there.

We are in contact with it although this contact is not realized at every moment; even if it is, it is not the most crucial focus of our attention. Second, when dealing with practical matters, we lose contact with the body; we ignore it because we are usually in a hurry, have specific things to do, are making a career, and are running away from the here and now (Leder 1990). We ignore it even when the body signals something (pain, discomfort). We have developed a specific habitus of overlooking the body in our lives. We live mainly in the mind.[9] In addition to managing the body, we can be alienated from it by feeling foreign, false, or hostile (Rosa 2020: 202).

When we practice hatha yoga, the minimal self about feeling the body becomes the point of concentration. I am here in practice, with my body moving in a certain way and striving to perform a particular position. The body, or I, performs these movements and positions. Paying attention to other bodies is also related to the attention focused on my body. The body returns to favor; I become friends with it; it is mine because I feel it fully, in pain, stretching, limitations, pushing the limits, and achieving the unattainable a moment ago. I become aware that it is no longer an absent body with a so-called "minimal self."

4 Conclusions

According to Merleau-Ponty's philosophy, the mind of our interaction partners is not hidden and inaccessible to us. It is observable and accessible to us through the actions of the Other, and it exists "between" our body and our interaction partner. Mutual understanding in hatha yoga is made possible by this interaction of bodies and my reflexive I. This interaction is also made possible by the body giving me signs of possibilities for action and performing specific actions to others. What we could see at the beginning of the paper in my description of responses to bodily practice in hatha yoga. Therefore, we can expand the interpretation of bodily interactions by Merleau-Ponty by adding our input on the contemplation of practice that starts with the self-observations we proposed in our research. The pre-reflective reactions could be followed by post-reactive reflections that became active and still bodily interpretations of what happened just before when we had reacted spontaneously without minded aware focus on the moves of our body. We can see it thanks to the research through self-observations and self-reporting, and

9 As Rosa (2020: 93) wrote, this type of lifestyle is a consequence of "acceleration."

contemplative memos on self-reports. Our reflection can influence the future reactions of our body to the bodies of the Others, so the prereflective could also become a reflective dimension. It could also be the conscious background of changing our body schema and, at the same time, our interpretation of the events in the lifeworld, of selves and of Others. We can see it thanks to the research by self-observations and self-reporting and contemplative memos on self-reports (Konecki 2022a).[10]

The transformation of the perspective of the world is changed through changing the body schema. The hatha yoga space could become a resonance space when we react to the other and meet the other to create an authentic intersubjective space of understanding "I" and "Me" in society (Rosa 2020). Contemplating it becomes the basis of reflective transformation (Rehoric and Bentz 2008).

Intersubjectivity arises when bodies interact. Intersubjectivity in hatha yoga is possible through resonant space (Rosa 2020: 196); we respond to another body while still being ourselves because we are in contact with our body. I draw on the theoretical and sociological findings of Hartmut Rosa. He talks about the search for resonant spaces that would enable us to move away from the social idea of continuous growth and modes of dynamic stability that are filled with competition and are in a constant state of accelerating production, new technologies, and lifestyle changes, all of which lead to depression and burnout (see also Han 2015).

This resonance would allow us to avoid alienation, obtain the much-desired recognition in the eyes of others, and enter into a resonance mode with others, including the natural world. It can happen in many bodily practices, including yoga, meditation, and contemplation in walking, running, hiking, climbing, and cycling, among others. Let us add the following to Hartmut Rosa's conclusion: the categories of bodily interaction, the recognition of our pre-reflective perception of the body, reflection on the body and its use as an object for oneself and others, and being a bodily object for others when this perception does not influence us. This would allow us to be fully and consciously in the world,

10 The body schema could change by consciously concentrating on the breathing, for example:

"During the practice, I noticed that I have more strength, and the positions that require it turned out much better than last week. I tried to use as much conscious breathing as possible. As soon as my attention slipped away, some exercises became more difficult. It seemed I was already exhausting myself; I quickly returned to my breath consciousness and tried to adjust it to the asana. As soon as I started to breathe consciously, I noticed that my body fit better, and the body was gaining a new energy supply" (woman, exerciser, research collaborator).

or instead, one should write, "to be toward the world" (Maciejczak 2001: 73), where history, language, and culture, together with the body, have a role in getting to know the world and the self and understanding others.

Bibliography

Badiou, Alain. 2001. *Ethics. An Essay on Understanding of Evil.* London, New York: Verso.

Barber, Michael. 2002. "Alfred Schutz: Reciprocity, Alterity, and Participative Citizenry". In: *Phenomenological Approaches to Moral Philosophy. Contributions to Phenomenology*, vol 47. Dordrecht: Springer. https://doi.org/10.1007/978-94-015-9924-5_21.

Bentz, Valerie M., Jeremy J. Shapiro. 1998. *Mindful Inquiry in Social Research.* London: Sage.

De Beauvoir, Simone. 2010. *The Second Sex*, C. Borde and S. Malovany-Chevallier (trans.), New York: Alfred A. Knopf. Beauvoir.

Churchill, Schott D. 2022. *Essentials of Existential Phenomenological Research.* Washington DC: American Psychological Association.

Collins, Randal. 2004. *Interaction ritual chains*, Princeton, Princeton University Press. NY.

Fontana, Andrea and Richard Van De Water. 1977. "The existential thought of Jean-Paul Sartre and Maurice Merleau-Ponty" In *Existential Sociology.* Eds. J. Douglas and J.M. Johnson. Cambridge: Cambridge University Press. (pp. 100–129).

Gallagher, Shaun. 2005. *How the body shapes the mind.* Oxford: Oxford University Press.

Heidegger, M. 1996. *Being and Time.* New York: State University of New York Press.

Krzysztof T. Konecki. 2005. The problem of symbolic interaction and of constructing self, in: *Qualitative Sociology Review*, Vol. 1(1), 68–89.

Konecki, Krzysztof T. 2008. "Touching and Gesture Exchange as an Element of Emotional Bond Construction. Application of Visual Sociology in the Research on Interaction between Humans and Animals" [93 paragraphs]. *Forum Qualitative Sozialforschung / Forum: Qualitative Social Research*, 9(3), Art. 33, http://nbn-resolving.de/urn:nbn:de:0114-fqs0803337.

Konecki, Krzysztof T. 2008. "Dotyk i wymiana gestów jako element wytwarzania więzi emocjonalnej. Zastosowania socjologii wizualnej i metodologii teorii ugruntowanej w badaniu interakcji zwierząt i ludzi." *Przegląd Socjologii Jakościowej*, Tom IV Numer 1, 71–115. (http://www.qualitativesociologyreview.org/PL/volume6_pl.php).

Konecki, Krzysztof T. 2022. *The Meaning of Contemplation for Social Qualitative Research. Applications and Examples.* London, NY: Routledge.

Konecki, Krzysztof T., Aleksandra Płaczek, Dagmara Tarasiuk. 2024. *Experiencing The Body in Yoga Practice. Meanings and knowledge transfer.* New York: Routledge.

Legrand, Dorothee. 2007. "Pre-Reflective Self-Consciousness. On Being Bodily in the World." *Janus Head*, 9(2), 493–519.

Leder, Drew. 1990. *The Absent Body*. Chicago: University of Chicago Press.

Maciejczak, Marek. 2001. *Świat według ciała w fenomenologii percepcji M. Merleau-Ponty'ego*. Warszawa: IFiS PAN.

Mead, Georg H. 1934. *Mind Self and Society from the Standpoint of a Social Behaviorist*. Charles W. Morris (ed.). Chicago: University of Chicago.

Merleau-Ponty, Maurice. 2005. *Phenomenology of Perception*. London: Routledge.

Morley, James. 2001. "Inspiration and Expiration: Yoga Practice Through Merleau-Ponty's Phenomenology of the Body", *Philosophy East & West* 51(1), 73–82.

Moustakas, Clark. 1994. *Phenomenological Research Methods*. Thousand Oaks, CA: Sage.

Rehoric, David A., and Valerie M. Bentz. 2008. *Transformative Phenomenology. Changing Ourselves, Lifeworlds, and Professional Practice*. Lanham, MD: Lexington Books.

Rosa, Hartmut. 2020. *Przyspieszenie, wyobcowanie, rezonans. Projekt krytycznej teorii późnonowoczesnej czasowości.* (*Beschleunigung und Entfremdung. Entwurf einer Kritischen Theorie spätmoderner Zeitlichkeit* – translation from German to Polish by Jakub Duraj, Jacek Kołtun) Gdańsk: Europejskie Centrum Solidarności.

Samudra, Jaida K. 2008. "Memory in our body: thick participation and the translation of kinesthetic experience." *American Ethnologist* 35(4), 665–681.

Strauss, Anselm. 1988. "The Articulation of Project Work: An Organizational Process." *The Sociological Quarterly*, 29(2), 163–178. http://www.jstor.org/stable/4121474.

Schütz, Alfred. 1972. [1932]. *The Phenomenology of the Social World*. London: Heinemann.

Schütz, Alfred. 1970. *On Phenomenology and Social Relations: Selected Writings*. (H. Wagner, Ed.). Chicago, IL: University of Chicago Press.

Schütz, Alfred. 2011. *Collected Papers* V. *Phenomenology and the Social Sciences. Edited by Lester Embree*. Dordrecht, Heidelberg, London, New York: Springer.

Strauss, Anselm L. 1997. *Mirrors and Masks. The Search for Identity*. New Brunswick, NJ: Transaction Publishers.

Strauss, Anselm. 1993. *Continual Permutations of Action*, New York: Aldine.

Tanaka, Shogo. 2014. "Creation between two minded-bodies Intercorporeality and social cognition." *Kvarter*, Vol. 09, 265–276.

Tanaka, Shogo. 2017. "Intercorporeality and aida: Developing an interaction theory of social cognition." *Theory & Psychology*, 27(3), 337–353. https://doi.org/10.1177/0959354317702543.

Tanaka, Shogo. 2018a. "Bodily Basis of the Diverse Modes of the Self." *Human Arenas* 1, 223–230. https://doi.org/10.1007/s42087-018-0030-x.

Tanaka, Shogo. 2018b. "The Self in Japanese Culture from an Embodied Perspective." In *Challenges in Cultural Psychology, Historical Legacies and Future Responsibilities*.

Edited by Gordana Jovanović, Lars, Allolio-Näcke, and Carl Ratner, London: Routledge.

Tanaka, Shogo. 2018c. "What is it Like to Be Disconnected from the Body? A Phenomenological Account of Disembodiment in Depersonalization / Derealization Disorder" *Journal of Consciousness Studies*, 25(5–6), 239–62.

Tarasiuk, Dagmara. 2023. *Ciało doświadczane i ciało doświadczające. Socjologiczna analiza praktyki hatha-jogi.* ("The experienced body and the experiencing body. A sociological analysis of hatha-yoga practice." Ph.D. Thesis) Rozprawa doktorska. Łódź: Uniwersytet Łódzki.

Van Manen, Max. 2015. *Researching Lived Experience. Human science for an Action Sensitive Pedagogy*. N.Y.: Routledge.

CHAPTER 3

Who Am I When I Am Teaching? Self in Yoga Practice

Who am I?
When I break conventions
Unexpected thoughts come to me
Body sensations are different
I am full of joy
Full of energy
Create
I am myself
Only when I don't have
The social corset that suffocates me
Binds my body
in a sadistic weave
And my heart
is filled with saliva spit out on me
with their longing feelings

A poem by the author

∵

1 Introduction

The chapter[1] can be considered a critical contribution to sociology, highlighting the diversity of social reality and the complexities of the relationships between roles and identities at the individual level (Badiou 2001). Identifying patterns that explain social order and the social conditioning of identity formation is often challenging. Numerous situational, methodological, pragmatic, and consciousness factors must be considered to adequately explicate

1 The chapter is a revised version of the published paper: Konecki, Krzysztof T. 2022. "Who Am I When I Am Teaching? Self in Yoga Practice." *The Qualitative Report*, 27(11), 2623–2658.

how and why certain events occur. Therefore, the researcher needs to perform a critical self-analysis, which can be our input to critical sociology.

First-person reports, such as self-reports, diaries, and autoethnography, show that descriptions of situations and experiences are also a creation. The objectivity of these descriptions may be the narrator's goal; however, self-analysis indicates that achieving this objectivity is entangled in many cultural, linguistic, and rhetorical meanders. There is also self-presentation of the subject (see Kubica 2002: 5–6), and the goal of self-analysis may be to work on oneself (Kubica 2002: 20, 26; Malinowski 1989). Writing can transform the writer, which is why it is vital to show this process of knowledge production from the inside. Telling a personal history of knowledge production allows you to discover what is usually hidden (Kacperczyk 2020: 73). It will enable us, at least partially, to question the habits and thinking patterns present in our previously learned scientific procedures and the basic assumptions adopted in the academic world (Szwabowski 2019; 2021).

In the following self-analysis, we will use the first-person narrative, but we will also use the third-person convention to stand by the side of our lived experience. On the one hand, it will provide a different layer of perception of one's own experiences (Rambo 1995), the first-person report. On the other hand, it will allow for third-person observation in the form of paraphrasing the analysis of what the narrator experiences. The voices of the main narrator and the author of the text will be joined by his research collaborators to show that knowledge is also produced collaboratively, even when one person's voice is present or dominant in the narrative and analysis (cf. Ellis & Rawicki 2013; Pławski, Szwabowski, Szczepaniak, & Wężniejewska 2019).

The participants of the research, discussion, and analysis learn from each other together. It is an attitude of "learning together" or "leregogy" (Rehorick, & Bentz 2017; Bentz & Marlatt 2021: 10). The student becomes the teacher; the teacher becomes the student. This often happens in a case assessed as new, chaotic, and full of contradictions (Rehorick & Taylor 1995; see also Appendix 1 and 2). The acquired knowledge is partial and situated (Denzin 2013: 355) but also "knowledge is experienced and expressed in sensuous terms ..." (Denzin 2019:454). There is consent to chaos and contradictions. We usually look for signs and patterns of social order in observed situations in social sciences. However, the order can be partial or temporary. Order, according to Denzin (2019: 455), is an ideological term that can justify the interpretative practices of science.

There are possible moments of silence and downtime (Rehorick & Bentz 2017: 27). Joint maturation is associated with hatching knowledge gradually, though sometimes eruptions and illuminations of new perceptions, reflections, hypotheses, and concepts are possible. It is vital in contemplative research to record and share thoughts (Rehorick & Bentz 2017: 33) and go beyond what is taken for granted. Writing reveals what has been experienced and can be reflexively processed, and it can lead to a transformation of views, attitudes, and/or identity (Rehorick & Bentz 2008; cf. also Pławski, Szwabowski, Szczepaniak, & Wężniejewska 2019; Rehorick & Taylor 1995). The internal review of interaction ritual chains, our meetings with teachers and significant others could be done through self-reflection (Collins 2004: 397, note 9).

This chapter examines the self-observation of sessions led by a hatha yoga instructor, revealing the transition between different identities: teacher, trainee, student, and researcher. Self-observation is a first-person presentation of my feelings about the practice and teaching of hatha yoga, and the chapter presents extended narratives from self-observation (Konecki 2018: 228–230). However, the author will also carry the self-analysis from the first-person, third-person, and impersonal perspectives. It will, in a way, be an external look at one's own experiences, although it must be remembered that this view is made by the person producing the records of lived experiences. The third-person and impersonal analysis experiment makes it possible to be detached from assumptions, e.g., the view that direct and first-person stories about situations and experiences are the only available truth about lived experiences because they come from incidents immediately described.

The attempt at self-analysis is juxtaposed with the reflection of the co-researchers of the main narrator. The analysis is carried out in the convention of contemplative sociology (Konecki 2018; 2021; Bentz & Giorgino 2016; see also Rehoric & Bentz 2008).

In this convention, researchers make self-observations and record them immediately after experiencing a particular situation. We try to be close to our past experiences. We write about the lived experiences described in the self-reports and contemplative notes (Konecki 2021), which are a paraphrase and, at the same time, elements of explication of our lived experiences (Richardson 1992).

They are also records of experiences from the moment of explaining the written auto-reports. Experiencing and communicating about them is a source of knowledge, not only empirical materials (Denzin 2013: 355). In this explication, we also look for explanations from other sources and from our colleagues, students who at this point become our teachers (cf. Rehorick & Taylor 1995).

•••

In yoga, the relationship between teacher and student is significant. They were initially called guru-siṣya (guru-disciple) relationships. The apprentice would practice with his master for an extended period. It was a direct relationship; the contact was face-to-face, and it was also an individual relationship – one master and a student who was constantly under his influence. Choosing a qualified guru was crucial for success in yoga (Mallinson & Singleton 2017). It was not advisable to have other teachers, so there was a solid and direct relationship between the student and the master. The thread of power appears here; the master somehow decided about his student's worldview, lifestyle, and relationship with the world. However, as early as the 20th century, such relationships began to disappear. Now, in the 21st century, they are sporadic: "The guru-siṣya (guru-disciple) relationship is often considered an essential aspect of imparting yogic knowledge. However, at the beginning of the 21st century, intensive teaching of yoga, one on one, from master to student, is unique" (Newcombe 2014: 147). There was intensive teaching of yoga in groups, which completely changed the relationship between teacher and student.

In the second half of the twentieth century, the institutionalization of hatha yoga appeared. A guru who usually has charisma, which was also the result of interacting with students, turned the relationships with pupils into formal training that sometimes ended with the bureaucratic approval of competencies to teach yoga. There is no individualized teaching, yoga is conducted in a group, and there is usually no continuous and prolonged contact with the teacher daily. Moreover, the practitioner is never sure if the practitioners are performing the asanas correctly (Sarbacker 2014: 292).

The guru's charisma[2] is almost mystical; the guru brightens up the darkness; *gu* is darkness, and *ru* is removing this darkness (Williamson 2014: 222). However, according to Max Weber, any charisma ultimately formalizes what Weber calls "charismatic routine," especially when a charismatic leader enters the modes of an organization or creates it himself. The institutionalization of charisma occurs then (Newcombe 2014: 148; Weber 2012: 367–373). Governance takes the form of rational power/authority, standardized by-laws, and formal regulations.

Institutionalized yoga has its benefits. It is undoubtedly safer when rules related to the health of practitioners and their safety are formalized. The emphasis on safety and avoidance of bodily injuries has been exceptionally high in Iyengar's school (Newcombe 2014: 158).

2 Charisma is understood after Weber as having unique personality traits that are the basis of achievements, and unique insight into reality, as well as an enormous influence on others, thus gaining power over them based on authority (Weber 2012: 367–373).

Secondly, there is also some formal safeguard against abusing guru practitioners. Often these relationships were very tense, and sometimes they were even violent on the part of the master (Singleton & Fraser 2014: 103, see also footnote 3 below).

It is therefore difficult to talk about the existence of a guru-disciple relationship today, especially in Western countries. The teacher is replaced by an instructor who has received the appropriate certification from some organization to teach a specific type of yoga, and these certifications replace charisma. However, the lineage is still relevant here, i.e., where these certifications come from. This change of roles, from a charismatic teacher in a direct relationship with the individual learner to an instructor, raises many questions.

Are we dealing today with a teacher or instructor of hatha yoga? Who is the instructor today during the hatha yoga sessions? Are they a practitioner or a teacher? Probably both. But which accents prevail then? When do they pass from one identity to another? Are they also a teacher imparting some aspects of traditional yoga knowledge?

How is the knowledge about yoga transmitted according to the first-person narration? How the mind of the teacher works? What role do they take on? Are they only a teacher, or maybe they also learns from his pupils? Is the knowledge that comes from the masters embodied? I would also like to show how the knowledge on yoga practice is collectively produced in the research project? I want to show it by experimenting with the first-person and third-person narration and receiving the comments from collaborators in the project. The evocative expressions of the subject are commented by the third person comments used by the subject to make the distance to the role of the teacher.

From the self-observation presented below, one can see that the identities of the instructor and the practitioner are fluid. They are social constructs connected with ordering reality, but this is from the point of view of an external observer, not a practicing hatha yoga instructor at that moment. I am describing my engagement in yoga as a practitioner-here and now-instructor. Therefore, in yoga sessions, I switch between two identities. I am never tied to one self-identification for too long.

There is also another significant identity, that of the student. The teacher also learns by teaching others. By observing practitioners' reactions, getting feedback during and after classes, she/he learns and changes the way she/he leads the pupils and her/his behavior is also meaningful here; she/he introduces new elements, becomes cautious, and learns to recognize the weaknesses of others. This third identity, being a student while learning from pupils, is at work. It is not always made aware. An analysis of my auto-reports reveals this phenomenon. It should also be emphasized that the frequently criticized subjectivity of statements and self-reflection may be an advantage of the researcher because they often reaches unspoken feelings, and the subject is a socialized unit. Writing about oneself is also writing about others (Gunnarsson 2021: 105).

Moreover, writing itself changes us; it is a transforming element (Rehorick & Bentz 2008). The record is a performance of what has been experienced; it shapes our testimony of the experience and makes it available. The notation, writing style, phraseology, and vocabulary are given, but the choice of words and writing style is individual. The experience with the record is an expression of our relationship to the world here and now. Does writing change our experiences? It changes and does not change at the same time. It is part of a holistic experience of the world. Even anticipating what will be written during self-observation is a holistic experience. Predicting what will be written, evidence of the writing, and the written report itself, if used, are parts of the process of experiencing the world.

It is also vital "who writes and for whom"? (Denzin 2019: 462). What is described below was written for the author himself and the hatha yoga practitioners to better understand what is going on in hatha yoga. It is best to understand together in the process of collective learning from your own body and your own and shared practice.

And when does an instructor become a teacher?

The teacher can also introduce spiritual threads, and then they become a kind of quasi-guru, a spiritual teacher if that is what the practitioners define it.[3] However, in general, the latter role and the identity assigned to it seem to be rarely introduced into the practice of hatha yoga (Konecki 2015). If this happens, it enters unnoticed, slides in with the help of single words, phrases, gestures, or the names of certain Sanskrit positions (e.g., the name of the asana;

3 However, the title of guru is reserved for very significant yoga teachers. Either they create some school or some yoga lineage. Usually, they are big names, and I will mention just a few: Swami Vivekananda, Shri Yogendra, Krishnamacharya, Pattabhi Jois, and B.K.S. Iyengar. These figures have had a tremendous influence on the formation of yoga practice in the modern world and they have also influenced the justifications of yoga practices in the past. However, in contemporary society, the role of the guru is changing as a result of adapting to the new cultural, social, economic, and technological conditions in which yoga is taught (Singleton & Goldberg 2014: 1–3). It comes closer to the role of an expert based on scientific evidence about the effects of yoga on the mind and body than to the guru's philosophy, i.e., traditional religious and ethical justifications (Singleton & Goldberg 2014: 6–7).

savasana that means corpse position).[4] This name can be perceived by practitioners in an aura of some mystery, heralding something extraordinary, out of the ordinary, or supernatural. But it requires this interpretation on the part of practitioners and the yoga teacher's unique personality traits and authority among the practitioners.

This interpretation occurs automatically, and it is not always consciously controlled by the instructor/teacher who transmits the knowledge that she/he once mastered and which is simply about performing asanas and naming them in a specific and long-established way. Moreover, having certain personality traits and authority, they influence the behavior and knowledge of others.

2 Self-Observations and Their Self-Analysis

In the text below, I analyzed 25 of my self-observations (Konecki 2018) from January to September 2020. To begin with, I would like to present one of the self-observations from when I conducted a yoga session and gave instructions on how to perform specific asanas.[5] It is a self-observation that includes, in my opinion, the most critical elements of my yoga practice. Then I will try to analyze what I did during these sessions. I carried out this analysis eight months after the self-observation, so I no longer remember what happened during the session; I only relied on the written text. Generally, when I look back now, without the help of the following self-observation records, past events and feelings merge into one proceeding, with no clear markers to remember more than a week, or at most, two weeks back, what happened during the yoga session.

I analyze first-person documents mainly in the first-person style of narration, sometimes impersonally, from the point of view of a third person – although it is still me (my interpretation of first-person appearances). Referring to yourself in the third person is an interesting rhetorical maneuver in many types of texts, such as in a diary. It can also be a psychotherapeutic treatment when the subject tries to distance himself by referring to the self as a stranger. In the literature on the subject, this procedure is known as illeism.[6] This treatment is also used in jñana yoga to get out of the body and look at it from an

4 The use of asana names to refer to the traditions of Hindu culture and religion was, for example, for Iyengar, a form of discursivizing his origin from the old masters/gurus of hatha yoga. This tradition was evoked precisely through the language and names, as well as the legends, stories, and myths to which they relate (Smith & White 2014: 125; De Michelis 2004: 256).

5 I am a certified instructor of physical recreation in the hatha yoga specialty.

6 https://aeon.co/ideas/why-speaking-to-yourself-in-the-third-person-makes-you-wiser [retrieved September 20, 2020].

external perspective. It is the perspective of the eternal soul (Ataman) being freed from the body. They are free and look at the lifeworld from a distance. We will use this yogic inspiration here in our yogic research project. This analysis will also try to look at ourselves from an external perspective, writing about ourselves impersonally or from an imaginary third-person perspective. It is an experiment that allows us to see direct first-person auto-reports from the point of view of the first person because they are constantly speaking; it is the same subject, but with the use of a thought experiment, i.e., imagining himself as a stranger. We omit here the esoteric aspects of this procedure, using only its epistemic advantages, i.e., the possibility of the subject distancing himself from himself and, in the same account, discussing his own experiences. In addition, it is also important not to get attached to the assumptions and the desire that first-person reports are the only truth about experiences because they come from almost immediately described first-person experiences.

3 "Self-Observation/Self-Report – Krzysztof T. Konecki – January 28, 2020; Conducting a Session

In practice, we opened the throat chakra (*Vishuddha*). I made a short introduction to the chakra, which is responsible for communication and self-expression, that the color blue is essential and affects the thyroid gland. We started in *badha konasana*, then with our arms back.

I usually think briefly about the session in advance. It is usually generally planned. But in the process, new items come to mind that match the previous one, and I turn them on. For example, they fit the opening of the chest and throat.

The three most important positions for opening the throat chakra that I have used are *halasana*, *salamba sirsasana*, and *matsyasana*. We also made a warrior directly from the rider's position – lots of a dog facing down. There was also a lot of stretching. Stretching relieves tension.

– The writing about everyday life in the third person helps in a more rational approach to life. This is the conclusion from psychological research:

"The current work showed that wisdom is not the purview of just a few fortunate individuals. Utilizing the ancient practice of distanced self-reflection, we demonstrated that referring to oneself in the third person during repeated reflections on daily events affords a more expansive self-focus, in turn facilitating wiser reasoning. The results from two field experiments suggest that training distanced self-reflection can bolster wise reasoning in everyday life" (Grossman et al. 2019: 29).

I felt a lot of choking in the candle pose. I compared it to the old days when I always felt a stranglehold, but not as much as today.

Halfway through the class, I looked at my watch, 6:35 PM (the session lasts from 5:30 PM to 7:00 PM). There is still time to do a few exercises while lying down. So, I control not only the positions of the participants but also the duration of the session. Arch position, hip extension to the sides. I have the impression that careful control of everything happening in the room is part of the instructor's job. His attention is outside, sometimes only on his own body. When I stay in a position longer, I can only turn inward for a moment.

As I read the self-reports of the project participants, these readings began to influence me as a teacher. I began to pay more attention directly to individual participants. I helped with the poses, paid attention to detail. However, I still give general instructions on asanas, and I practice with others. I also want to exercise myself, influence my own body with asanas. However, I pay attention to the exercisers, but from my place on the mat. This, of course, interferes with focusing on my own body; but still being on my mat and not moving, the positions can be done by me, and the positions of others can be corrected and controlled. I talk a lot, pay attention to details in poses. I repeat the same thing every class with the same positions. I shouldn't be talking that much. One day I have to do wordless classes without talking and without this technical chatter. But it's too early. I must teach them more.

Finally, we did savasana. I turned off the light. There was a better mood than usual with the light. I controlled the time and looked at the clock twice to finish at 7.00 PM and not exceed this time. Dagmara was leaving early, and I wanted her to end together with everyone else. There were 10 minutes of savasana in total. Time passed very quickly. During savasana, I was very agitated. I felt high blood pressure, which could be because I forgot to take my blood pressure pills in the morning. However, the stimulation could also result from the intensity of exercise and stimulating asanas. And before that, a double espresso.

I concentrated on my breathing, counting to ten. I could focus quickly, although it felt like giving myself a firm command: count and do not pay attention to anything. I felt strength and determination in my body. Not in my mind. I counted on and off. I paid attention to the stimulation of the body. I was aware of this. Body sensation: ready to act, to spring, the whole body alert, muscles prepared to contract at any moment, but mainly the sense of agitation passed into the head and the hearts. It's hard for me to describe it. One universal word comes to my mind, agitation. What is it really? Does everyone feel the same?

Finally, after completing savasana, I ask: how are we feeling? Usually the same answers: good. For one of the participants, it took a long time. Cezary was also excited; he told me so. Me too … So a community of experiences, expressed verbally and openly, though for a moment and with one person …"

4 A Note Summarizing the Main Topic of the above Session: "Concentration on Instructions and the Transfer of Technical Knowledge"

The yoga session is usually thought out. I know what I'm going to do, though not exactly; there's a bit of spontaneity to it. And if the plan is not prepared, I have my scheme in the "stock of knowledge at hand," which I usually use then. This knowledge is obvious to me, and it results from my biography as an instructor. The scheme is based on the "Sun Salutation" sequence, but it is more elaborate and accurate, and slow, with long stops in individual positions.

Even though I sometimes put into the session esoteric threads, such as the knowledge of chakras, in my self-observation of practices in which I am a teacher, I see a lot of technical descriptions: What have I done? How and what can I improve? So I am mainly an instructor, but in self-observation, I call myself a teacher. This name appeared naturally, although now analyzing my notes, I can see that I am probably only an instructor, not a teacher. However, in these moments, I am also a student because I am learning from practitioners; they make these corrections.

Esoteric and spiritual threads are not the most important things. I watch asana practitioners. I wonder what they are feeling. I infer their feelings from my feelings, but I'm not entirely sure if my intuitions are correct. There is also controlling the time of the session, primarily devoted to specific phases of the yoga session, to *pranayama* and *savasana*. In addition, I keep wondering how to improve the practice ("I shouldn't be talking so much."). I try to leave a few minutes for *savasana*, which I consider an essential element of the practice, physically and mentally closing and summing up what we have achieved during the asanas. There are few references to observing my feelings. Only when any problems arise (choking in the plow position).

Moreover, during *savasana*, I am aware of my feelings; then, I can only observe my feelings, not focus on others, although sometimes I think about what they are feeling at that moment. There is generally no time for this during the session. My thoughts are on what I do and how to do asanas concerning the individual practitioners and their possible reception of the instructions and demonstration.

An interesting observation in the above self-observation is *that one's psycho-physical state may influence the course of the session*. The instructor's intense stimulation may affect the so-called "Hard practice," in which he offers exercise and long-term asanas to be performed. Also, if the instructor does not feel well, the practice is conducted differently than usual. Here is an example of such a situation from another day:

> "Today, I was right after a massage. I decided to have a massage because my spine and lumbar region have been hurting for several days. It turned out that I still have tension in the area of the shoulder blades and a painful lumbar region. During my practice, I was tired from the massage.
>
> I did a short introduction about meditation and pranayama. I said that you have to prepare yourself technically well for exercises (aids, space, etc.), especially meditation, so as not to get distracted during the practice.
>
> So, the session was light. I did not make any twists or postures that involved tilting the spine. I informed the practitioners about the light practice. In the tutorial, I talked about being light in doing asanas, not tensing up, and doing it freely and lightly. Which I also used to do."

4.1 *I Turn On Third-Person Mode for Analysis*

If Konecki felt and remembered what he wrote above, his body must have had *intense bodily sensations*. So, it could have been his stomach ache, pain in his backbone, or some other part of his body, but they were also remembered in the context of his instruction and knowledge of the practice:

> Today, I did the forward bends again. I ate two and a half hours before my yoga session. I also drank some water before practicing. And I started my session with bending. I was pressing on my stomach, and I felt sick, just like I thought it would be ☹
>
> I also had the impression that I had made a mistake and did not do one batch of exercises on one side. But I wasn't sure; it occupied my attention for a while.
>
> I still feel my stomach full – no more eating before a session. Four hours' break minimum! (Self-report, May 12, 2020)

At the end of the session, Konecki usually asks the question, "How are you feeling?" He expects practitioners to share their impressions and reflections with him. Practitioners usually share casually, responding that they feel good, and sometimes respond more broadly, as in the first example above, when Konecki was told about the distortions in the perception of time and stimulation during the hatha yoga session.

A similar concentration of the instructor on instruction occurs in the breathing exercise, *pranayama*. The instructor is still in the role, and his mind becomes that of the instructor. Here is an example confirming this observation from Konecki's yoga session on another day:

> I did pranayama. As usual, introductory *ujjayi* followed by *viloma* with breath-hold for two times on inhalation and four times on exhalation. The following pranayama was inhaled four times and exhaled twice. I recommended lightness when inhaling, which I used to do. I felt a lot of relaxation during and after the pranayama.
>
> Then I did the meditation (19 minutes) for those who wanted to meditate, and those who wanted to lie in savasana were doing savasana. I gave some instruction again to savasana and meditation. I saw that only K. was sitting. The rest of the people were in savasana.

5 Need for a Response, Need for Interaction

I see the need for practitioners to react to what I say and do, especially in online hatha yoga. Since March 2020, I have been running an online course due to the Covid-19 pandemic. We could not meet, so we were in contact via the Internet live using Zoom or Skype platforms. In the following self-observation, *I focused on the issue of perceptions and reactions* without being sure what they are. I expressed this in a comment summarizing my self-observation.

> While giving the asana instruction, I couldn't see my performance or the performance of the participants. I tried to talk a lot and give precise instructions so that the participants would follow them and do the asanas correctly. Due to the lack of interaction, I asked Dagmara twice if I was online and visible. In general, I trusted the zoom.us technology, but I did not trust my router because the wi-fi range in the small room where I was doing the online session is not very good.
>
> Conducting the hatha yoga without any response was a bit of a challenge for me ...
>
> And the whole online session was focused on one thought: Do they hear or see or exercise? The lack of direct contact is a severe limitation to the teacher. When I compare it with yesterday's online meditation, when I saw the instructor and I was only a participant, it was much better for me to meditate. (Self-observation, Krzysztof T. Konecki, March 17, 2020)

Asanas were a bit difficult for me because I was already practicing yoga from noon, and I was a bit tired. In addition, I lack self-vision and

> confidence if they see me, and how do they see me? And the second thing, I don't see the participants, which also bothers me. They had their cameras on today, but I didn't see much anyway. The biggest problem with online classes is the lack of direct contact in the same physical space. And it bothered me. (Self-report, Krzysztof T. Konecki, online session, April 7, 2020)

One day, in online hatha yoga,[7] I decided that all of the practitioners should have their cameras turned on. I wanted to see them, and *I had a strong need for eye contact with them*. I wanted to know what they were doing at a given moment:

> I asked the practitioners to turn on their cameras because I do classes better when I see the practitioners. And it was true; there was contact, I felt it. Of course, I didn't see exactly how they perform the positions, but I saw what point of the pose they are at. And it was a great help for me. For example, I could wait for Luiza to bring exercise accessories. (Self-report, online session, May 12, 2020)

The need for eye contact with the instructor may result from the didactic requirements, and it *ensures total participation* of individual people in the exercises:

> I asked them to turn on the cameras so we could see each other. Being in a group motivates; the awareness that others can see us is also a form of control during meditation. We are not supposed to move, sleep, or go to the toilet if we do not have the camera on.

Sometimes the response and the observation of the face can be disturbing, for example, in the transmission of knowledge of the spiritual aspects, although in this case, described below, they related to doing asanas anyway. I had some concerns about whether the narrative of hatha yoga philosophy would be well received when certain spiritual aspects were discussed. I was aware of the cultural differences regarding the perception of hatha yoga (Singleton 2010a, 2010b). Full of apprehension, I joined this lecture at the beginning of my yoga

---

7 Some people positively evaluate the development of technology and its use in yoga practice, e.g., in Bhakti yoga. The internet allows you to stay in touch with a guru-teacher. Practitioners can express their bhakti to the guru by frequently interacting with him (Warrier 2014: 309). This contact is vital for the practitioners to adhere to the guru.

session. Without seeing faces, and thus the reception of my mini-lecture, I was able to lead it freely, even if the reception was not very favorable. This is how I made it up. But I wasn't sure if this perception was negative or positive until the end. I kept thinking about it. I didn't see the faces of the practitioners:

> Today, I did the classes online again, this time with a lecture on *Yamas* in yoga (*Ahimsa, Sathya, Asteya, Brahmacharya, Aparigraha*) and doing asanas and physical exercises to relax the cervical and thoracic spine.
>
> I mentioned *Yamas* with some reserve because I do not know if this thread of the Eastern philosophy and spirituality of yoga will discourage the practitioners. However, I did this to show that asanas are just a fraction, 1/8 of yoga. Moral principles are fundamental, and they can also be exercised in asanas. I was applying certain principles to some examples of asanas. For instance, greed is not yogic; that seeking pleasure in yoga and following the pleasure principle is not hatha yoga. Ahimsa is about not hurting others or ourselves. Also, we do not do anything by force during the hatha yoga sessions, but according to what the body tells us (according to the truth of the body – *Sathya*). These principles, applied in doing asanas, can be carried over into the routine of everyday life.
>
> I have never given such a lecture, but I decided to introduce yoga to the practitioners at some moment. Maybe the fact that I didn't see their expressions and faces was not discouraging for me, and I had more courage to pass this knowledge directly. (Self-report, Krzysztof T. Konecki, April 7, 2020.)

> A brief introduction to *Ishvara pranidhana*. I did not want to talk about God, so I was talking about humility and surrendering to fate. This can also be done in asana by surrendering to the body, observing it, and following its signals. It is a preparation for humility and submission to fate. (Self-report, May 12, 2020)

5.1 *Moving to the Third-Person Perspective*

Krzysztof Konecki's reactions to the asana performance are somewhat subdued, and he never scolds the participants. He tries to talk generally about asana techniques. In the course of the yoga session, it also communicates possible psychophysical states regarding the feelings of the body and mind. He tries to show the relationship between body and thinking. In addition, at this point, based on his observations of the work of other instructors or teachers and his own, he may state that there are different styles of doing hatha yoga. It may be, for example, an authoritative or subdued style. So, he shared it and thought that his style of conducting hatha yoga is subdued; it is not known if he believes it himself, but at the moment, he thinks so:

> I generally avoid intense and individualized corrections. I don't want to scare the participants. I typically say how an item should be done. I also mention body sensations and the relationship of different feelings to each other in different parts of the body. I presented two tactics of dealing with the tensions and resistance of the body, mainly the psyche. Smiling and focusing on your breathing helps to break your body's resistance. The relaxation that comes from the head relaxes the muscles. Although I do not know how it happens, it helps to forget about the body's resistance that arises because the mind says, "I can't," "it will not work." The body and mind relax at the same time and contract at the same time. A smile is essential for this. Tightening the facial muscles tenses the mind simultaneously, and the mind tenses the muscles. If the whole body is tense, it will not do the asana well. (Self-observation, Krzysztof T. Konecki, February 11, 2020)

•••

Now I would like to present the interpretation of my self-observation made by my collaborator, Aleksandra Płaczek. It draws attention to the teacher's uncertainty and his distance from the practitioners. This reflection drew my attention because keeping this distance was natural for me but not perceptible (cf. Zerubavel 2018). The second thing that caught my attention was Alexandra's use of the form professor. Using this form of address in this context indicates a specific relationship with the tutor. It may indicate the social distance between the teacher and the practitioner (participant of the research project), but it may also be a power relationship.[8] My third observation here is that I am giving

8 When I asked Aleksandra, who is both a colleague in the study and a student, about the matter, she found that using this form of address was helpful to her in replacing the consistently appearing wording from the teacher. This would indicate that the power relationship was not directly perceived by it, but that does not mean it was not there.

After a second question, there was a reflection on this. It turned out that power relations do exist. I also asked if this distance affects how she is describing my feelings. Aleksandra wrote back to me as follows: "I think [the power distance] might have been disturbing at the very beginning of the collaboration, the hatha yoga sessions, and writing self-observation. But soon, any embarrassment faded away. My reports are honest, and I describe without hesitation what I feel and think. I feel very comfortable when writing reports because I know that nothing will be taken wrongly, and it is such a moment that allows for even more

a choice of how to close the session of yoga, either savasana or meditation. So, in a yoga session, there is a certain freedom of choice, although it is generally carried out according to my exact instructions and within certain limits.

I give the voice of my co-workers here without commenting on what one of them wrote because it is an analytical note, which is also a paraphrase of my self-observation and self-analysis (see Richardson 1992): *Let the note speak for itself*, although it will never speak for itself, because there is a narrator behind it, talking in a particular context:

> *A professor as an instructor.*
> While reading the professor's self-observation, what immediately came to my mind was thinking about others, caring for others. The professor, as the lecturer, pays a lot of attention to the transfer of knowledge beyond physical knowledge, apart from the asanas themselves. He wants to precede his yoga session with lectures on his philosophy of living in accordance with his body and mind. I noticed that the classes were not introduced at the beginning of the teaching, but after a series of sessions, after getting to know the participants and gaining confidence, exploring the group's ground. Nevertheless, the professor is still reluctant to say everything, and he shortens some lectures for fear of alienating the participants. This means that there is still some barrier and uncertainty between him and the participants. In speeches and statements, he is helped by the form of the classes, i.e., online yoga. He does not see the complete reactions of the participants, so he feels more confident and does not feel embarrassed during the speech, pointing out that in the case of live hatha yoga, this uncertainty could take a deeper, more abundant form. The set of asanas is selected by the teacher mainly in terms of his well-being. If another effort precedes it, or if the tutor does not feel well, the practice is lighter, less demanding.
>
> The yoga session is planned, usually directed to the specific needs of the body/health. During the exercise, the tutor adds new items that suddenly come to his mind and are related to the lesson's theme. So, the plan of the session is flexible and not rigidly held.
>
> The tutor focuses on what is outside during the yoga session – he observes the participants, space, and time. Time is constantly monitored, even during the relaxation, the calming part of the session. The leader

colloquial expression of thoughts. It is more about learned distance in addressing each other, but it does not significantly affect the content of the auto-reports." (e-mail communication, October 18, 2020).

cares about the atmosphere of the meetings and also adjusts the lighting to them. This prevents the tutor from focusing on himself, his body, and his mind. Attention is drawn inward only during longer kept asanas. However, the facilitator expresses the need to focus on oneself.

Asking the participants about their well-being during and after the sessions establishes understanding and contact, which results from the need for a sense of community. When one of the participants presents similar observations as the tutor about body sensations and emotions, the instructor becomes confident and focuses on it.

The instructor tries to discuss all the positions and give tips to the practitioners – how they should feel during the asanas, how they should breathe. Sometimes he offers participants a choice of the form of exercise, the phase of the session, so that they can adapt it to their well-being (the choice between *savasana* and meditation).

During online hatha yoga, the cameras and the tutor-practitioner contact are of the utmost significance. The facilitator feels uncertainty during the yoga session when the practitioners have their cameras turned off. The lack of interaction makes the teacher ask about the technical aspects of the practice (whether they can see or hear it). He recognizes that being on the other side is entirely different, and it is easier for the practitioner; it is not such a huge obstacle. The active cameras give the presenter a feeling of confidence. Hence, the request to turn on the cameras becomes an indispensable part of the exercise.

The instructor avoids individualized corrections – it results from reflecting on the well-being of the participants, not wanting to scare them, harm them, or embarrass them (Aleksandra Płaczek)

6 Individual Practice and the Teacher as a Participant

Individual Practice

6.1 *Moving to the Third-Person Perspective*

He was practicing individually, without an instructor, alone. Then Krzysztof Konecki tries to return to himself, to his body. He observes the sensations, but he also plans how to do the following session when he is the facilitator. In general, individual practice is necessary for him to feel the taste of yoga, its strength, peace, and mood, which combines all the elements of this world. Through the body, he can feel a connection with the material and animate world. He often does it to lighten the mood and even try to get out of depression (see the contemplative memo below, which he wrote after practice).[9] Frequently, his body chooses specific asanas and ignores some. His body is the subject of the activities. What he does and what happens during the hatha yoga session is described in a reflection note.

> **Memo – reflection after individual practice – January 1, 2020**
> Today, while practicing hatha yoga at home, I made my Sun Salutation the starter kit as usual. These are slow-motion Sun Salutation positions made from different variants of this traditional Sun Salutation. However, the sequence of asanas and their logic is generally preserved and can be found in different versions (*namaste* and *tadasana, urdwa hastasana, uttanasana, ashva salanchasana, kumbhakasana, chaturanga dandasana, bhujangasana, adho mukha svanasana, ashva salanchasana* again, *uttanasana* again, *urdva hastasana* again, *tadasana* and *namaste* again). I composed this set myself, although, as I mentioned, it is based on the Sun Salutation sequence. I perform this sequence very slowly, extending the duration of a single asana. The entire sequence takes up to 10 minutes or more. Performing this set stretches muscles and tendons well, elevates my mood, exercises my strength, and gives me confidence. These are my conclusions from my observations. I work well with this set in the morning afterward.
>
> Today I was doing other asanas first, and I wanted to skip this sacramental set of mine, but I was drawn to doing it. And at the end of the yoga session, I finally did it.
>
> Recently, I have had difficulties motivating myself to do yoga. It was hard for me to bring myself to hatha yoga. You could say, in short, that I had a severe mood drop.
>
> After doing this set, I found a bunch of asanas for depression on the internet today. It turned out that of the six proposed asanas, four are in my collection (*urdva hastasana, adho mukha svanasana, bhujangasana, uttanasana*), while the other two are always in my set of asanas (*virabhadrasana II, balasana*) – *balasana* before the basic set and after it, and *virabhadrasana* always after the basic set. I composed this set of mine long ago, and I always use it when teaching hatha yoga. It works great

9 There is some evidence from medical research that hatha yoga has therapeutic value in combating depression, although further research is needed to fully confirm this hypothesis (Uebelacker et al., 2010).

> for your well-being and prepares you for further exercise. I checked it on myself and later on the exercisers. And it works; these are my reactions from people who have been exercising for many years.
>
> It turns out that my body made the choice I made a long time ago because I was practicing what helped me feel better. This is what I liked the most. Somehow these asanas popped up naturally in my individual practice. They are exercises that require a lot of physical effort, build endurance (hence my rather long positioning). They also are asanas for relaxation, such as pranayama and meditation at the end of the yoga session. My body chose this sequence (wishing to exercise and stay in shape); the mind merely followed those choices (wishing then to relax and calm down). I didn't realize it. Although in yoga, I was mainly looking to calm my mind and develop my knowledge about the Eastern techniques of working on the mind (motives in-order-to), it turned out that this body guided my choices. Although these asanas were given to me on a tray, their order and "manner" (I mean focusing the mind on certain parts of the body, the length of time in a position, breathing, and concentration on breaths) were almost entirely invented by me, albeit with some borrowings, from what I read and learned from X and other teachers.
>
> However, it also comes to mind that there are generally asanas in hatha yoga that help with all ailments and that are suitable for all developments of the body, mind, and heart (emotionality). However, the body may have selective attention here and make choices about the type of exercise. This may also be choosing the teacher or leaving some teachers/trainers. Perhaps there is a question about tuning the same sensitivity of bodies or their states at any given moment.

In individual practice, Konecki has a better focus on the sensations of his own body, and he may better name these sensations, even if they are atypical, which is what he usually experiences:

> Today, when I pulled my arms back, lacing my thumbs on the back, I felt the stretch of my muscles across my chest. As if a piece of paper was being stretched across the chest. From the breastbone to the sides of the body. Weird feeling. (Self-observation, Individual practice at home, August 18, 2020; 8.30 PM.)

By practicing, Krzysztof himself can observe what "stretching" is and penetrate it deeper. It is not enough for him to name the feeling; he wants to fully understand it.

These unusual feelings are even mystical for him, for example, when he feels that his mind is stretching. But this can only be noticed when he is practicing alone and is strongly focused on what is happening in him:

> When I bend my cross leg forward, I feel the muscles and tendons on the back of my hips really stretching – almost painful stretching. But by staying in this position for a long time, I think that I can bow lower and lower, and move forward with my upper torso. This stretching is getting deeper and more demanding, and I feel it expanding my range of possibilities. As if the back and the muscles on the hips were longer. I can feel the length of these muscles, joints, and tendons.
>
> But I also have a different feeling. It is not only the body that increases its capabilities; the mind also stretches. It becomes more stretched, more comprehensive, longer. It reaches somewhere where there is no physical space, but there is a mental space or some other space which I don't know much about. (Self-observation, Stavros, Crete, September 7, 2020).

•••

At the end of this section, I present the interpretation of my descriptions of individual practice by one of the co-researchers in the project, Aleksandra Płaczek.

> In self-observations concerning individual practice, the issue of thinking about others and focusing on what is external disappears. On the other hand, there is a focus on the inner sensations of the body and mind, which is evident in the descriptions of feelings. They are detailed; the professor surprises himself and discovers new things in his body and thoughts. The descriptions are full of reflection, and reflectivity also becomes the motive for development. By being aware of your own body and mind, both issues are expanded and developed. The professor feels every exercise within himself, and he selects each subsequent one for himself. He sets up a plan, a set of exercises in advance, and they differ from each other; he likes to repeat one sequence he knows. It turns out that the sequence was created in response to the needs of the body. The body thought before the mind. Sometimes it also happens during the conducted session, but there are limitations in other practitioners and their needs, and everyone has different ones. This makes one reflect that only the individual practice of an experienced yogi with knowledge allows him to meet these needs. The need to turn attention inward, to focus on one's "I" is also satisfied here.

> Could this lead to the reflection that the fullness of yoga goodness can only be achieved with some selfishness? Here, the ego "I" refers directly to the body. The body is the authentic self, and the mind is its derivative and, at the same time, the response and modifier. When we listen to the body, we listen to our real needs, not artificially created ones. At this point, reflecting on the professor's reflections, I recall the theories of real and false needs. False needs are those imposed on an individual while using particular social processes to repress him. These processes have a social content and function and are determined by external forces that the individual has no control over. Marcuse and Freud asked what real needs are. There is intense concentration during practice, a fusion of the body with the mind – a feeling of enormous stretching of muscles and tendons bordering on pain. Mind-body fusion, responding to sudden sensations, increasing the range of possibilities, self-awareness, and the feel of your own body and its components. Then, despite the reality surrounding us and numerous stimuli, we can separate the external from the internal and feel and respond to our own real needs. It is possible when yoga is advanced, and we don't need instruction. (Aleksandra Płaczek)

Aleksandra pointed to discovering what the body feels and needs during the yoga session. She used theoretical reflection to define and understand this phenomenon. Here, she tentatively used psychoanalytical concepts related to the division of needs into false and actual needs. False ones are socialized; real ones are hidden deep in a person's body and mind and do not come from society. Discovering these needs is possible during hatha yoga. This can be especially true during individual practice when we do not focus on others if we are instructors or co-participants if we practice with others. We then observe and recognize our bodies more precisely. It is "muscle awareness" that allows us to discover our needs. It is pre-text knowledge, which we later verbalize or write down (Hastrup 2018). This reflection complements observations and thoughts, which I have stated, and it is an essential note for my self-awareness as the instructor. By writing these notes, we get to know each other during and outside the yoga sessions. I learn a lot here. There are layered explanations, where one interpretation and description builds upon another to understand more (Rambo 1992). I also learned how another person could read my report on my stream of consciousness. The person whom I exercise with gives me a feeling that understanding someone else is faster and more complete when there is a community of experiences. I can see it in Aleksandra's descriptions. The community of yoga practice is essential here, and the community of those who write about experiences and reflect on those experiences. The writing culture and the writing subculture are environments where certain conventions for describing experiences are produced, including the subcultures of contemplative research, autoethnographic research, and phenomenological research (see chapter 1). In general, language is the basis of science and human studies (e.g., the categories and types of needs in Aleksandra's notes). These writing subcultures provide categorical foundations to describe the world, but also the ability to play with and operate on language to express what can be directly said and what has thus far not been possible to tell.[10]

6.2 "Me as a Participant"

Often in hatha yoga, *as a participant*, as in individual practice, Krzysztof has a more significant opportunity to focus on his bodily feelings and more time to think about what is happening to his body and what are the causes of certain states of his body:

> There were a lot of asanas for stretching the backs of the legs. I noticed I had very tight hamstrings on my hips and immobile hip joints; I struggled to lean forward with my spine straight in a sitting position. Pain in the hips. Surprise at this pain. It occurred to me that it was from sitting at the computer for a long time yesterday. (Self-observation, Krzysztof T. Konecki, Yoga in Park Źródliska, August 15, 2020, 12.00–13.00.)

The hatha yoga in which *Krzysztof is a participant* usually comes down to *observing the work of the instructor*. He highlights those elements that can bring something new to his sessions and teaching and that he can use in his approach and education of others.

> At the beginning, the instructor told participants to retract their eyeballs while standing in tadasana, to look inside rather than outside. Yoga was exercised – 1.5 hours of exercise. Plank, sides planks, alternating between two sides – direct transition from the dog facing down to the Lounge pose and the Warior I pose, Triangle. I noticed that the instructor was talking about withdrawing his head once we were in position. *Ardha candrasana*, I also noticed that the instructor was talking about withdrawing the head

10 "Even the words freeze the contents." Any literary form imprisons lived experience; yet, without form or structure, it would be impossible to convey any experience." (Rambo 1992: 123).

> once I was in position. (Self-observation, Krzysztof T. Konecki, as a participant, yoga on the grass, Park Źródliska, August 8, 2020, 12:00, Intense heat, 30 C)

Krzysztof also draws attention in self-observation to those elements that are different from his practice, i.e., when his mind enters *the comparison mode.* The participant's perspective is mixed with the instructor's perspective. It isn't easy to be just a participant. Although he tries not to judge these differences, as can be seen in the author's report below, *there is a hidden note of judgment in the background*:

> After the yoga session, I felt powerfully energized. There was relatively no relaxation; I felt a surge of energy that was not used up and found no release or calming down. I also felt tired but full of energy, a lot of self-confidence, and even aggression. Instead, I have a different goal in yoga: relaxation, withdrawal, focus, concentration, and meditation. (Self-observation, Krzysztof T. Konecki, as a participant, yoga on the grass, Park Źródliska, August 8, 2020, 12:00, Intense heat, 30 C)

> For me as an instructor, it was interesting that the stretched triangle was done as in gymnastics. This is probably the first time I have seen something like this – quick entry and exit. Bam! Bam! Bam! Likewise, bends with arms raised, rapid change. (Self-observation, Krzysztof T. Konecki as a participant, Yoga in Park Źródliska, August 9, 2020)

Sometimes the assessment comes directly from comparing his practice and his philosophy of hatha yoga. There is a perspective of assessment that he is aware of during the exercises:

> The lady in charge did a very short *savasana*. We entered savasana from *badha konasana*. After doing this, we had to lie on our back with the soles of the feet still touching and then extend the legs to *savasana*. *Savasana* lasted only a minute. In my opinion, you shouldn't do that. You cannot accumulate the good currents and energy of the whole practice in such a short relaxation time. (Self-observation, Krzysztof T. Konecki, Yoga in Park Źródliska, August 15, 2020, 12.00–13.00.)

> I like to participate in the session when someone is conducting it. I don't have to overthink. I follow the instructions. However, the judgmental attitude and the instructor's attitude keep turning on for me. The instructor

> talked a lot, and he made a mistake in the name of the item once. It does not inspire confidence. Even though he was better stretched than me, I still think I do yoga better in a didactic sense, not only from him but also from many other instructors (apart from X and Prof. Sz.). However, I have noticed that the asana sequences selected by the instructor are similar to mine. Maybe he has the same motor and body sensation habitus. He did the bends as I did to rest after the positions of the warriors and the stretched triangle. However, I was surprised that he made the chair pose almost at the beginning of the session when we were not warmed up yet. (Self-observation, Krzysztof T. Konecki, participant, Yoga in Park Źródliska, August 16, 2020, 10.00–11.00.)

Krzysztof's instructor perspective constantly appears, even the compulsion to compare his practice and teaching, looking for similarities and differences. Even if it takes place in a geographically and culturally distant site (Kathmandu, Nepal, where he also practiced), it should arouse respect and acceptance of the knowledge about hatha yoga. The participant's perspective stops in the body because the body responds to instructions, while Krzysztof's instructor mind turns on the comparison mode:

> We found the school through an advertisement on a poster, in the street. It was close to where we were staying in Thamel, Kathmandu.
>
> I felt a little excited – what the session would be like, almost at the source of yoga, under the Himalayas? The host trainer explained the meaning of her name, "ongoing love" or something like that. She announced the exercising of asanas in the convention of ashtanga yoga and pranayama (*kalaphati*) and meditation/relaxation. I immediately had the feeling that I was doing this too, three things – asanas, pranayama, and meditation. In Poland, it is rare to do these three things in one yoga session.
>
> We started chanting the mantras. They were in Sanskrit; I had a hard time repeating them, but I sang them. It was a little embarrassing not to be able to repeat them.
>
> Then there was a Sun Salutation, done differently than what I do. There was four-point support instead of *chaturanga dandasana*, but with the chest on the floor, followed by a direct transition to *bhagujasana*. There was no pushing the pace.
>
> After practicing asana, there was pranayama, *kalaphati*, rapid inhalations, and exhalations with the diaphragm. At one point, the teacher left.

> Which I noticed, and the judgment immediately arose that she should not be doing it.
>
> We also did pranayama by plugging the nose (Nadi Sodhana). I do it a bit differently. There was no support of the right elbow with the left hand so that the right hand (for right-handers) would not get tired at the face. In a more simplified way, I suggest holding the left hand's fingers without hiding the middle and ring fingers. Open hand, the thumb blocks the hole in the right and the left ring finger. The teacher explained that this pranayama balances the left and right hemispheres of the brain; the right one is responsible for intuition and creativity, the left one for logic and planning. I also explain this in my classes; I had such a thought. I had a moment of wanting to use Sanskrit words for the two energies coming through the nostrils (*Ida* and *Pingala*) and wanted to say it out loud but decided not to. (Self-report, Krzysztof T. Konecki, Kathmandu, Nepal, "Sambodhi Yoga Home" School, March 11, 2020)

This perspective of assessment, and being aware of it, prompts Krzysztof to make an effort to remove it because yoga with a continuous assessment mode is not authentic yoga, an experience here and now. The comparisons refer to his past practice and the future; when Krzysztof thinks about how he will do hatha yoga and how he will not do it, he always does so regarding how hatha yoga is experienced and evaluated here and now. Ultimately, he decided to suspend these assessments in the session described below, and he used it consciously and practically; *it was his epoché*:[11]

> Then she asked us to lie down and to relax. She did not use the word *savasana*. She was talking all the time and relaxing. She talked a lot. The instruction at the beginning dealt with the tension of the muscles of the whole body, from the bottom of the body upwards. She listed different parts of the body. Then she asked us to let go of that tension. She was talking all the time, extending the syllable: reeeeelax. It made me laugh a little. I smiled and laughed inwardly. I felt pressure in her voice to make

11 The *epoché* of practice generally refers to the philosophical suspension of one's assumptions, prejudices, and acquired knowledge about a given phenomenon or even the world. Of course, the *epoché* used here is a modification of a philosophical procedure to deal with a specific mental problem in a given situation. Of course, this is not a methodological procedure as understood in phenomenology, but an inspiration to be applied in everyday life (see Schütz 1967).

> me relax. But after a while, the thought came, accept it, let go of your prejudices. I figured I needed an epoché. This is precisely the concept that came to mind. And I did it. And I only heard the sounds of her speech, not the content. (Self-report, Krzysztof T. Konecki, Kathmandu, Nepal, "Samobodhi Yoga Home" School, March 11, 2020)

The comparison also applies to cultural issues if the practice takes place in a different cultural setting. After one of the hatha yoga sessions in Nepal, Krzysztof reflected that "the main difference between the Nepalese style in the Sambodhi school and in the Polish schools is that mantras are sung here, and music with mantras is played more often than in Poland. There seems to be a greater tolerance for religious, para-religious, and spiritual threads involved in yoga":[12]

> I was looking at her asana performance because I didn't understand all the instructions, and the instructor's accent disturbed my understanding. We started chanting the mantras and then did the *Surya namaskara* sequence. Each position in the "Sun Salutation" began with a mantra that the instructor spoke about first, and then we sang together. I had a problem with the mantras, with repeating the mantras …
>
> At the end of the session, we got up and sang the mantra that closes the session and om and shanti, shanti. (Self-report, Krzysztof T. Konecki, Nepal, March 13, 2020)

Krzysztof also perceives and compares the way he does yoga regarding *performance, self-presentation,* and unique facade (Goffman 2000: 53–54), which the performing instructor brings with him on stage and partially arranges. There is the outfit, and the body is a kind of physical capital (Rossing, Ronglan and Scott 2014: 349), an exterior, and a manner that can be gentle or decisive. Doing hatha yoga can be seen in terms of a performance that has particular aesthetic values and evokes certain emotions in the audience (Singleton 2010a, chapter "Demonstrations. Yoga as spectacle.")

---

12 Here is my self-observation note when I was practicing in Poland: "We were working on the crown chakra. Responsible for spirituality. I haven't talked much about spirituality because I don't want to discourage people who are not motivated to achieve the spiritual elements of yoga from practicing yoga. I am careful here; I give this knowledge slowly and in moderation." (February 11, 2020. Krzysztof T. Konecki) (See also Konecki, 2015; Mallinson & Singleton, 2017). In general, yoga is more secularized today, and its teaching is more adapted to the values of Western society (Singleton & Goldberg 2014: 1–3, 5).

Krzysztof conducts his hatha yoga in a relatively gentle manner, and his *decorations* are subdued, inconspicuous. Therefore, he drew attention to these differences and described them in the self-report below:

> Today's yoga in the park was led by instructor X. He was undressed, only in underpants. He had tattoos on his right leg and left arm; the tattoos on the left arm extended the tattoos on the right leg. In the beginning, X very decisively (with a strong voice) gave orders regarding the mat placement. He said they should be pointing at him and arranged concentrically. He told me not to have a backpack in front of me because he must see me. I found that I was straightening the mat with my bag. And he said, 'Take it off!' Me: 'I took it off ...'
>
> Then he explained for a long time how to do tadasana. He talked a lot. And he paid attention to details and each exerciser. That was my impression. He noticed the feet not connected; then he shouted to this person: "put your feet together, blue T-shirt connect your feet!" "Bridge up!", Knee-patches up, 'Cap up!'
>
> We held our arms in the star position for a long time in preparation for the *utthita trikonasana* position. Mr. X laughed when someone lowered his arms and said: 'You are cold, so we warm up, triceps to the shoulder, we hold tight. It's getting warmer.' And he smiled ...
>
> The instructor also gave the command at the beginning to roll up two-thirds of the mat and sit on it straight, but with one leg lying fully on the mat and the other slightly raised. The practitioners expressed their surprise because the grass was wet and the mat was also wet: 'Don't be afraid, nothing will happen to you, you can just get your shorts wet. When one exerciser later wanted to wipe her daughter's (about ten years old) feet with a handkerchief, the instructor exclaimed: "What is this?! Nothing's going to happen; a little wet won't hurt.' The instructor was very vigilant; he saw everything and reacted immediately ...
>
> Overall, I was satisfied with the session. It was intense for me because I had had a break. I was a bit tired but happy to meet such an original instructor. (Self-observation, Krzysztof T. Konecki as a participant, yoga in Park Źródliska, August 29, 2020, 12.00–13.20)

After writing the self-report above, Krzysztof wrote a note summarizing his perception of how to conduct the instructor's practice. This perception is, of course, his interpretation of the practice by someone else. However, he was taking the role of an instructor all the time:

> I had the impression that by shouting and giving orders, Mr. X. was playing a role, the role of a yoga sergeant. At first, I wouldn't say I liked it. I thought that the people from my group in the project would not accept such guidelines with this tone and directness. But over time, I accepted it, and it made me laugh.
>
> I had the feeling that X had to control everything. His raised voice and shouts built the authority and probably also the power over the bodies of the other exercisers. I was surrendering to that authority. There were, on his part, many games, but games with an attitude of dominance over the rest. The instructor was almost naked, clearly different from us. There was little time for contemplation; it was a time for permanent concentration, here and now, on physical exercise. I wonder how he conducts meditation.

In the perspective of Konecki's comparison, he is sometimes surprised by the way he performs the asana sequence, e.g., with the pace of moving from one asana to the next:

> There was also *Pradaritta Padottanasana*, with a quick change to the side, to *Parsvottanasana* to one side, and back to *Pradaritta Padottanasana*, and then to the other side, to *Parsvottanasana*. It was done at a high pace. I've never done anything like this. I do not know why such a pace; after all, tendons and joints will not have time to stretch with such a rapid pace of position change. (Self-observation, Krzysztof T. Konecki, Yoga in Park Źródliska, August 15, 2020, 12.00–13.00.)

Krzysztof goes through a chain of thoughts in the process of comparing to get emotional energy for his practice (Collins 2004: 202–03). It is based on participating in ritual interaction chains, i.e., the sequence of yoga sessions with different teachers. He tries to build the internal solidarity of his self to be a better yoga teacher.

6.3 *I Come to the Relationship from the Point of View of the First Person*

The description below is about the relationship with the teacher, so I want to describe it as "I am talking."

Interesting observations appear after practicing with my *first instructor*, who I can also call *the yoga teacher* who shaped me and whose understanding of hatha yoga I have acquired, and who is still close to me.

I haven't seen my teacher for a long time, and I still respect him (code – respect for the teacher). M runs so-called "strong practice." Therefore, intense practice causes fatigue in the body. Here is my reaction when I went to a hatha yoga session in a park without knowing who I would meet there:

> M is my teacher. He has always exercised very intensively. He did not pay much attention to the mental or physical condition of the practitioners. He demanded a lot from them. I always liked that, apart from those sessions when I couldn't handle it. I learned the most from M. I was making significant progress. He greeted me:
>
> 'I saw that you had had a long journey.'
>
> 'Yes, I had a long trip to Nepal. I managed to leave at the last minute and return to Poland. The borders were closed soon afterward (because of pandemic).' (Self-report, Krzysztof T. Konecki, Participant)

Although there were concerns about the teacher's grades, which he never expressed openly, I was pleased to meet him. Among other things, I like his sometimes playful and distant tone that he reveals during the exercising:

> It was a bit cramped in the pavilion. We arranged the mats concentrically directed towards the instructor. However, we were very close to each other. The distance was about 20 cm. M and one practitioner said that the epidemic was over. It was all in the convention of a joke. (Self-report, Krzysztof T. Konecki, Participant)

In addition, I liked his unconventional methods; it was difficult to get bored with him. M did not need not to talk as much as other instructors. He spoke as much as necessary; it allowed us to perceive the sensations of the body and our movements and to contemplate them:

> Then we exercised as we wanted, we chose the position we wanted, the position our body wanted. That's how X led us. It was a lovely lived experience. Our body exercised us with minimal choice by the mind. At the end of this session, we sat down and went to meditation. There wasn't much talking. M told us to take a deeper breath to the top of our heads and exhale to our hips. We were supposed to watch what was happening with our exhalation and our body. We were not to get attached to the sensations of the body. We were supposed to accept what was happening and observe.
>
> I liked it very much. Not a lot of talking, but a lot of observing yourself and your own body and mind. (Self-report, Krzysztof T. Konecki, as a participant)

6.4 *Third-Person Perspective*

After the session, Krzysztof wrote down his feelings and reflections about his first teacher. He tried to understand why he liked yoga with M so much, even though it was difficult. He returned to the past and early socialization related to the habits of physical effort – accepting, breaking, and enduring it during fatigue:

> I was delighted and even touched when I returned to practice with M. I'm thinking of going back to his school. This is an excellent teacher, and I can feel his practice. M jokes a lot, is at ease, has a perfect voice, inspires confidence, and has the authority to do so. His jokes are pretty mild and do not hurt my feelings. There are a few teachers like this. I appreciate them. Perhaps it matters that he was my first teacher, who taught me a lot. It is also essential that he exercises intensively, does not spare the body. Perhaps my habitus, taken from hard physical work in the countryside and in factories, where the body was heavily used and exploited, is also essential here. I don't regret my body; I often exercise when my body is frail and resisting. This is when the most remarkable advances are made. This is my conviction, and it is based on my past experiences. Without pain and hard work, there is no progress. To this, M also adds work to the mind. It's not that he only works with the body. Breath is also crucial for M. He is a pranayama instructor. He knows what breath is and how to use it. He is also experienced in meditation. (Self-report, Krzysztof T. Konecki, Participant)

My teacher, M, whom I admire, was criticized by one of my collaborators, Dagmara Tarasiuk, however. She expressed it in an emotional contemplative note. She also showed me my hidden assumptions about hatha yoga as a patriarchal system of teaching. The system has had implicit assumptions that the masters and teachers (usually men) should not be criticized, and we should accept their behaviors and teachings because "this is the yoga." She also connected it with the educational and academic system, where the patriarchy dominates, and which I am part of. I felt discomfort reading it, but ultimately, I had to agree with the opinions. I try to escape from the hierarchy and patriarchy. The problem is that both sides of the interaction have difficulties running from the system. Another side of the issue is that when we lay the theoretical structure of the external theories or concepts onto yoga practice, we are trapped twice: by our cultural ideas and by our ideological ones, which evoke strong emotions (see Appendix 2 in this Chapter). We internalize social life, and it becomes part of our thinking processes. Our individual subjective experience is based on memories of past participation in interactional rituals, for example, the lectures in sociology that taught us that we are a social product, or the yoga sessions that taught us that we should listen to our body and emotions. All of these situations become a part of the thinking process. The internalization of external voices means that they slowly become internal ones (Collins 2004: 186–89). The thinking process has the character of an internal conversation (Blumer 1969; Bakker 2005), with words and phrases and the images and schemes of the body's moves. We remember the words and pictures of our yoga master's performances from the past in the individual yoga practice.[13] The thinking chains are consequences of the chains of the experienced interaction rituals.

•••

At the end of the session description as a participant, I would like to present the reflection of another collaborator, Aleksandra Płaczek. She notices a problem with chanting the mantra in Sanskrit. This is a significant observation because it indicates linguistic issues and my reluctance to recite texts that have a religious or para-religious flavor.

Aleksandra also states that there is a comparison and evaluation of the hatha yoga sessions conducted by other instructors. This confirms my feelings and problems related to concentrating on the practice and the body when someone else is leading it. Aleksandra ends her reflections with the statement that only self-practice can help one focus well on one's feelings, and I partially agree. Sometimes, I get an insight into my feelings when someone else is practicing, e.g., my first teacher. But it is related to his authority and my trust in him as my master:

---

13 My teacher wrote similar things on Facebook after the death of his teacher: "We both experienced Guruji's departure very much. Then Slawek told me that when the Master leaves the body, all his knowledge and wisdom flows onto his disciples. The feelings that accompany me now are even stronger because Sławek was my first teacher. He is with me in every asana, in every yoga-related memory. I will continue the work that he started to the best of my strength and ability." (https://facebook.com/story.php?story_fbid=6487535197954805&id=100000951677392&ref=content_filter, retrieved on 14.11.21). We incorporate the gestures of our masters. They become part of our repertoire of movements in hatha yoga practice. We are the heirs of their traditions in a literal, embodied sense. A similar situation can happen even in academic work when the gestures of our masters are often imitated.

Contemplative Memo – 'I' as a participant in a session conducted by another person

In the role of a participant who obeys the instructions of another instructor, the tutor is repeatedly surprised by the form that the classes take, the exercises themselves, and their impact on his own body (unexpected pain, difficulty, tendon strain occur). In self-observation, there is an element evaluating and comparing how classes are conducted to the way one does it oneself. The assessment is often negative; the Professor assesses his practice better, and the instructions are more understandable and extensive. He prefers his ways. The Professor's description focuses more on commands and observation of what is around, not on the feelings of the body or mind. So there is less self-reflection in it, only minor reconstruction of feelings. The way classes are conducted that the Professor prefers should be geared towards giving practitioners space, i.e., fewer descriptions of the teacher, the possibility of focusing on oneself. It is an element that is consistent with the reports of one's practice and the role of the instructor when the Professor draws attention to his inability to focus on himself. According to the Professor, the ideal instructor should be colorful, aggressive, and firm. He values people who do not spare practitioners and who force them to make a lot of effort. The Professor claims that this is due to his habitus of a person taught hard physical work (in the village and factory).

In Nepal, the Professor was a practitioner with much less self-confidence. He felt resistance to speaking and to repeating mantras. Here, language and the linguistic barrier play a significant role. Asanas can be presented by showing them a physical outfit. Mantras are a component of speech and dialect, so good pronunciation and understanding are essential to understand and repeat them. The problem of pronouncing mantras is therefore insoluble, and one cannot use only eyesight, following the movements of the lips, and the sound of the voices pronouncing them.

His practice gave the Professor a feeling of fulfillment and fulfillment of the body's needs. When this practice is being conducted by someone else and another person chooses the asana set, the results may be contrary to expectations and desires. The Professor is looking for relaxation and withdrawal, and during one of the practices, he obtained a substantial inflow of energy. This prompts me to reflect again that only in our doing hatha yoga are we able to get what we expect and need. The body determines the needs that the mind locates and satisfies secondarily.

7 Conclusions

What do these various self-observations (from the participant, teacher/instructor, student) have in common? There is one integrating thread here, sometimes openly expressed, as in the descriptions of the online sessions: receiving instructions and controlling the course of sessions. For the role of the instructor, the interactive context is essential, as is the feedback, which is expected either through observing the body movements, facial expressions, and sounds made by practitioners, or after sessions in the statements and comments of practitioners. The teaching of hatha yoga is interactive. It can often be perceived as a performance where we seek confirmation for our message and are interested in how we came out in the eyes of others.

In practice, considered "individual," a person exercises and observes his body and mind. However, most practitioners are usually under the supervision of an instructor and follow his instructions. Moreover, even when there is no instructor or teacher, we hear (in our memory) his instructions, his voice, or remember what we learned when under his supervision.[14] He is a significant other, remembered in our body and body responses through his communicated body movements, sensations, and experiences (Rossing, Ronglan, & Scott 2014: 345). We hear his voice (I listen to it) even when practicing individually. The embodiment of the instruction and knowledge is vital; that's how I remember it and feel it right now. This knowledge somehow enters the habitus of practitioners (Bourdieu 1977). Therefore, the production of knowledge in the course of practice has its origins in primary socialization and also in the chains of situations in which we participate in our life, here in yoga sessions (Collins 2004: 183, 186).

During my apprenticeship with my first teacher, I noticed the importance of primary socialization in teaching how to use the body. Two aspects seem essential to me here. *The first is related to my teenagers' habits*, heavy physical work, body and endurance, and physical perseverance during hard work

14 Krishnamacharya drew attention to a similar mental phenomenon of remembering what the teacher said or did: "He was known to declare, 'I don't say anything, I close my eyes and it is the guru in me who says all those things'" (Singleton & Fraser 2014: 90). The interactional rituals, as yoga sessions, during the socialization in yoga practice, become part of the internal conversations in mind. Chains of thought are chains of symbols that were part of interaction rituals in the past. We think using pictures and physical moves, and sounds. Rituals appear in our minds. (Collins 2004: 183–5). The sociology of thinking, according to Collins, shows the connection of inner processes of thinking with the external world.

and strenuous physical exertion. *The second aspect is related to socialization in hatha yoga*, learning from the first teacher/instructor who has been accepted as a master – maybe not in the traditional sense as a guru, but as a teacher who provides instruction and knowledge about what yoga is. This primary socialization influences the further perception of yoga and how it is performed, and in the situation of being an instructor, how it is instructed/taught. The first experiences with various practices of using the body are crucial for developing its biography and treatment in life.

Another important theme of the self-reports above is *taking the teacher/instructor's perspective into hatha yoga as a participant*. Being in practice led by other instructors, I still compare it with my way of conducting sessions. This perspective of comparison appears automatically. It is accompanied by astonishment, an indication of the diversity of cultures and evaluation categories. The instructor's perspective is dominant in teaching and practicing, which seems natural. But even when it is possible to concentrate on your own body and mind, for example, during "savasana," the instructor's perspective comes on. This does not mean that the judgmental attitude is tiring or in itself that it interferes with our perception of our feelings. I perceive my feelings, and I am aware of them. Assessment is accepted, as this is the practice of the instructor. Similarly, the perspective of acceptance comes into play when I deal with a practice with my first and respected teacher, who is an authority on hatha yoga for me. All sessions with him were like chains of interactional rituals that built my emotional energy and motivation to do yoga (see Collins 2004); The internal dialog concerning yoga is done with him all the time. (Blumer 1969; Bakker 2005)

The body is an instrument of teaching through the display and discussion of body movements. How practitioners perceive this teaching is, in my opinion, the most crucial element of this type of practice, practice in teaching hatha yoga, and possibly other bodily exercises. It is the reception of the teacher's instruction, not necessarily his hatha yoga philosophy or his philosophy of life. This is how I can generalize these last two phrases in my practice and teaching. The rest is up to the practitioners themselves to evaluate and reflect on.

Finally, I would like to present a contemplative note of my research colleague who offered the following reflection after analyzing my self-reports. It is a view from the outside and from within our practice and from within the research process itself. It is another perspective that tries to understand what is happening here in this dynamic research project, in which analyses are intertwined with contemplative reporting (Konecki 2018; 2021; Bentz & Marlatt 2021) about data already analyzed as well as the analysis of new data. What happens in a research project where the research subjects are also the researchers themselves?

> Strong relationship with the first teacher and a certain reluctance towards the other teachers. The practitioner puts his first teacher as the first important person, then himself and other teachers. He often emphasizes that he would have approached his classes differently, that he would have changed something, that he would not like something in the style of the classes. High expectations of how others conduct classes – constantly comparing and evaluating. In the practitioner, the schedule of classes is firmly rooted, taken from the activities undertaken by the favorite, first teacher, and those undertaken by himself. Surprisingly, the class of the practitioner (K. Konecki) is very different from that of *the guru. The guru's* style, and thus the practitioner's favorite way of conducting classes, is intense and effortless. It doesn't spare the body, which is what the practitioner's body knows, having spent a large part of his life in the countryside and factories working physically. When assuming the role of a teacher, the practitioner's style is matched to the needs of the participants. It is characterized by gentleness, empathy, and respect for their bodies. During the classes, the practitioner does not suggest content that may discourage participants (such as aspects of spirituality in yoga), does not force their bodies, and perhaps due to the delicacy mentioned above or even conservatism, avoids touching the students' bodies. Although he does not like chatter during classes, the practitioner explains a lot and talks about the practice. He focuses a lot on students, not concentrating on his training during this time, which he emphasizes. He controls the situation and all participants. That is why he feels so uncomfortable during the online sessions; when deprived of this control, he cannot observe all the participants accurately. The teacher does not see their entire body shapes and body configurations during the position. The limitations of online classes – spatial, technical, and visual – depress the tutor and distract him. (Dagmara Tarasiuk)

I learn from my colleague, who is also my student. The observations that confirm my conclusions and those that I am not fully aware of are valuable for me. For example, I differ significantly in my teaching from a teacher whom I admire and appreciate, emphasizing a more contemplative attitude than just a physical one. The second observation is the contradiction in my reluctance to "overtalk the practice" and the actual and frequent verbal explanation of many things in yoga. This reflection of hers and mine, in turn, allows me to become more aware of and see from the outside what I write about my practice and teaching.

Generally, many of Dagmara comments are consistent with my observations and self-analysis. A lack of incoherence could be due to two things:

1. Common and collaborative knowledge production. Together with the research team (two co-workers, Dagmara and Aleksandra), but also with the participants of the project practicing with us, we learn together and from each other. This is a co-production of knowledge that lasts over time (Bentz & Marlatt 2021; Davidson, Decker, & Tarasiuk 2021; Rehorick & Bentz (Eds.) 2008; Rehorick & Taylor 1995). The conclusions of the analysis also come from conversations, exchanging correspondence, agreeing on meanings, expressing emotions and disagreements, being online together, and most of all, joint practice (see Appendix 1 in this Chapter). The common perspective appeared unnoticed, and the initial incoherencies and doubts were forgotten.
2. It may also result from using an adopted sociological perspective (contemplative social research, Bentz & Georgino 2016; Rehorick & Bentz 2017; Konecki 2018) and the collaborative research and analytical techniques that generate a specific type of knowledge. Descriptions are derived from observation and self-observation of body sensations, reports on emotions and thoughts that arise during the yoga sessions. By using a similar perspective, language, and shared experiences, you can come to common and similar conclusions.

The joint production of knowledge in the first-person narrative perspective is emphasized in collaborative autoethnographic research (Elis & Rawicki 2013; Ellis et al. 2018) or in a study in which we deal with the attitude of "learning together" ("Leregogic", Rehorick, & Taylor 1995; Rehoric & Bentz 2017: 8, 26–27, 33; Bentz & Marlatt 2021: 10). In this type of pedagogical or research situation, research participants learn from each other. A hierarchy based on previous academic or expert degrees is suspended in favor of open discussion and joint conclusion. However, overcoming the hierarchy may encounter difficulties with both sides of the interaction (the professor-student relationship in our study). Tradition and habits play a role in preserving the hierarchical process of knowledge transfer. However, the collective learning approach is dominated by the joint construction of knowledge. It occurs thanks to a deeper understanding of relations, emotions, and everyday situations and overcoming the incoherence of learning through discussions. Authenticity and openness to the direct experience of the world by another become values and, at the same time, the basic assumptions for the production of knowledge. Astonishment/surprise is not rejected but is accepted and processed reflectively. It is a value, not only cognitively fertile but also one that gives joy to discovering new layers of social connection and awareness of social relations. They most often have the nature of "we relations" (Schütz 1962; Schütz & Luckmann 1973: 85), which take place in the entire presence of interaction partners here and now, where there is a mental and bodily coexistence. A unique and direct here-and-now exchange of knowledge occurs, and ultimately, the merging and compilation of the research participants' knowledge and their inclusion in the mutual learning process.

I dealt with such a situation in the self-observations that I described above. I would not have seen myself without my colleagues and research participants' presence, reaction, reflection, and self-observations.

Appendix 1

Contemplative note – after reading the professor's text on self-analysis by Aleksandra Płaczek

Reading the text brought new inspiration and focused your thoughts on your chapters or papers. I notice threads that I have already touched upon, or I can mention them in my texts. This way of exchanging views and exchanging the content we have created complements each other's knowledge and ideas. Still, it is pretty risky at times – I fear that the chapters I have written may not be revealing, and I will unconsciously recreate what I read in texts, papers, chapters, and notes from other researchers.

The professor writes about himself in the third person. Dagmara and I read this content as other third parties – this gives me the feeling that I am reading the text from the perspective of "growing something, layer by layer" and with the feeling that at least nine people are working on the text: we participants (3), we researchers (3), and we personalities (3). One by one, the project participants' knowledge, experience, and roles grow into the text being read at a given moment. Everyone has the perspective of their own emotions and feelings, as individuals (non) researchers, and as private individuals. The smooth interpenetration of roles overlaps throughout the text and the empirical materials, like layers of earth or a cake, making me feel chaotic and uneasy. I look at the text with the feeling of having a dissociative identity disorder. On the other hand, this is what it should be like during the research process. This causes anxiety to arise, but it is immediately suppressed by the sense of rightness. When writing notes, analyzing the materials, I ask myself who I am now, what role, or rather, what glasses do I put on or should wear at a given moment? A practitioner's glass? A sociologist's? A psychologist's? Should I take these glasses off for a while and take the perspective of someone entirely outside? Despite being grateful for the experience gathered during the project, I would like to undo the product, gain new knowledge, and sit in front of the empirical materials as someone new, without accumulated memory. To be like a blank page.

Even so, I now have a feeling that I can deepen my analysis, look further. The collected remarks and the repeated reading of the materials allow us to notice what may have been unattainable before. The boundaries of the mind expand. This is good for the results of the work, but it hampers the research process itself. There are many questions, thoughts, and clutter that I try to clean up and sort.

Here is my reaction to the contemplative note expressed in an e-mail to Aleksandra Płaczek:

Good morning,

An excellent contemplative note.

The fear of repetition and not being innovative is always with us. This is normal in the research process.

The interpenetration of roles always occurs in the research process. We reveal it. The remark about nine people is excellent!!! So, there is a lot of us in this project, and only three people are paid. :)

Project experience is another cognitive filter. It must be remembered and suspended (epoché). But the willingness to be like a blank slate proves the awareness of the determinants of perception.

In my text, adopting the perspective of different people concerns the act of writing itself. In the process of writing, we discover new things and perspectives of our practice, and we even generate categories. In explication, as an analyst, I am always a third person. In writing, we can also express ourselves from the point of view of the first person. We probably have the problem of intersubjectivity when we analyze our auto-reports, but thanks to your notes, I can see it again from the outside. "Dissociative identity disorder" is an intended strategy here. I think there is more order in this disorder than in the "collective tinkering" of Szwabowski and his group (see Kaczmarek, Madys, Pławski, Szczepaniak, Szwabowski, and Wężniejewska, 2020). But I don't know if this is better or worse for a text meant to break up the precise structure of traditional sociological texts. Generating knowledge may come precisely from the dissociative approach to writing what we are going through. For example, you are experiencing disorder and chaos, which could best be expressed with a poem or a jagged analytical text. Let's do it!

Besides, the inspiration for Illeism, writing about yourself from the point of view of a third person, also comes from jñana yoga. ☺ We are also here at home. In addition, we also get a therapeutic effect.

There is another problem, the authority of the teacher or also the power. In English, authority is also power. His (male) influence on thinking can also be

a problem in terms of subordinating to his thoughts, the way of thinking, and opposition to what he represents.
I learned a lot from your notes! Thank you! 🧘 🧘 🧘 🧘
Regards,
Krzysztof T. Konecki 😇

Appendix 2

Contemplative note by Dagmara Tarasiuk:
This is a contemplative note after reading a newspaper interview with Paulina Młynarska, in which I write on the topic of hierarchy, usually male style yoga, and the abuses related to it were discussed.

The interviewee is against forced corrections, pressure, or touch during practice. She sees universal consent to this touch in the automatic permission from others to manage her own body, which is characteristic of women, who are socialized from childhood to occupy a lower position in the hierarchy.

In one of my project interviews, the interviewee complained about the classes with X, who pressed the students without asking for permission to touch them. During one of the practices, he injured the interlocutor by pushing her to the ground. It took many years for her to recover from the injury, but she never went to the instructor about it. She never demanded compensation, which now seems to me to clearly show the patriarchal, i.e., hierarchical system in the student-teacher relationship.

What is extraordinary is that our leader and, at the same time, the grant manager [KTK], when discussing this case, did not seem to sympathize with the interviewee who directly wrote that she was hurt. The professor often emphasizes that X conducts intensive practice, which the professor is particularly pleased with. A smile often accompanies storytelling about it. The professor also often emphasizes how important the teacher was in the process of educating him. After reading the interview and writing a chapter on hierarchy, I started thinking more about this case.

I wonder if the professor's reaction stems from a) sympathy for his teacher, b) a solid master-student relationship, which does not allow the professor to look at his master critically, c) the subconscious pattern that Młynarska talks about – a patriarchal attitude that does not allows the grievances of a participant in his master's classes to be taken seriously.

I experienced this fragment of the interview very much. I remember that I felt enormous anger towards Mr. X, the more so because the same story was repeated in another interview with another of his students! M., a participant in our project, was also damaged by Mr. X's aggressive working methods. That is why I did not want to interview this teacher, and while reading the interview conducted by Alesandra I felt disgusted and aversion, even though the content was not repellant; indeed, at some point, Mr. X even apologizes to his students, whom he might have hurt in the past. Interestingly, it seems to me that I did not articulate my anger towards this teacher on an ongoing basis precisely because my male teacher is his student and admires him. I did not want to undermine his master's authority. So, I remained subordinated to the power of my professor, not voicing my doubts.

I think this case shows the strength of a hierarchical structure based on a power relationship, both in the case of yoga practice and academic classes.

•••

My reply to Dagmara note (sent simultaneously to Aleksandra Płaczek):
Interesting note. Very emotional. I understand. And I also understand this tension.

Remember that you have "real/authentic" contact only with me (a bit of conceit is also useful :)). Other teachers are beyond your reach of reliable and open communication. They isolate themselves, distance themselves, only create the appearance of direct contact because such contact is emotionally and communicatively demanding. You can tell me many things; which other teachers can you do this with at our university?

I suspected that [a feminist article on the patriarchal structure in the yoga world] would spark some threads for reflection on the practice. And it happened. I sent it on purpose. So am I entering the patriarchal structure again because I wanted to achieve a specific effect? I am trying to create conditions of equality. If I leave the role of teacher, who am I in our relationship?

Did you come out of the patriarchal rhetorics? If so, who are you at present? What identities can be attributed to us? "Leregogy" can be helpful (Rehorick, Taylor 1995; Rehoric, Bentz 2017: 8, 26–27, 33; Bentz, Marlatt 2021: 10). These notes help us to learn from each other and go beyond the patriarchal structure.

Again, the note is precious … because it is sincere and evocative.
Regards,
Krzysztof T. Konecki

Acknowledgments

I am grateful to my students and close collaborators in the project, Dagmara Tarasiuk, and Aleksandra Płaczek. The research project has been sponsored by National Science Center in Poland, Opus, grant number 2018/29/B/HS6/00513.

Bibliography

Badiou, Alain. 2001. *Ethics. An Essay on Understanding of Evil*. London, New York: Verso.

Bakker, Johannes I. 2005. The Self as an Internal Dialogue: Mead, Blumer, Peirce, and Wiley. *The American Sociologist*, 36(1), 75–84. http://www.jstor.org/stable/27700414.

Bentz, Valerie M. & Jim Marlatt. 2021. *Deathworlds to Lifeworlds. Collaboration with Strangers for Personal and Ecological Transformation*. Berlin: De Gruyter.

Bentz, Valerie M. & Vincenzo Giorgino. 2016. *Contemplative Social Research. Caring for Self, Being and Lifeworld*. Santa Barbara: Fielding University Press.

Blumer, Herbert. 1969. *Symbolic Interactionism. Perspective and Method*. Berkeley: University of California Press.

Denzin, Norman K. 2013. "The Death of Data?" *Cultural Studies ↔ Critical Methodologies*, 13(4), 353–356. https://doi.org/10.1177/1532708613487882.

Denzin, Norman K. 2019. "Grounded Theory and Politics of Interpretation, Redux." Pp. 449–469 in *Current Developments in Grounded Theory* edited by T. Bryant and K. Charmaz. Los Angeles: Sage.

Davidson, Lori, Jennifer Decker & Dagmara Tarasiuk. 2021. "Overcoming Deathworlds of Addiction, Self-Injury, And Stress." Pp. 205–224 in Bentz, V., Marlatt J. (Eds.) *Deathworlds to Lifeworlds Collaboration with Strangers for Personal, Social and Ecological Transformation*, Berlin, New York: de Gruyter.

Ellis, Carolyn & Jerry Rawicki. 2013. "Collaborative Witnessing of Survival During the Holocaust: An Exemplar of Relational Autoethnography." *Qualitative Inquiry* 19(5), 366–380. doi:10.1177/1077800413479562.

Ellis, Carolyn, Arthur Bochner, Carol Rambo, Keith Berry, Hannah Shakespeare, Craig Gingrich-Philbrook, Tony E. Adams, Robert E. Rinehart, and Derek M. Bolen 2018. "Coming Unhinged: A Twice-Told Multivoiced Autoethnography." *Qualitative Inquiry* 24(2), 119–133. doi:10.1177/1077800416684874.

De Michelis, Elizabeth. 2004. *A History of Modern Yoga Patanjali and Western Esotericism*. London: Continuum.

Goffman, Erving 1959. *The Presentation of Self in Everyday Life*. Garden City, New York: Doubleday.

Gunnarsson, Nina V. 2021. "The Activation and Restoration of Shame in an Intimate Relationship: A First-Hand Account of Self-Injury." *Qualitative Sociology Review* 17(2), 104–121.

Hastrup, Kirsten B. 2018. "Muscular consciousness: Knowledge-making in an Arctic environment." Pp. 116–137 in *Pre-Textual Ethnographies: Challenging the Phenomenological Level of Anthropological Knowledge-Making*. Edited by T. Rakowski, & H. Patzer. Sean Kingston Publishing.

Kacperczyk, Anna. 2020. "Autoetnograficzna inicjacja." ("Autoethnographic initiation.") Pp. 43–78 in Kafar M. & Kacperczyk A. (Eds.) *Autoetnograficzne "zbliżenia" i "oddalenia." O autoetnografii w Polsce*. Łódź: Wydawnictwo Uniwersytetu Łódzkiego.

Kaczmarek, Paweł, Agnieszka Madys, Marcin Pławski, Colette Szczepaniak, Oskar Szwabowski & Paulina Wężniejewska. 2020. "Kolektywne majsterkowanie albo zmiana, która nie nadchodzi." ("Collective tinkering or change that is not coming.") Pp. 161–206 in Kafar M. & Kacperczyk A. (Eds.) *Autoetnograficzne "zbliżenia" i "oddalenia." O autoetnografii w Polsce*. Łódź: Wydawnictwo Uniwersytetu Łódzkiego.

Konecki, Krzysztof T. 2015a. *Is the Body the Temple of the Soul? Modern Yoga Practice as a Psychosocial Phenomenon*, Lodz: University of Lodz Press/ Krakow: Jagiellonian University Press.

Konecki, Krzysztof T. 2018. *Advances in Contemplative Social Research*, Lodz: University of Lodz Press/Krakow: Jagiellonian University Press.

Konecki, Krzysztof T. 2021. "Contemplative Grounded Theory: Possibilities and Limitations." Pp. 151–186 in Denzin N.K., Salvo, J. and Chen, S.-L.S. (Eds.) *Radical Interactionism and Critiques of Contemporary Culture, Studies in Symbolic Interaction, Vol. 52*. Emerald Publishing Limited, Bingley, pp. 151–186. https://doi.org/10.1108/S0163-239620210000052010.

Kubica, Grażyna. 2002. "Wstęp." ("Introduction", in Polish) Pp. 5–35 in *Dziennik w ścisłym znaczeniu tego wyrazu* (*The diary in the Strict Sense of the Term*), Bronisław Malinowski. Kraków: Wydawnictwo Literackie.

Malinowski, Bronisław. 1989. *A Diary in the Strict Sense of the Term*. Stanford: Stanford University Press.

Mallinson, James & Mark Singleton. 2017. *Roots of Yoga*. London: Penguin Books.

Newcombe, Suzanne. 2014. "The Institutionalization of the Yoga Tradition: "Gurus" B.K.S. Iyengar and Yogini Sunita in Britain." Pp. 147–167 in Singleton, M. & Goldberg, E. *Gurus of Modern Yoga*. N.Y.: Oxford University Press.

Pławski, Marcin, Oskar Szwabowski, Collette Szczepaniak, and Paulina Wężniejewska. 2019. "Friendly Writing as Non-inquiry: The Problems of Collective Autoethnographic Writing About Collective Autoethnographic Writing." *Qualitative Inquiry*, 25(9–10), 1002–1010. https://doi.org/10.1177/1077800418809134.

Rambo Ronai, C. 1992. "The Reflexive Self Through Narrative. A Night in the Life of an Erotic Dancer/Researcher." Pp. 102–124 in Carolyn E. & Flaherty, M.G. *Investigating Subjectivity. Research on Lived Experience*. London: Sage.

Rambo Ronai, C. 1995. "Multiple reflections of child sex abuse. An argument for a layered account." *Journal of Contemporary Ethnography*, 23(4), 395–426.

Rehorick, David A. & Valerie M. Bentz (Eds.). 2008. *Transformative Phenomenology. Changing Ourselves, Lifeworlds, and Professional Practice.* Lanham: Lexington Books.

Rehorick, David A. & Valerie M. Bentz. 2017. *Expressions of Phenomenological Research: Consciousness and Lifeworld Studies.* Santa Barbara: Fielding University Press.

Rehorick, David A., & Gail Taylor 1995. "Thoughtful Incoherence: First Encounters with the Phenomenological-Hermeneutical Domain." *Human Studies*, 18(4), 389–414. http://www.jstor.org/stable/20000253.

Richardson, Laurel. 1992. "The Consequences of Poetic Representation: Writing the Other, Rewriting the Self." Pp. 125–140 in Ellis, C. & Flaherty M.G. (Eds.) *Investigating Subjectivity. Research on Lived Experience.* London: Sage.

Rossing Hilde, Lars-Tore Ronglan & Susie Scott. 2016. "'I just want to be me when I am exercising': Adrianna's construction of a vulnerable exercise identity." *Sport, Education and Society*, 21(3), 339–355, DOI: 10.1080/13573322.2014.920316.

Schütz, Alfred. 1962. *Collected Papers* I. Edited by Maurice Natanson The Hague: Martinus Nijhoff.

Schütz, Alfred. 1967. *The Phenomenology of the Social World.* Evanston, IL: Northwestern University Press.

Schütz, Alfred and Thomas Luckmann. 1973. *The Structure of the Lifeworld.* Evanston: Northwestern University Press.

Smith, Frederic M. & White Joan. 2014. "Becoming an Icon: B.K.S. Iyengar as a Yoga Teacher and Yoga Guru." Pp. 122–146 in *Gurus of Modern Yoga*, edited by Singleton, Mark & Ellen Goldberg. N.Y.: Oxford University Press.

Singleton, Marc. 2010a. Yoga Body. *The Origin of Modern Posture Practice.* Oxford: Oxford University Press.

Singleton, Marc. 2010b. Translations, belief frameworks and modern yoga practice. The Magazine of Yoga; http://themagazineofyoga.com/blog/2010/10/12/conversation-mark-singleton (accessed: 4.09.2020).

Singleton, Mark & Goldberg, Ellen. Eds. 2014. *Gurus of Modern Yoga.* N.Y.: Oxford University Press.

Singleton, Mark & Fraser Tara. 2014. "T. Krishnamacharya, "Father of Modern Yoga." Pp. 83–106 in *Gurus of Modern Yoga*, edited by Singleton, Mark & Ellen Goldberg. N.Y.: Oxford University Press.

Sarbacker, Stuart R. 2014. "Swami Ramdev: Modern Yoga Revolutionary." Pp. 351–371 in *Gurus of Modern Yoga*, edited by Singleton, Mark & Ellen Goldberg. N.Y.: Oxford University Press.

Szwabowski, Oskar. 2021. ""Shame on You!": An Autoethnography Poem About Being an Autoethnographer Who Writes Autoethnographic Poems." *Qualitative Inquiry.* https://doi.org/10.1177/10778004211039161.

Szwabowski, Oskar. 2019. *Nekrofilna produkcja akademicka i pieśni partyzantów. Autoetnografia pracy akademickiej i dydaktycznej w czasach zombie-kapitalizmu.* (Necrophilic academic production and partisan songs. Autoethnography of academic and didactic work in the times of zombie-capitalism.) Wrocław: Instytut Pedagogiki Uniwersytetu Wrocławskiego.

Uebelacker, Lisa A et al. 2010. "Hatha yoga for depression: critical review of the evidence for efficacy, plausible mechanisms of action, and directions for future research." *Journal of psychiatric practice* 16(1), 22–33. DOI: 10.1097/01.pra.0000367775.88388.96.

Warrier, Maya. 2014. "Online Bhakti in a Modern Guru Organization." Pp. 308–323 in *Gurus of Modern Yoga*, edited by Singleton, Mark & Ellen Goldberg. N.Y.: Oxford University Press.

Weber Max. 2012. *Theory of Social and Economic Organization*, translated by A.R. Anderson and Talcott Parsons, N.Y.: Free Press.

Williamson, Lola. 2014. "Stretching toward the Sacred: John Friend and Anusara Yoga." Pp. 210–233 in *Gurus of Modern Yoga*, edited by Singleton, Mark & Ellen Goldberg. N.Y.: Oxford University Press.

Zerubavel, Eviatar. 2015. *Hidden in Plain Sight: The Social Structure of Irrelevance.* Oxford, New York: Oxford University Press.

CHAPTER 4

Can You Stop Your Mind and Your Daily Activities? An Analysis of Meditation in Yoga Practice

1 Introduction

Although it seems to be a passive activity, meditation is an active activity in the mental sense; it requires attention and concentration. The meditator concentrates on "the projects and task plans." (Schütz 1962a: 213)[1]

That planned task is meditation. However, it is not a task in everyday life, and the plan is not very clear. The subject decides to start meditation, and entering meditation allows him or her to enter another reality, the reality of meditation, where there is passivity and focus on the here and now, without carrying out any practical tasks or plans related to everyday life. Concentrating on the "object of meditation" helps focus the mind. (Desikachar 1999: 113) The body or breath can also be the object of meditation (Desikachar 1999: 117). During meditation, the mind merges with the object of meditation, and the meditation process becomes inner and deep. (Desikachar 1999: 114; see also Cope 2006, chapter 13)

This project is aimed at breaking the mind out of everyday life.[2] However, it is still immersed in it, and it is also a reference point for realizing where the attention is currently located and what consciousness is directing it to. But this immersion is moderated by the meditation "bubble." Therefore, meditation is a paradoxical project of everyday life that takes place at its very center, suspending the individual's involvement in it, thus referring to a temporary rejection of this world (everyday life). Finally meditation stops the work of the mind and the practical activities of the meditating subject. So, it is challenging to create and then describe meditative states when the mind is turned off. It is not easy to research these meditative states scientifically (Sparby 2019: 131).[3]

---

1 "... within its acts and its attention is exclusively directed to carrying its project into effect, executing its plan" (Schütz 1962a: 213).

2 The chapter is a revised version of the published paper: Konecki, Krzysztof T. 2024. "Can you stop your mind and your daily activities? An analysis of meditation in yoga practice." Kultura i Społeczeństwo, 68(3):169–203.

3 We treat the term meditation broadly. The practice of mindfulness also falls within the scope of our analysis, as it concerns the practice of mindfulness in sitting, observing the breath, and the reaction of impulses that come from the body. We are still dealing with an attempt to

Sociology has tried to capture meditation from an external perspective (Collins 2004, 2011), and reference has been made to religious practices. Collins treated meditation as an interactional ritual that occurs in the individual's mind; a person engages in an internal conversation between the social aspect of the self and the individual. There is reference to Mead's (1934; Blumer 1969; Prus 1996) concept of the self. Interpretations of meditation can also be inspired by the sociology of Durkheim (2008/1912) and his analysis of the elementary forms of religion, and by Gidden's (1991; cited in Pagis 2019) description of the individualization of modern societies. The classic sociology usually concerns the motives and explanations for undertaking activities and their social embeddedness, the networks, and the collectives that they promote. In addition, there is a reflection on meditation's place in contemporary spirituality and how philosophies and elements of Eastern religions are adapted to the Western world (Singleton 2010; Pagis 2019; Newcombe 2019; Newcombe and O'Brien-Kopp 2020).

From the perspective of critical sociology meditation and mindfulness practice can be viewed as a form that supports the existing power and domination in contemporary corporations. The practice is mainly meant to increase productivity and the rhetoric of a calm and free mind, and cover up the real goals and effects of meditation practices (Islam, Holm, and Karjalainen 2017). It may even justify and stabilize contemporary consumer capitalism (Purser and Loy 2013; Carvalho 2021; Chen 2022; Purser 2019; see also Anālayo's (2020) critique of this thesis) and how "contemporary liberal-capitalism is felt and lived with" (Coleman 2020). Critical and political interpretations tend to be made from *a priori* positions; prior categories of analysis are superimposed on processes that are not familiar to critical analysts from within. A kind of data forcing takes place (Glaser 1992), and different conclusions could come from broad empirical research. (see: https://theconversation.com/yoga-versus-democracy-what-survey-data-says-about-spiritual-americans-political-behavior-187960; Kucinskas and Stweart 2022; Steensland, King, Duffy 2022.). The goal of the research is to look and describe the meditation practice from the inside without making any assumptions about what can be found in the situation under study; it is a contemplative study of the minding rather than a detailed description of the space where the thinking/not

disconnect from everyday life and to get to "a point" of concentration. If meditation is used in pain therapy, individuals can distance themselves from the body and lose ownership of sensations, and finally, there is a perceived reduction in pain intensity (Riegner, Posey, Olivia, Jung, Mobley, Zeidan 2022).

thinking takes place. Contemplative research is inspired by phenomenology, so we are also under its influence (Bentz and Giorgino 2016), and inspirations come from Buddhism Zen (Janesick 2015; Konecki 2018: 43–53).

We researched and analyzed the meditation using the contemplative grounded theory methodology. The empirical materials are based mainly on self-observation, self-reports of the research participants, and unstandardized interviews. Empirical materials are analyzed according to contemplative coding procedures with contemplative memos done in the context of coding and analysts' assumptions. The reflective process is opened and objectified by writing and often analyzed (Konecki 2022, see Chapter 2).

The practice sometimes seems homogenized when we look from the external perspective; however, it is firmly experientially individualized. We do not take a deterministic perspective in which liberal capitalism is supposed to be the structural basis for the experiences and feelings of individual consciousness in meditation practice or mindfulness practice (see Coleman (2020) for a discussion of this issue).

In addition, there is interest in the micro-perspective, where the analysis of the relationship between the self and social situating finds its place in the sociological perspective (Pagis 2010, 2015; 2019). We, as Pagis, want to describe meditation from a micro perspective, from the practitioners' point of view, and from the embeddedness in the situation, including the occasional first-person account of the author of this text. The sociological perspective is used minimally here, although it exists in the background of the analysis, for the practice of meditation does not take place in a social vacuum. It takes place in *the situation*, but, as we shall see, it nevertheless tries to isolate itself in the face of social pressures, including the burdens of working life (Schütz 1962a). As sociologists, we want to cross the borders of the social determination of the process and explicitly show how the mind creates reality, which is supposedly constructed by social factors. Inspired by phenomenology, we want to show how crossing the border of *provinces of meaning* looks like, crossing from everyday life reality to the realm of meditation (Schütz 1962: 231). There could be a collision between two visions of reality, two different *finite provinces of meaning* (Schütz 1962: 229–234).

> We speak of provinces of meaning and not of sub-universes because it is a meaning of our experiences and not the ontological structure of the objects which constitutes reality. Hence, we call a certain set of experiences a finite province of meaning if all of them show a specific cognitive style and are – concerning this style – not only consistent in themselves but also compatible with one another (Schütz 1962: 230).

We do not concentrate *on the essential features of the finite provinces of the meaning of meditation* but want to show how entering it happens. Although we can not say it is ethnographical research, it is similar to that concerning the detailed description of the situation occurring in the minds and bodies of beginning meditators.

•••

This article follows a qualitative and contemplative analysis style and will describe the components of entering a meditative state in a concrete physical and social situation. How do (primarily) beginners in hatha yoga and meditation deal with this state? What do they feel? The purpose of the analysis is to explore and list the conditions that influence entering into the meditation process and isolate the meditation elements that arise in the *beginner's mind* (Suzuki 2010). We do not adopt any model to describe meditation experiences (Preston 1981: 48). We try to get as close as possible to these experiences and reflect their meaning and understanding as they appear in the practitioners themselves (Prus 1996; Giorgino 2014) in crossing the boundaries of the realm of everyday life and meditation.

Some of the elements of the external and the internal environment are disturbing to meditation. We want to list and interpret them, and see how practitioners deal with these obstacles – what tactics do they employ to eliminate them or redirect attention and include them in the background of the main point, concentration?

Our analysis will mainly focus on self-reports provided to researchers from self-observations made by participants in the research project (in self-observation and self-reporting see Konecki 2018: 229–231).[4] Self-reports or journaling could be a good way of coming out of the meditation or breathing exercises (pranayama) and integrating the stillness of the mind with the life-world. Moreover, we still remember what happened during the writing process directly after meditation. It is also the material to work with the Self. "The challenge in recording these experiences lies in finding the language to capture their subtlety on the page." (Kempton 2011, chapter 10; compare also Rosen 201: chapter six).

The research project in which we tried to describe, among other things, meditative states, concerned the analysis of the experience of hatha yoga and

4 The main self-reports will be cited below; it will be indicated wherever there are quotes from interviews.

the transfer of bodily knowledge.[5] Meditation is one of the elements of yoga practice, so we also dealt with it in the abovementioned project, but meditation was not the central theme of the research project. While it is usually not strongly emphasized in commercial hatha yoga practice, it is traditionally an indispensable component of yoga (Eliade 1997: 20–21; Iyengar, undated). The mere physical practice of hatha yoga is a form of meditation in motion. Still, *Dhyana* – concentration on an object – is both a separate and an inner element in the practice of hatha yoga. As yoga masters and teachers claim, you cannot practice yoga without meditation (Iyengar 1990; Desikachar 1999). There are also some proposals or instructions, which are more or less general, on how to meditate, coming from other than yoga traditions:

> The same way works for you yourself as well. If you want to obtain perfect calmness in your zazen, you should not be bothered by the various images you find in your mind. Let them come and let them go. (Suzuki 1995: 32–22)

In our yoga sessions, we tried to introduce meditation practice at the end of the session, after practicing asanas and breathing exercises (Rosen 2011). Or we tried to do separate meditation sessions to study how our mind functions while meditating and what changes occur in our perception of the world as a result of meditative concentration in general. We were also interested in connecting the work of the mind (thinking) with the body's sensations. There is no contemplative research on minding without describing the body's feelings (Konecki 2022; Konecki, Płaczek, Tarasiuk 2024). How did the body react to still sitting, and what signals did it send to the mind? What did the mind do with it? What emotions did you feel while sitting? And how were they dealt with? These questions accompanied us when analyzing the self-reports that the project participants prepared immediately after the practice. Self-observation was conducted under instruction, and the self-reporting was preceded by instructions (descriptions of these research techniques can be found in Konecki 2018: Chapter 10).

The study consisted of 17 self-observing participants in hatha yoga, pranayama, and meditation sessions each week (we obtained 532 self-reports).

---

5 The article is based on the research project: "Experiencing corporeality and gestures in the social world of hatha yoga. Meanings and knowledge transfer in body practice". Sponsored by National Science Center in Poland [Opus, grant number 2018/29/B/HS6/00513]. A book published after the project's realization describes the knowledge transfer process in yoga bodily practice (Konecki, Płaczek, Tarasiuk 2024).

There were 44 meetings, held every week from October 21, 2019, to June 1, 2021. Additionally, we had yoga and meditation sessions with 67 Erasmus students (2020–2022), who also provided self-reports from their self-observations (520 self-reports). Most of the project participants were hatha yoga beginners. Furthermore, we obtained 50 interviews with practitioners and teachers, seven hours of audio-video recordings of hatha yoga practice, and 70 hours of participant observation. Informed consent was obtained from the study participants to use the textual data and video recording for analysis and publication. This paper mainly concerns the self-reports and interviews done during the research.

The University Ethics Commission accepted the research project.

2 What Is Meditation?

Below we describe experiences from meditation sessions, which took place during our project, usually at the end of the hatha yoga practice, after the breathing exercises. The meditation was about sitting, and here we were inspired mainly by the sitting instruction from Zen Buddhism practice (Konecki 2018: 50), although there are stated similarities between yoga and Buddhism, especially in the realm of meditation (Cope 2006). The instruction was to sit still in various positions, with your eyes fixed on one point, and observe your breathing, all the body's reactions, and the work of your mind. The material elements that create the atmosphere, e.g., mats, blankets, meditation cushions, and the bell, are also added to the instructions. Through sound, the bell creates a unique atmosphere and borders with the outside world (Carvalho 2021). We did not question what might appear while sitting. We were also not concerned with the effects of sitting and yoga practices, such as attaining enlightenment (Preston 1981).

Let us now answer this question from the practitioners' point of view: What is meditation for them?

Practitioners often ask themselves, what is meditation? It is unknown whether we are in a meditative state or only in mindfulness (Nhat Hanh, Thich 1976). This meditative state does happen, some yoga practitioners say. Sometimes, while observing the racing of thoughts, we are aware of what is happening inside us, and we remember different stories, what we were doing earlier and what we are doing now, and how our mind works. This is mindfulness. However, yoga is a mindfulness practice with the body as the first mindful object (Vicente and Stuhr 2022). Sometimes, participants of meditation sessions say that there are gaps between thoughts. And then there is an inner "calmness," peace and joy, and inner beauty (Pagis 2015, 2010). There are also doubts about what meditation is. There is often no language to define meditation. Even yoga teachers, who have been practicing for 20 years, mention that you can only sometimes get insight. The following quote from an interview with a yoga teacher shows many of the qualities that practitioners can attribute to meditation:

> I try to sit every day. So, I usually sit in silence, or sometimes I turn on a mantra, choose positions and asanas for sitting, those that are stable for me, sometimes you can sit on a chair. Usually, I sit on the ground. So, what does it give me? Silence inside. Silence is also easier because it is not always possible; what is meditation? This happens to us, right? Usually, there is a storm of thoughts in the head, but these thoughts are also needed because you can see what we have, what we do, what our mind is doing, and where it is going. Sometimes stories come to mind. And sometimes there are gaps between thoughts, and then we are close to that deep, inner peace. And sometimes, after meditation, your eyes shine, and you know it was something. You feel such deep joy and peace. And although I sit every day, I have something to do with myself in the spiritual and internal spheres. Because sometimes ... I can say that I don't know if it is meditation. It is a very inward state of profound peace, such inner beauty. But sometimes, it's just a thought, a storm of thoughts, or a storm of emotion. Sometimes the body hurts, and we want to change the position, and sometimes we want to run away from it. It means running away, not doing it, because the body hurts, and this state is shortened when a certain amount of time has been allocated. It also happens that there are ups and downs, right? Along the way of this practice. (interview with a yoga teacher, woman)

The difficulty of describing the meditative state is sometimes indicated (see also Shear and Jevning 2002: 191). It is, in a way, a different world, and this other world has no language. Language is from the lifeworld. Meditation is a generally non-linguistic world. We want to disconnect ourselves from thinking, and thoughts are language; they are *inner conversations* (Mead 1934). And this other world should be deprived of that. So, it isn't easy to describe. This difficulty is related to its *essential feature*, the fact that it is a beyond-language reality, *it is extra-language state of being*. Of course, one can conclude from Wittgenstein that we must remain silent about what cannot be said. We do not want to be silent because silence is also significant for our entanglement in the world of life. Its description is a continuation of this paradox of immersing the world of meditation in the world of practical activities through the intention to cut ourselves off from the world of thoughts, names, categories, and actions:

> Meditation takes me into another world, into another dimension. I really like this feeling; it's hard for me to describe it. (exerciser, woman)[6]

> It clears my mind somehow. I don't know how to explain it, but my body and mind felt lighter. (exerciser, woman)

3 Preparation for Meditation

Well-conducted meditation requires explanation and preparation by practitioners. Therefore, the role of the teacher is essential. He/she must explain the basic principles of meditation and what may happen during it. However, after some time of the practice explanations are not so much needed. Teachers usually leave practitioners a lot of room for discovery, although they sometimes explain the situation if they expect difficulties on the part of the practitioners:

> In my last practice, I had wanted to do a 20-minute meditation. I explained a lot about how to meditate. However, without interpretation of possible feelings. But what is meditation? I thought and said that meditation was an essential part of yoga. Asanas and pranayama and pratyahara are preparation for meditation. I said that practicing asanas today would be easy.
>
> I was doing the meditation, starting with the bell. As it should be, I also gave out instructions on the meditation paper. We were doing the meditation on a chair. We don't have pillows, and it is probably better on a chair because sitting on the floor would be more of a challenge without cushions. Pain in the legs, knees, and spine could occur in inexperienced practitioners.
>
> I explained a lot by talking about meditation because I was afraid of the reaction in the process. I know that the race of thoughts is a pain in our times, and it is difficult to fight it after a hard day's work. (author)

6 We use two terms here: exercisers and practitioners. Exercisers are people who have systematically attended hatha yoga for less than one year. On the other hand, practitioners are people who have systematically attended classes for more than one year.

The caption "author" under the quotes refers to the researcher and author of the paper who is both a practitioner and instructor of hatha yoga.

It is vital to prepare the position and place for meditation, e.g., to avoid falling asleep:

> During meditation, I was half asleep because I was alert, and I knew what was happening around me, even though I fell asleep. That 20 minutes passed by incredibly fast. I was sleeping, and now and then, I woke up thinking about what I still had to do, especially at work. These thoughts did not last long, and I fell asleep again. I chose the chair on purpose, hoping to avoid such a situation. (exerciser, woman)

It is also important to prepare to lower your body temperature:

> I was too cold last week, so I prepared two blankets for meditation. Happily, the guided meditation has focused on the feeling of warmth passing through the body, along with the feeling that it is heavy. (exerciser, woman)

4 Meditation as a Challenge: Pain, Negative Emotions, and Sleepiness

Often meditators struggle with *the limitations of the body*. They fight pain, numbness, body inertia, and recurring pains ... There are also particular feelings of the body, e.g., leaving the body, the *body feels foreign or external*, and the practitioner loses control over it:

> I was looking at one point on the mat. This inertia made me feel like I had come out of my body. It felt like it was foreign. I looked at my hands; they looked like they were made of wax and seemed dead. It did not cause any emotions in me. I felt nothing. (exerciser, woman, research collaborator)

Some obstacles due to *body physiology*, such as a throat irritation, can interfere with meditation:

> In the end, I almost succeeded [at focusing in meditation]. I closed my eyes and listened to my breathing, but my throat bothered me because my throat was irritated. And in the middle of meditation, I had to stop and drink something so as not to cough up ☹. (exerciser, man)

Sometimes, the pain during meditation is so severe that *anxiety and emotions of fear and sadness* arise, and the practitioner has to stop meditating. After relaxing your body, you can go back to counting your breath and continue until the end of your meditation. Meditation can be a severe challenge to beginner practitioners:

> When I saw the feet of the other participants and the lack of any movement on their part, I felt even more overwhelmed. It was a strange feeling. I wouldn't say I liked it. After a while, I felt very scared. I was scared. Anxiety awoke in me, the source of which I did not know. I had no visions, and I felt fear and a little sadness ... The pain was over immediately, and I relaxed. I felt that I was back in my body; I was comfortable and well. I was breathing calmly, counting to 10. Suddenly the gong sounded. (exerciser, woman, collaborator of principal investigator)

Feelings of uneasiness and *dread* associated with the feelings of the body may arise during meditation. Existential anxiety appears, the fear connected with the issue of death. It is accompanied by body sensations (e.g., tightness in the stomach). The practitioner fights negative thoughts by recalling positive ones:

> After about half of the meditation, which is 10 minutes, I felt a sudden fear and stress. There was a sudden tight knot in my stomach, anxiety, and a loss of sense of security. Thoughts about death began to appear in my head, the image of someone's funeral, a coffin. I became instantly anxious, and started to fight these thoughts, trying hard to recall positive, kind thoughts. After a while, the negative thoughts disappeared. (exerciser, woman, research collaborator)

Pain during meditation (pain between the shoulder blades) is a severe obstacle to concentration and a challenge for the practitioner. The pain was the cause of distraction, but at the same time, the focus, *the conscious perception of pain, was a moment of mindfulness*. It was not a "glorious pain" (Lev 2022) but a very useful pain. After the meditation is over, there is a sense of relief, no pain, and a surge of energy. So, the practitioners see the positive effects of meditation:

> During the meditation, an increasing pain between the shoulder blades returned. Whenever my thoughts focused on the pain, I quickly tried to shift them to a single point on the floor. My vision was blurred. I couldn't hear sounds from other rooms; the only thing that made me distracted from time to time was pain. At the end of the meditation, the pain was so excruciating that I began to ask in my mind for the gong to ring out. When I heard its sound, I smiled gently (or so I thought) and felt relief

> and a sudden burst of energy. The pain between the shoulder blades stopped. (exerciser, woman, research collaborator)

Meditation, as already mentioned, can be *a severe challenge* to beginners, as well as those who are advanced in practice. During meditation, intense thoughts about work may arise that are not easy to break free from when meditating *after work*. Concentration is difficult, although it may occur, as in the following example at the end of the meditation:

> I had thoughts about work all the time because I had been working intensively; I had online meetings, phone calls, and much correspondence. Work, work, work ... It was challenging to focus on the breathing, the stomach, and the navel. It was easier for me to focus on the breath in my nostrils. I could hear my breath, making it easier to focus. I counted breaths to ten. It was only towards the end that I could fully immerse myself in meditation. I was in the here and now, almost without thinking. A single chime rang out and ended the meditation. It surprised me, as there were always three rings. (author)

As you can see, the meditation challenge for advanced people concerns *the strong tension of consciousness* in the lifeworld (Schütz 1962b; Sebald 2011; Konecki, Płaczek, Tarasiuk 2024: 247–249). It is difficult for them to enter the world of meditation and stop, or they are not careful enough to enter meditation because they are not adequately prepared physically and mentally. We can see also how the author wants to accommodate the lifeworld in the regime of working life.[7] Changing the reality (cognitive style) is not easy:

> During meditation (on a chair), focus on breathing. Departures from thoughts about work. About today's scientific degree committee. About the phone talks. And work talks that come along always make me uneasy. But I dissolve it with meditation. Focus. I feel a pain in my back, a 'pain

7 Maybe the author becomes the self-helper and tries to accommodate liberal capitalism, which strongly exploits him, within himself (Purser 2019; Han 2015; Rosa 2020). However, this reflection was only possible after reading the external interpretation of the cultural processes of introducing mindfulness to the capitalist system (see also Coleman 2022). However, after some other readings, we could incorporate another perspective, and see that "mindfulness might turn out to be a crucially important resource in facing the ravages caused by neoliberal capitalism" (Anālayo, 2020). Practicing mindfulness in every moment can do more to change the conditions of suffering than merely having a critical stance. In this space, critical sociology meets contemplative inquiry.

> belt' on my back; on the right side, I felt pain. I was leaning against the chair. But then I was lethargic, close to falling asleep. Again, I went back to the erect spine, and the pain I had noticed before came back. Concentrating on the breath, on the stomach. Repeating the word 'focus' while inhaling; 'focus' on the exhale. Without counting. (author)

Thinking about work (working life as *the finite province of meaning*) can also be interspersed with *entering a state of falling asleep* (the border of another *province of meaning*, sleeping and dreaming); on occasion, there is a disturbance in the perception of time (the essential feature of *province of meaning* – the specific time perspective, Schütz 1962).

> The strangest thing is that I really don't know if I fell asleep. On the one hand, I think I didn't because I heard the leader ending the meditation. On the other hand, I completely lost track of time. (exerciser, woman)

Planning is one of the many activities of the mind that is busy working all day, in the province of working life. Meditation is an opportunity *to master your racing thoughts*:

> During meditation, especially at the beginning, my head talked to me a lot, planned and created potential dialogues and situations. Then, as if I remembered what this part of the practice should be, I started counting inhalations and exhalations to ten. Thoughts tried to penetrate me, but they weren't as intense as they were at first. (exerciser, woman)

Observing others as you meditate and comparing yourself to them can be a hindrance, but it is also a focus on the here and now. Thus, *a rule of comparison* is taken from everyday life (Brown 2021). But observing others also shows that meditation in a group is a collaborative practice; we try to find ourselves in this group, adapting to others to harmonize our sitting and breathing (another feature of the finite province of meaning is the *form of sociality*):

> By looking at the same point all the time, I started noticing other participants in the practice. My attention was drawn to the swaying sideways of my friend sitting in front of me, and I began to wonder why she was swinging so much, why I wasn't doing it, and if it had a calming effect. Later, I saw another friend's toes move, bend and straighten. (exerciser, woman)

Below is the perspective of the person sitting next to the practitioner who wrote the statement above. Similarly, we are dealing with observing others and trying to compare ourselves:

> Often, with my eyes closed, I used to open them to see how meditation is going on in others or if they have their eyes closed. And when someone had their head tilted down, I wondered whether that person was meditating with their eyes closed or half-open or fully open; it was such a mystery for me to decipher. However, I remembered what the professor said so that we would not stay on a given thought for too long, so I stopped trying to solve the answer to the question I had asked. (exerciser, woman)

Meditation can also be a challenge when we have prepared ourselves inadequately. For example, if *we did not follow a diet* and ate a meal just before meditating. This, along with a *difficult day at work*, can be a severe obstacle to focus:

> During meditation, my stomach was full, and I was after lunch. Physical fatigue is felt throughout the body. The whole day of work and online contact with colleagues. Preparation for classes at the university. (author)

According to one yoga teacher, the remedy for overcoming the obstacle in the form of the presence of others and other obstacles is *accepting* what is outside and focusing on what is inside. Focusing on small things can help us transform our view. (Cope 2006, chapter 13). Accepting attitude differs from the critical and analytical cognitive attitude in working life. Asana practice can help in getting acceptance of the outer world and concentrating on the inside world of meditation:

> So, really, again, you can look for a lot of obstacles and say, 'Oh, I don't like the color here.' And it might happen that someone in the room will say, 'Well, but this light bothers me.' And they distract me, as if they are running away from what is going on inside and looking for such obstacles outside. And this change, through the practice of asanas, makes it easier for us to accept what is outside and turn our attention inward. (interview with a hatha yoga teacher, man)

5 Self-Knowledge

Meditation is also a way to observe the *mind's work and to distance yourself* from your thoughts and the process of thinking itself. It is a process of self-knowledge and recognizing your own mind's work. Thus, mindfulness is involved here, as we realize what we think and how we think (Nhat Hanh, Thich 1976: 7–8). There may also be epiphanies, certain revelations that resolve matters of everyday life. But most of all, we observe our thinking and distance ourselves from it. This self-recognition as a result of meditating can keep you motivated to continue your practice and distance yourself from the current situation and yourself, which in turn can help stop your thoughts from racing, that we usually experience in the working life:

> Well, that's what it is for me: learning to not pay attention to everything that's going on in your head. That's where all the thinking is going on, the pondering, the wondering, the embracing, the planning. And meditation is learning not to pay attention to that, that your brain will do whatever it wants anyway and get you into different scenarios. And such a success in meditation is not to stop thinking at all, because that is very, very, very difficult ... as I talk to people who meditate every day, it's just a super hard thing to do. Rarely does anyone succeed, rarely anyone [can do it] for more than half a minute, but what is a great success is being aware that you are thinking about all the things and learning that, 'OK, this is how it will always be, I don't have to. And in meditation, various interesting visions came to me, created by my brain. And also, thanks to that, I reconciled with my father because, suddenly, I had some kind of epiphany that maybe he didn't want to hurt me X years ago. (practitioner, woman).

During meditation, in this case, walking meditation, we also learn about our weaknesses and be mindful of the body:

> When meditating, walking in circles, at first I was focused on my breath, but the longer I kept my feet in the air, the more I had the feeling that with each step, they were getting a little heavier, and I was thinking about getting them on the ground. I felt that I was not very patient if I wanted to quickly put my feet on the ground. (exerciser, woman)

Self-recognition can also relate to the mind's and body's work of *recognizing the amount of time that passes*; the realization of a working intuition is startling:

> At the end of the meditation, 20 minutes. We sat with the cameras on, I was also aware of seeing each other, although I was not looking at the practitioners, concentrating on the point in front of me. I was drowsy, but I returned to observing the breaths by straightening up and taking deeper breaths. A stillness came over me in meditation. A little different from that in pranayama, not as joyful but isolating from daily life activities.
>
> I knew exactly when the bell would ring to end the meditation; it's incredible how the body senses the passage of time during meditation. (author)

Another property of self-cognition may be *a greater awareness of specific states of mind, such as the location of pain and the suspension of the mind.* Concentration enables one to perceive these phenomena and report on their existence. The body awareness is sharp and vivid in the meditation province of meaning, in opposition to the working life province:

> During meditation, the sun was shining brightly. I could feel it in my eyes and on my face. I liked the sensation. I also felt pain in my stomach and back. I knew precisely where, behind my shoulder blade, my back hurt. This location was highly accurate. Through meditation, I was able to notice these pains. In everyday life, I would not notice what hurt; I would overlook the sensation.
>
> Despite a moment of actual suspension, I had these perceptions, full awareness in a still body and mind. It lasted for a short time, but I felt it very clearly. (author)

> It cleared my mind (even after that, I looked a bit confused and sleepy). I felt a lot of peace. (exerciser, woman)

Concentration also makes it possible to see that certain phenomena are not perceived, e.g., the non-perception of sounds. In the self-reports below, while practitioners heard while sharing self-reports after meditation, the reports of other meditators' feelings said that they did not notice the sounds some practitioners perceived. People who went deeper into the meditative state were excluded from observing the environment and they went to the state of "deep self" (see Scheff 2014):

> Entering the room, you could hear a chirping sparrow through the open window. While meditating, I didn't notice it at all. As if it had disappeared and reappeared. I didn't hear it even though I liked its chirping very much, and it appeased me. (exerciser, woman)

There may also be a state between *wakefulness and sleep during meditation.* It is a state of full consciousness but in a passive form. The phenomenon also happens in the savasana state of mind, the yoga pose preparing for meditation (Konecki, Płaczek, Tarasiuk 2024: 258–260). It is then that the position of the observer appears, who is aware of the existence, although his reflectiveness is blocked. The state of "don't know" appears in meditation:

> I drifted away several times – I felt as if I was dreaming while awake; I did not know if I was sleeping and I dreamed it, or if it was just thoughts appearing in my head. (exerciser, man)

6 The Course of Meditation – Racing Thoughts, Visions, Achieving Peace

The influx of loosely coupled thoughts that interrupt the focus on *the object or point* of meditation (e.g., breath, a point on the floor) has already been explored. These thoughts emerge at specific times, usually after losing touch with your body, followed by particular body responses, distractions, and changing points of attention (Petitmengin et al., 2017).

During meditation, various observed phenomena flow from the mind and are observed by the practitioner. It could be the observation of *a sequence of related thoughts, loosely related thoughts, racing thoughts, or multiple visions.* The sound and the thoughts floating around it quickly affect the sense of hearing:

> I focused on the sounds outside the window, the noise of cars and trams. There were thoughts, but I very consciously did not go into them. This is probably the first time I've experienced thought observation. Although I don't know if this is observation; it is just letting one thought flow very smoothly and even abstractly into a second thought. It amused me; more loose associations came, but it was a collection of random thoughts. Unfortunately, I don't remember which ones. With time, more and more, I entered the noise outside the window, which was "massaging" my head; I thought of this noise as something abstract, heavy, as something that has a form. And ... I don't know what happened next. (exerciser, woman)

6.1 *Chasing Thoughts*

> For the meditation, I tried to adopt the most comfortable possible position on the chair. I prepared a blanket to be placed in the lumbar region. I put my foot on the ankle, although I admit that I did not count on being able to concentrate, and indeed it did not happen. All the time, I kept getting 'reminders' about work, about not thinking, about my health, about past meetings, about how my thoughts are more like a roaring noisy streetcar that distracts everyone as it passes by and not like clouds that should flow through my head without occupying my attention. (exerciser, woman)

The racing of thoughts during meditation usually concerns *everyday matters* and working life. In addition, memories and emotions, often negative ones, emerge. The awareness of these emotions is revealed precisely during the practice of meditation. Working life is still in the awareness, and to live it can create difficulties:

> Since the classes were held shortly after I submitted the correction of my tax report, thoughts came to me about 'total earnings,' 'income,' and 'due taxes.' I let go of the thought slowly, and after some time, another quite strong feeling came to me, which surprised me: I remembered summer, just before the beginning of the second grade of elementary school, I had knocked out two upper teeth (true story). I was learning to skateboard, and I fell onto the curb. I have to admit that I do not remember the pain of the day, but I do remember the big confusion later on (the visit to the dentist, the checkup, parents rushing, considering x-rays, etc.). I don't know why it was during Tuesday's yoga that a completely different feeling came to me that day: being left unattended, almost neglected (and I am a spoiled only child, so the feeling of neglect never arises when I think about childhood). It was surprising because there was also the anger: 'Why was I left unattended?' This is nonsense, of course, because this accident could not have been prevented. (exerciser, woman)

6.2 *Visions*

There are also visions. The mind uses the sense of sight to represent specific thoughts. All of this can lead to reflecting on the creative power of the mind and arouse the need for deeper insight into what is happening while sitting.

There are *visualizations*, and various images, often very clear (cf. Preston 1981: 52). The visions mean that we are entering another realm. In everyday life, they happen rarely. An attempt is made to explain, for example, visions, where they come from, and why:

> During the second class, it happened to me that I 'saw' the outline of a man's face appearing for a moment under my eyelids with my eyes closed. This aroused my interest so much that when, after 20 minutes, the bell signaled the end of the meditation, I wanted to go back for a moment and recognize who it might be. It was a male face that I still can't recognize, which only appeared on the left side for no more than 2–3 seconds and then disappeared for another 5–10 seconds. (exerciser, woman)

> In meditation, I was relatively focused on one point on the floor. I also saw the shape of the face – a pattern of faces formed from dots on the wooden floor. Whether I opened my eyes wider or not, the front remained; I knew that these were only points on the floor and that I was creating (my mind creates) the shape of the face from these points.
>
> So, the mind is a demiurge ... (author)

Visions may repeat in subsequent meditation sessions, and *facial images* may appear, although sometimes they are shapes that are difficult to identify:

> During meditation, it happened to me once again that an image of a male face appeared to me on the left side while taking a breath. You can't recognize anyone you know in this face or any particular symbolism. (exerciser, woman)

The facial images can be startling and disturbing. The images change and disappear after a while:

> One of them reminded me so much of someone that I held my breath, and the saliva stuck in my throat; I was a little scared. The look on that face was mocking. The sight of various faces appearing lasted for about 3 minutes; then, I saw figures of medieval people (a man and a woman) on the wall against the background of a forest with a path as if the painting stopped them in conversation. Then the patterns on the wall seemed to form a clown. (exerciser, woman)

Visions can also appear while meditating in nature. They are associated with shifting the focus to various objects, which may move into the background. This phenomenon can be called "bokeh" in photography, and it is associated with focusing on the main object of the photo while everything around it appears in a blurred background. In the example below, meditation is also associated with feelings of unreal and slower thoughts. It can be said that after meditating, there is a "bokeh of thoughts." Concentrating on an object occurs slowly when everything that arises around a thought goes into the background:

> But in the last few days, I have practiced meditation sitting in the woods several times, so I thought I would write about this meditation instead of the previous yoga practice. I sit on my favorite clearing, on a hill, and where I sometimes walk around wild boars. A small clearing covered with moss and pine trees around. According to meditation tips, I choose one point to look at. Usually, it is some leaf on a bush. There are lots of little trees with fresh leaves around, and as soon as I start meditating, a kaleidoscope turns on. It is exciting what happens with my vision because one time, only the leaves sharpen, another time it could be branches, and sometimes it's clumps of grass. Even if I shift my gaze to something else for a moment, when I return to my fixed point, the surrounding immediately becomes a kaleidoscope again. Additionally, I feel heavier, and I feel where I touch the ground. My breathing slows down a lot. After meditating, sometimes I think unrealistically; even when X starts talking to me, I have to digest it longer as if I were sitting in a bubble and things were reaching me more slowly. [That's] the great thing about this sitting meditation in nature. (practitioner, woman)

6.3 *Peace*

Correctly performed meditation gives *the feeling of peace* and lightness to the body. The following elements are essential: a straight spine, counting breaths, and concentration. The body sometimes loses balance, but a focused mind allows it to return to an upright position. In the following meditation, a safe space can be conducive to a well-executed meditation, i.e., one that brings calmness and lightness to the body:

> I began as always by concentrating on a straight and stable spine and counting my breaths. I closed my eyes and observed my body and mind. Thoughts kept popping up, but I tried not to focus on them; I let them

> drift away. After a while, I felt myself relaxing, my arms and head becoming light, and my body gently leaning forward. When I lost the sense of an upright posture, I started again. But I did not feel any anxiety. I straightened my spine again without losing the lightness of my body. I was in a safe space, my own home, which undoubtedly contributed to my feeling of peace throughout the practice without being distracted. (exerciser, woman)

7 Effortlessness

Achieving peace and slowing down the body's work is a kind of introduction to effortless meditation. Effortlessness is an essential feature of meditation (Sparby 2019; Shear and Jevning 2002) as a cognitive style (finite province of meaning Schütz 1962: 230). Making efforts, overcoming weaknesses, and pushing forward are usually appreciated in working life.

Here is an example from guided meditation. After meditating, the practitioner feels the body *slowing down. She also feels calm* and fluid in body movements:

> But when I heard the leader's voice informing me that we are coming to an end, I suddenly came to my senses. Then I realized that I was not fully aware of what was happening around me. However, I was still awake. It's hard to describe this state. It is a bit like leaving my body and only controlling my mind. It sounds pretty abstract, and maybe I'm exaggerating in describing it this way, but I can't put another word to it. After meditating, I felt my body slow down. My movements were slow, calm, and smooth. I thought that I was prepared for sleep, and if I had wanted to, I could have fallen asleep after a while. (exerciser, woman)

Sometimes, *a slight change in position* allows you to get more comfort from sitting and reduce the tension caused by concentrating. This can make meditation *effortless*. Here is my (author) self-report on the self-observation of meditation that I conducted myself:

> When I had a straight back, I felt a tension in my back, and therefore I still had such tense energy focused on my abdomen/navel. So, attention was focused on a specific point, but it was done with great effort.
>
> And at one point, I leaned against the back of the chair, and then I felt tremendous relief, a sudden change, and no effort. This sudden change

> was striking. Relief! I felt effortless meditation, which gave me great pleasure; I could see that concentration was already going naturally, and I wouldn't get out of it if I sat like this … I was sitting very well.

In the above description, I used the phrase "I was sitting very well," but this is not my formulation; it is a formulation heard from others. My teachers. When summing up the meditation, some teachers often ask, "well, how was it with sitting?" The practitioner replies, "It was very comfortable sitting." And nothing else needs to be explained here. This shows that entering the phase of full meditation, which is already effortless, does not cause pain or difficulties; if difficulties are accepted, they are relegated to the background (Sparby 2019: 140). We do not drift away from the space of concentration at a given time.

> I liked the guided meditation very much; it seemed to me that I very rarely 'talk' to myself so tenderly and wish myself something nice, and it was delightful. (exerciser, woman)

According to the yoga teacher quoted below, meditation is *an effortless concentration of the mind* (see also Sparby 2019: 143; Shear and Jevning 2002: 93). He compares the mind to a crystal that is always transparent, no matter what color of light passes through it:

> Meditation is a state where the mind's object of concentration is held effortlessly in your mind. So, it's as if this mind were suddenly occupied with an object, but it would be effortless. And here, science gets lost because we cannot measure effortlessness. But now, what the good old yoga scriptures say is that your mind is like a crystal. A mountain crystal, and if you illuminate this crystal with colored light, it emits that colored light, but this crystal is not colored. So, your mind is as if it were occupied with this object of concentration, but at the same time, it does it effortlessly. Just as you illuminate a crystal, and it may be red, it may be blue in a moment, it doesn't care.

8 Self-Perception

Deep meditation is often associated with *distortions in self-perception*. It is not easy to place yourself in reality of working life only as "I" without the partner of the dialogue, ME (Mead 1934; Blumer 1969; Prus 1996). Disturbances can also be related to body sensation and awareness of the current reality, whether you are in sleep mode or still awake. However, when awareness of what is happening is maintained, it is possible to return slowly to the fundamental reality, to the lifeworld:

> I heard everything, I knew where I was, who I was with, but I didn't feel myself. It's hard to describe this feeling. I was with myself at the same time, not being. My eyes were so tightly closed that I didn't feel that they were closed. I didn't know my position or if I was sleeping, but I was aware. After the bell, it was strange for me to come back to myself. I had to slowly gain a connection with my body, legs, and hands. (exerciser, woman)

Nature can also be visualized during meditation when we are not in the bosom of nature; at the same time, *there is an impression of depersonalization*, looking at ourselves from the outside, the self disappears, and the observer appears, which rarely happens in working life:

> By focusing on the correct breathing, I first moved my mind to the great mountains as if I were sitting on one of the peaks at sunrise. I felt a chill go through my whole body. I was sitting on one of the peaks, sitting in Turkish style. There was still snow on the peaks, as if the dominant season of the year were not summer but winter. It was supposed to be me, but at times I had the impression that I was in someone else's body, despite the awareness that I was watching my breath. (exercising, woman).

We can see a phenomenon close to an "out of body experience":

> I felt like I was on a beach, totally relaxed. As if my body were the sand, firm, and my feelings – the waves of the sea, up and down, coming and going, and my mind – the sun, from above, observing everything. It was as if I had come out of my own body and was feeling my body, emotions, and mind separately. I loved experiencing this because it had never happened to me. I had managed to relax, but I had never reached this level of connection between body, soul, and mind. (beginner, woman)

We can see the phenomenon as an "out of body experience." The meditation associated with observing the breathing, the body, and thoughts can create a kind of bilocation that is the cognitive consequence of solid attention on self-observation. It is an exciting experience; here (in the quote above), disconnection is called connection. It is an experience of the bilocation of the mind that sees the body from the outside. Emotions and the mind are observed from the outside.

Meditation can be *thought-provoking*. While meditating, "wrong thoughts" may also appear, and they may remain with the practitioner after meditation. However, there may then be *a reflection* on whether it is worth focusing on the specific issues that caused negative thoughts and emotions during the meditation:

- *After the end of such a meditation session, for example, when you cried, what did you think when it ended? Were these negative thoughts and emotions interrupted, and were they still with you?*
- They were there, of course, they were. It's not that meditation will cure everything; you have to start talking to yourself and consider whether you need it in your life. Does it make sense to worry so much about certain things because some of them are simply beyond our control? Sometimes during meditation, I find an answer to whether what causes me so much pain in some life situations is worth later crying over, or being in a bad mood, or being upset because of it. And that's how it is. (interview with a practitioner, woman)

9 Perception of the World: Changes in Perception of Being in the World

During meditation, various thoughts and perceptions about reality arise. There is often a feeling of losing control of time; it can also be a feeling of time passing quickly (*specific time perspective* – a feature of the finite province of meaning of meditation realm), but also of losing control of ideas, as well as struggling with sleep:

> While meditating, I quickly lost track of time. I think I managed to stay conscious for quite a long time, but the signal to stop caught me when I was on the verge of waking and dreaming. Torn from this place, I remembered that my thoughts were already spinning out of control. They did it on many different topics and were quite chaotic. The signal instantly brought me out of this state and restored my sense of time and awareness. (exerciser, man)

> I was shocked that 20 minutes had passed; I thought ten, maximum. (exerciser, woman)

Disturbances in the perception of time are part of a specific process called "*entering an altered state of consciousness.*" Despite the most frequently indicated difficulties in describing what happens during meditation, we sometimes find in retrospect a very accurate naming and description of the feelings that arise during that time. Here we are dealing with a form of numbness (see the quote below). And coming out of this state, we also feel that the passage of time changes. The feeling may be that time has passed quickly, but the passage of time is imperceptible during meditation, and there may be a feeling of timelessness (Coleman 2022). There is a feeling of complete detachment from everyday life and a sense of "being," and thus a feeling of existing in an unavoidable suspension of reality. *The sense of being comes from the body.* Even from the flesh (numbness), for a moment, we can get to the pre-reflective awareness of being and not being. We can be aware of our awareness. (Bauer 2019: 84–85, 92)

In this state, it is possible not to feel the chill that appears immediately after coming out of the meditative state, and thus realize that it was not there while sitting. There is also "non-thinking," which is the actual meditative state. In this self-reflection about the meditative state that occurs, the thought of doing nothing arises. This is a critical thought because sitting or being in a *savasana* pose makes it possible to break away from everyday activities and do nothing. The whole experience is, in the summary of the narrator's statement below, interpreted as attractive, and the description of the perceived reality indicates a kind of unreality:

- *Mm-hmm. And what did you feel during the meditation?*
- Well, this is where the strangest things happened, because we had our eyes closed and so on, there were some images that we saw or something. It was a bit like psychedelia and stuff like that. Well, I tried not to fall asleep there a couple of times, I didn't manage, but I don't know, time sped up. It was a bit like pressing the spacebar in strategy games, you know? I lay down, and now I control my breathing and close my eyes, and suddenly, after that moment, time usually went by faster. It was like, that's it! Such a snapping out of a state of numbness, like, I don't know, like you're levitating in space, and suddenly someone brings you down to earth. It was like that with me, that it was such a detachment from everyday matters, from what was going on around me, and being somewhere … It was a bit like being, but not being; being in non-being. Well, you touched the floor, all that, and so on, but on the other hand, you didn't feel it because I sort of didn't feel the cold. For example, I felt cold just after we had talked about what the professor had prolonged.

- *So now answer what you felt there.*
- That's when I felt cold; I was getting dressed then, and I saw that others were getting dressed too. But, for example, if I had been lying like that, I don't know, I would have had to lie down for a very long time to feel that I was cold. And also, if you didn't manage to think about anything, you seemed to be there, but you weren't because you didn't know about anything. Because you weren't thinking about anything. I mean, you were lying there doing exactly nothing. So doing nothing, doing exactly nothing, is hard. Because you're always doing something, and here you're doing nothing. That was so interesting too. (interview with an exerciser, man)

Disturbances in body perception may refer to the phenomenon of the "*unreal body*." It is perceived differently than in everyday life. In the world of meditation, the body is passive and generally does not move; this causes some disturbance in perceiving different parts or even the whole body, which seems to be something external to the conscious mind being here and now:

> Very quickly, I entered a state of relaxation, and after two minutes, my vision changed – I had a narrower field of vision, the shapes on the carpet swirled slightly, my hands lying on my thighs were unreal, as if I did not feel their weight at all, they seemed shorter and as if fused with my thighs. The professor's voice seemed to be floating somewhere nearby as if I heard it from another person, not myself. (practitioner, woman)

10 The Effects of Meditation: Reflections Afterward

We have already described the effects of what happens in the course of meditation. But let us summarize and point out how meditators perceive the effects of meditation after performing it. One effect that is often repeated is *inner peace* and *the removal of tensions*, an effect that has been mentioned before. In particular, it was referred to by practitioners (beginners), and although teachers and instructors mention this state, they do so less often; it is an obvious state for them:

> When we started meditating, I started to get rid of thoughts from my head. It was as if I was floating in space. There were no negative emotions. I felt a sense of relief. It was as if I was lying on the water on a summer's day, with the sun occasionally shining through my eyelashes. (exerciser, woman)

Central and integral to the other meditation effects and the yoga practice associated with meditation may also be a fusion, *a merging of body and mind, person and object of concentration* (coalescence; Sparby 2019: 140). When we enter a deeper meditative state, overcoming distracting obstacles, a change in our state of mind may occur. At first, we may feel irritated, but gradually we gain distance from our problems. This happens through concentration when we reach a state of no "mind-movement," and even the meditator disappears. The merging of body and mind occurs almost spontaneously; the state is achieved step by step; it does not appear immediately and finally we achieve the state of deep self (Scheff 2014).

Meditation cannot be taught to someone; learning occurs by experiencing and observing the experience. The following quotation summarizes many effects of meditation, the most important of which is the "merging and connecting," which can even refer to merging with supernatural elements. The distinctive mind disappears and also "the person who focuses disappears" (see quotation below). We can see how the mind can stop; it can stop and become one with the world if there is no distinctive thinking.[8] It happens thanks to yoga and meditation:

> Initially, my mind was restless, irritated, sometimes also just watching how others do it and I don't. This level of annoyance was very, very high; it was very, very high, which caused me to try to meditate basically ...
>
> Again, there are 8 degrees in this method. It says here ... Again, we may have different ideas about meditation, so first of all, meditation is not some state of flying away and finding in yourself an escape from reality. So, this meditation allows us to free ourselves from a situation and gain some distance, which causes the problem to resolve itself. So, it's really about merging – merging all these bodies that we have. They say it's a combination of body, mind, and soul. So, this work in asanas and balancing this anatomical body, that is, balancing these proportions between too much tension and too little tension, also causes this balance to appear at the physiological level, that is, the functioning of our internal organs.
>
> This communication between the brain and the rest of the body is then undisturbed, which causes our emotions to calm down. Then we have this body that is already so spiritual that suddenly we see that we are not just a collection of muscles, bones, or internal organs, that we are not also our intellect. Because it is known that all the contents of our heads

8 To stop distinctive discriminative thinking, so-called koans are used in Zen Buddhism and in Transcendental Meditation (Shear and Jevning 2002: 192).

> are also things that have been accepted, and now when we calm down, we have a chance to experience this connection, and this is the connection with atman, that is, with such a cosmic soul, where there is no division, and everything is unified. And that's also what this meditation is, that there is no such thinking at some point, so you could say that the gap between the thoughts that appear is lengthened ... Iyengar said you couldn't teach meditation because it is such a state of experience, and you can't tell someone about the taste of an apple, right? We can describe it, but it still won't have the right image. And it's the same with concentration. In this method, long-lasting concentration, that is, the lack of these movements of the mind, causes us to enter the state of meditation. So, by concentrating on a point, and here it can be our body, this body merges with the mind. The person who focuses disappears. The concentration itself, and the object of attention, it all merges. (interview with a hatha yoga teacher, man)

The effects of meditation also relate to strictly social aspects. Thus, there is the possibility of *improving one's relationships with others*. However, it is recommended that meditation be effortless and purposeless; it should not be associated with any additional emotional benefits, such as pride in having performed the meditation well. Such additions are sometimes mentioned by meditation Zen masters:

> Once you understand our innate power to purify ourselves and our surroundings, you can act properly, and you will learn from those around you, and you will become friendly with others. This is the merit of Zen practice. (Suzuki 1995: 37)

Although the benefits of meditation should be revealed, meditation is an autotelic activity, sufficient for itself. Its effects can at most be perceived by the mind outside the practice of meditation.

Some of the project participants also approached this attitude. It is the feeling itself that becomes essential rather than the linguistic interpretation of the practice:

> For a while, I accused myself of lacking focus or effort, but I felt this was an incorrect diagnosis. I began to question whether I was doing the practice well, why I was doing all this, and what tangible benefits were coming. The answer was short. The important thing is that I feel that it serves me to practice, so why put it into words and argue logically. (exerciser, woman)

11 Learning to Be in Meditation

Our research was about entering the meditation state of mind. We described the problems encountered by beginners changing from the realm of working life to a meditation finite province of meaning. Although one of our research participants stated that meditation could not be taught, the instructions for meditation have existed for a long time. Some guidelines on how to meditate are usually given in the practice of hatha yoga or meditation practice itself. In these descriptions and meditation instructions, you can also find common features, contemplative maps, and signs that indicate where we currently are in the meditation process (contemplative landmarks, Sparby 2019: 138). They can be given very briefly or be more elaborate.

Learning meditation is processual (Preston 1981), and we gradually reach the practice of free meditation (effortless meditation). *After mastering one of the meditation techniques* (e.g., counting breaths or repeating mantras), we gradually reach insights, *noticing something that appears in our mind.* We no longer perceive the disturbing elements, or we do not assess what emerges as problematic. It is challenging in our culture to switch to the do-nothing mode and accept this situation. It also has to be learned so that we can grasp techniques and the interpretation of certain states, e.g., the state of inactivity.

When this happens, *the judgmental mind disappears.* But it has to be perceived that we are just fully here and now. There is peace, and we notice things we did not see before and do not judge them. This learning process is individual, and detailed instructions are rarely given on what to do in a thought racing situation. Going back to breathing observation and/or breath counting is generally suggested. The teacher gives instructions on meditating and teaches meditation techniques, but rarely includes interpretations of feelings. So, we are learning a technique that can help control the racing of thoughts, whatever those thoughts are (usually from our culture and disturbing). Ultimately, however, the meditator himself has to deal with this problem:

> there is zazen meditation, in which breath is something that allows us to enter the state of meditation, and count the breaths from 1 to 10, saying in our minds 'inhale,' 'exhale' and so on, and start from the beginning. And how to be a person will get lost, because it is known that the mind starts to pull somewhere, so it starts all over again. This is the kind of meditation I started. And I will do it until, at some point, I don't need these breaths anymore. You enter this meditative state, at least that's how I feel, such a state of total emptiness. As if there was simply nothing in my head. Of course, at some point, emotion arises, there is some emotion,

> and often when this mind is so evident and calm as if there is such a void, such insights appear, but these insights are just like noticing something. This is also so amazing. (interview with a yoga instructor)

Meditation can also be viewed in the scientistic convention, when the medical perspective is invoked (Shear and Jevning 2002). The flow of electromagnetic waves in the brain can be checked with encephalography (Aftanas, Golosheykin 2005; Jensen, Kaiser, and Lachaux 2007; Moore, Gruber, Derose and Malinowski 2012) or respiration rate, oxygen consumption, blood flow to the brain or blood cortisol could be measured (Shear and Jevning 2002: 206–207). One of the yoga teachers, a scientist, takes this approach by presenting what meditation practice is:

> Well, now. How can I feel my departure if, for half a minute, I don't know what happened to me? Maybe I was in a meditative state, but I don't know if I was meditative; perhaps I took a nap? However, while concentrating on the mind, we can measure it again, and the frequency of the brain waves decreases. (interview with a yoga teacher, man)

The teacher plays a vital role in learning to enter the meditation province of meaning. They are also meditating, but their role is clearly defined; it is that of a teacher. It is often difficult for a teacher to fully enter a meditative state in this role. However, the suspension of the world does occur even though they are focused on preparation and conduct, time control of the meditation, and the participants of the practice. The teacher is balancing on the border of two worlds: the world of meditation and the world of practical activities. They are alternating between these two worlds. Meditation for a teacher is an excellent activity to achieve a specific goal, i.e., putting practitioners into a meditative state.

The teacher watches throughout the meditation. Although the practice is highly individual, the teacher's presence motivates and gives a sense of security, provides instructions, and determines the length of the meditation. The teacher, although meditating himself, is focused on what is happening around him:

> Generally, I am focused on the practice of yoga and the participants in the classroom. It was the same in meditation and when I was sitting. I was paying attention to what was happening in the hall. At one point, one of the meditation participants fainted and fell off his chair. I am afraid of this happening again. Everything is going well today. (author)

12 Conclusions

Our analyses are based on the first-person reports of meditation participants, including the researchers themselves. We did not adopt a simple critical perspective on meditation practices in the modern world (Purser and Loy 2013; Purser 2019) or other assumptions or models regarding entering meditation and the course of meditation (Preston 1981). As the subjects observe their body sensations, thoughts, and emotions, we watch how meditation develops mainly among beginners. We are closer to Carvalho's (2021) ontological approach, which observes what meditation does to an individual's subjectivity and self in a particular setting. It is a micro-research approach (Pagis 2010, 2015, 2019), kind of contemplative sociology (Giorgino 2014; Bentz & Giorgino 2016; Konecki 2018: 59–64), when the cognitive aspect of meditation is strongly emphasized along with the body aspect and the emotions associated with it (Konecki 2018, chapter 2; Konecki 2022, chapter 2; Janesick 2015). We also believe, like Berlant (2011), that "here and now" is considered in the context of the real situation of "*here and now*." We look at what appears in here-and-now meditation; even if it is difficult to express in language as in deep meditation, we want to see how this difficulty can be expressed. (Shear, Jewning 2002: 195). If one had not such experience (being in meditation realm), one could easily say it; if one had such experience, one could testify it. (ibidem)

Most of the meditation practices during our research were preliminary. Gradually, however, more and more awareness was acquired. In fact, for most practitioners, mindful sitting was precisely *the practice of mindfulness*, not deep meditation with objectless consciousness (see Nhat Hanh, Thich 1976; Desikachar 1999). First of all, many mental states, thoughts, emotions, and "*obstacles*" in entering the meditation realm were noticed. However, they were not obstacles at all, in fact, but an aid to realizing their state of mind, presence, or absence in a given situation here and now. The observation of the racing of thoughts, constant planning of the future, disturbances in the perception of time, pain, physical discomfort, negative emotions, sleepiness, and various reactions of the body that were unnoticeable in everyday situations were all helpful in the practice of mindfulness because they allowed meditators to gain awareness of the existence and course of multiple processes here and now, without the need for intellectual reflection. *Noticing obstacles is a state of the "beginner's mind"* (Suzuki 2010), which often sees more than the mind of an experienced meditation practitioner. It was one of the goal of our research to reconstruct the obstacles that become the aids of entering the meditation realm. The beginner's mind is often indicated as one that needs to be maintained over a more extended period to see things that are usually invisible to us. An experienced practitioner may lose the sensitivity that the beginner's mind possesses through the acquisition of experience.

We tried to reconstruct the minding process mainly from the perspective of the beginner. It shows how we look for the obstacles to stop our activity in some working life. However, noticing obstacles is a prelude to stopping the work of the mind and exiting activities in everyday life.

Crossing the lifeworld consists of an effort to overcome some obstacles. This is not overcoming by rejecting the elements that hinder the crossing of the world but by accepting them as elements that support this trespassing. This conclusion resonates with Alfred Schütz's theory of cognitive styles, especially concerning the delineations between finite provinces of meaning, which inherently possess cognitive aspects. The borders of worlds are traversed through the concerted effort of intellect, and emotion, intertwined with an awareness of how one's body reacts to shifts in perception of the world.

It is possible to stop the work of the mind and everyday activity, but it takes time and training, i.e., learning meditation techniques, perceiving the effects, and interpreting them. Sometimes, the "access meditation" state of mind was obtained in practice. This mind is associated with intensely concentrating on the object of meditation (the breath, the body, a point on the floor, etc.), overcoming obstacles, and finally accepting them. Finally, there is also effortlessness and focus on what is happening inside our minds (cf. Sparby 2019: 146). Most practitioners in our hatha yoga project were unable to achieve a meditative state when effortlessness and concentration accompany us throughout the day, apart from sitting on a meditation cushion (it is so called "absorption state," cf. Sparby 2019: 140). However, the struggle to achieve a state of concentration on one object and push obstacles into the background was a vital lesson for many practitioners and exercisers.[9] They gained temporal meditation insights and recognized the effects of meditation (e.g., disturbances in the perception of time, limitations of their bodies, emotions of anxiety or sadness, pain, thoughts about work, comparison with others, and racing thoughts). All this meant that perceptions of reality could change due to being distanced from it and seeing how much of this perception comes from our state of mind.

---

9 The issue of concentration in meditation is highly complicated; you need to concentrate on losing your points of concentration and the awareness of concentration itself: "Concentration is not to try hard to watch something. In zazen if you try to look at one spot you will be tired in about five minutes. This is not concentration. Concentration means freedom. So your effort should be directed at nothing. You should be concentrated on nothing. In zazen practice we say your mind should be concentrated on your breathing, but the way to keep your mind on your breathing is to forget all about yourself and just to sit and feel your breathing" (Suzuki 1995: 113; see also Shear and Jewning 2002: 195, 203).

Observing the reactions of beginners, we could also reconstruct some of the features of the finite province of the meaning of meditation. The feature is visible when the practitioner breaks the border of the lifeworld and meditation realm. This is the theoretical benefit of the research (see also the analysis of *Savasana's state of mind* in Konecki, Płaczek, Tarasiuk 2024: 258–277).

Becoming the observer is a feature of the meditation province of meaning. If we observe breathing or body reflexes, we see them from outside. Similarly, we can see ourselves from the outside and think; we become the observer of somebody who is the self but not the self. It is momentarily consciousness of the body or mind that can be reached when we enter the state of meditation. We can get the distance to ourselves.

The time perspective changes during the meditation. We can lose control of the time in everyday life. The time can speed up or slow down. It can be evaluated later on from the cognitive perspective of working life.

Another feature of the meditation realm is *effortlessness*, usually connected with peace of mind. Peace appears when the body is accustomed to the position of meditation and does not disturb the practitioner. This is possible for beginners, but it is still not easy.

Another feature of the finite province of the meaning of meditation is a *merging of body and mind, person and object of concentration*. It does not, instead, happen in the meditation practice of the beginners. There were signs of getting to this state of being, but the obstacles were the main point of concentration. This is the most challenging state of being for the beginners. Therefore, entering another finite province of meaning is processual and also needs some education and instruction, so it has some social background.

Educational effects on self-awareness were noticeable in the participants' self-reports. Even if we do the meditation practice with some effort and overcome our weaknesses, it ultimately benefits the practitioner and the practitioner: "So it is necessary for us to encourage ourselves and to make an effort up to the last moment, when all effort disappears. You should keep your mind on your breathing until you are not aware of your breathing" (Suzuki 1995: 37). So, the beginning, which involves an effort to face the challenge of meditation, is a normal state of mind in meditation. And it is, in a way, a condition for stopping the mind from working while meditating.

Practitioners often ask if they meditate correctly. It is difficult for a teacher to answer this question using the semantics available in language. Sometimes it is done in a roundabout way, using metaphors or examples, or by building specific associations. For instance, Buddhist master Seung Sahn said (1999: 12):

> If you do correct meditation, being sick sometimes is OK; suffering sometimes is OK; dying someday is OK. The Buddha said, 'If you keep a clear mind moment to moment, then you will get happiness everywhere.'

Not asking myself if I am meditating well is also a tactic to stop the mind from working. Answering such questions leads to an increase in the work of the mind during meditation. Realizing this is meta-awareness about stopping the activities of daily living. Learning this technique of meta-attention proves that people are advancing in meditation practice, for example, in the cognitive plane, which is extremely important for generating the appropriate motivation for meditation. It varies from person to person, occurring at different times in the practice. Each meditator deals with these interpretations individually. Some may withdraw from meditation because of discomfort or ignore it while practicing yoga. *Meditation practice is intensely personalized in terms of experience.* Some self-reports may show similar experiences; however, everyone experiences things differently and describes these experiences considering their biography, situation, memory, and physical and mental state in each situation and time. We stop the work of the mind individually, using proposed and collectively available techniques.

Research has also shown that the practice of hatha yoga is not often associated with meditation, although *dhyana* (meditation in yoga practice) is a crucial element of yoga philosophy. (Iyengar 1990; Desikachar 1999) Perhaps this rejection of meditation in our Western culture was related to its association with religion or spirituality, which practitioners do not always accept in the Western world. If you stop reflecting on whether meditation or hatha yoga is compatible with your value system or religion, you can enter the meditative state and limit the work of the mind while meditating.

For some philosophical and religious traditions, physical practice alone is not meditation, e.g., for Zen Buddhism (Seung Sahn 1999: 12). However, it must be admitted that traditional and contemporary texts on yoga philosophy do emphasize the role of *dhyana* (Iyengar 1990; Newcombe and O'Brien-Kop 2020; Desikachar 1999), which is increasingly being embraced by practitioners of hatha yoga.

The skill of stopping for a moment among the turbulence of the acceleration of our life (Han 2015; Rosa 2020) can be important part of understanding of the situation of Self in the lifeworld, and the starting point of critical stance towards the basic assumptions of our social system.

Funding

The author received the financial support for the research from National Science Center in Poland [Opus, grant number 2018/29/B/HS6/00513].

Bibliography

Aftanas, Ljubomir, and Semen Golosheykin. 2005. "Impact of Regular Meditation Practice on EEG Activity at Rest and During Evoked Negative Emotions." *Int. J. Neurosci.* 115, 893–909. doi:10.1080/00207450590897969.

Anālayo Bhikkhu. 2020. "The Myth of McMindfulness." *Mindfulness* 11, 472–479. doi:10.1007/s12671-019-01264-x.

Bauer, Rudolf. 2019. *Merleau Ponty: Subjectivity as the Field of Being within Beings. Awareness as Existingness*. "Revista Científica Arbitrada de la Fundación Mente-Clara" 4(1), 81–93 (61). doi:10.32351/rca.v4.1.61.

Bentz, Valery M., and Vincenzo Giorgino. 2016. *Contemplative Social Research: Caring for Self, Being, and Lifeworld.* Fielding Institute Press, Santa Barbara.

Berlant, Lauren. 2011. *Cruel Optimism.* Duke University Press, Durham.

Blumer, Herbert. 1969. *Symbolic Interactionism: Perspective and Method.* University of California Press, Berkeley.

Brown, Brene. 2021. *Atlas of the Heart: Mapping Meaningful Connection and the Language of Human Experience.* Random House, New York.

Carvalho, António. 2021. "Rethinking the Politics of Meditation: Practice, Affect and Ontology." *The Sociological Review* 69(4): 1260–1276. doi:10.1177/00380261211029457.

Chen, Carolyn. 2022. *Work, Play, Code: When Work Becomes Religion in Silicon Valley.* Princeton University Press, Princeton.

Coleman, Rebecca. 2022. "The Presents of the Present: Mindfulness, Time and Structures of Feeling." *Distinktion: Journal of Social Theory* 23(1), 131–148. doi:10.1080/1600910X.2020.1810730.

Collins, Randall. 2004. *Interaction Ritual Chains.* Princeton University Press, Princeton.

Collins, Randall. 2011. "The Micro-Sociology of Religion: Religious Practices, Collective and Individual." The Association of Religion Data Archives Guiding Paper Series. http://www.thearda.com/rrh/papers/guidingpapers.asp.

Cope, Stephen. 2006. *The Wisdom of Yoga: A Seeker's Guide to Extraordinary Living.* Bantam Books, New York. (ebook).

Desikachar, T.K.V. 1999. *The Heart of Yoga: Developing a Personal Practice.* Inner Traditions International, Rochester, Vermont.

Durkheim, Emile. 2008/1912. *The Elementary Forms of the Religious Life.* Courier Corporation, New York.

Eliade, Mircea. 1997. *Joga. Nieśmiertelność i wolność.* PWN, Warszawa.

Giddens, Anthony. 1991. *Modernity and Self-Identity.* Polity Press, Cambridge.

Giorgino, Vincenzo. 2014. "Contemplative Methods Meet Social Sciences: Back to Human Experience as It Is." *Journal for the Theory of Social Behaviour* 45(4), 461–483.

Glaser, Barney. 1992. *Emergence vs. Forcing: Basics of Grounded Theory Analysis.* Sociology Press, Mill Valley, CA.

Han, Byung-Chul. 2015. *Burnout Society.* Stanford University Press, Stanford.

Islam, Gazi, Marie Holm, and Mira Karjalainen. 2017. "Sign of the Times: Workplace Mindfulness as an Empty Signifier." *Organization.* doi:10.1177/1350508417740643.

Iyengar, B.K.S. 1990. *Joga (Yoga) Wyd. 1.* PWN, Warszawa.

Janesick, Valerie J. 2015. *Contemplative Qualitative Inquiry: Practicing the Zen of Research.* Left Coast Press, Walnut Creek, CA.

Jensen, Ole, Jochen Kaiser, and Jean-Philippe Lachaux. 2007. "Human Gamma-Frequency Oscillations Associated with Attention and Memory." *Trends Neurosci.* 30, 317–324. doi:10.1016/j.tins.2007.05.001.

Kempton, Sally. 2011. *Meditation for the Love of It: Enjoying Your Deepest Experience.* Sounds True, Boulder, CO. (epub version).

Konecki, Krzysztof T. 2018. *Advances in Contemplative Social Research.* Lodz University Press, Łódź/Jagiellonian University Press, Krakow.

Konecki, Krzysztof T. 2022. *The Meaning of Contemplation for Social Qualitative Research: Applications and Examples.* Routledge, London, New York.

Konecki, Krzysztof T., Aleksandra Płaczek, and Dagmara Tarasiuk. 2024. *Experiencing the Body in Yoga Practice: Meanings and Knowledge Transfer.* Routledge, New York.

Kucinskas, Jaime, and Evan Stewart. 2022. "Selfish or Substituting Spirituality? Clarifying the Relationship between Spiritual Practice and Political Engagement." *American Sociological Review* 87(4), 584–617. doi:10.1177/00031224221108196.

Lev, Assaf. 2022. "'The Glorious Pain': Attaining Pleasure and Gratification in Times of Delayed Onset Muscle Soreness (DOMS) among Gym Goers." *Journal of Contemporary Ethnography.* doi:10.1177/08912416221113369.

Mead, George H. 1934. *Mind, Self, and Society from the Standpoint of a Social Behaviorist.* University of Chicago Press, Chicago.

Moore, Adam, Thomas Gruber, Jennifer Derose, and Peter Malinowski. 2012. "Regular, Brief Mindfulness Meditation Practice Improves Electrophysiological Markers of Attentional Control." *Front. Hum. Neurosci.* 6:18. doi:10.3389/fnhum.2012.00018.

Newcombe, Suzanne. 2019. *Yoga in Britain: Stretching Spirituality and Educating Yogis.* Equinox, Sheffield.

Newcombe, Suzanne, and Karen O'Brien-Kop. 2020. *Routledge Handbook of Yoga and Meditation Studies.* Routledge, London.

Pagis, Michal. 2010. "Producing Intersubjectivity in Silence: An Ethnography of Meditation Practices." *Ethnography* 11, 309–328.

Pagis, Michal. 2015. "Evoking Equanimity: Silent Interaction Rituals in Vipassana Meditation Retreats." *Qualitative Sociology* 38, 37–56.

Pagis, Michal. 2019. "The Sociology of Meditation." In *Oxford Handbook of Meditation.* doi:10.1093/oxfordhb/9780198808640.013.50.

Pagis, Michal. 2019a. *Inward: Vipassana Meditation and the Embodiment of the Self.* University of Chicago Press, Chicago.

Petitmengin, Claire, Martijn van Beek, Michel Bitbol, Jean-Michel Nissou, and Andreas Roepstorff. 2017. "What Is It Like to Meditate?: Methods and Issues for a Micro-Phenomenological Description of Meditative Experience." *Journal of Consciousness Studies* 24(5–6), 170–198.

Preston, David L. 1981. "Becoming a Zen Practitioner." *Sociological Analysis* 42(1), 47–55.

Prus, Robert. 1996. *Symbolic Interaction and Ethnographic Research: Intersubjectivity and the Study of Human Lived Experience.* State University of New York Press, Albany, NY.

Purser, Ron. 2019. *McMindfulness: How Mindfulness Became the New Capitalist Spirituality.* Repeater Books, London.

Purser, Ron, and David Loy. 2013. "Beyond McMindfulness." *Huffington Post* 1(7), 13. Retrieved May 6, 2022. https://www.huffpost.com/entry/beyond-mcmindfulness_b_3519289.

Riegner, Gabriel, Grace Posey, Valeria Oliva, Youngkyoo Jung, William Mobley, and Fadel Zeidan. 2022. "Disentangling Self from Pain: Mindfulness Meditation-Induced Pain Relief Is Driven by Thalamic-Default Mode Network Decoupling." PAIN. doi:10.1097/j.pain.0000000000002731.

Rosa, Hartmut. 2020. *Przyspieszenie, Wyobcowanie, Rezonans: Projekt Krytycznej Teorii Późnonowoczesnej Czasowości.* Translated by Jakub Duraj and Jacek Kołtun. Gdańsk: Europejskie Centrum Solidarności.

Scheff, Thomas. 2014. "Role-Taking, Emotion, and the Two Selves." *The Canadian Journal of Sociology / Cahiers Canadiens de Sociologie* 39(3), 315–330.

Rosen, Richard. 2011. *The Yoga of Breath: A Step-by-Step Guide to Pranayama.* Shambhala, Boston and London.

Schütz, Alfred. 1962a. "Common-Sense and Scientific Interpretation of Human Action." In *Collected Papers* I, Edited by M. Natanson. Martinus Nijhoff, The Hague.

Schütz, Alfred. 1962b. *Collected Papers* I. Edited by M. Natanson. Martinus Nijhoff, The Hague.

Sebald, Gerd. 2011. "Crossing the Finite Provinces of Meaning: Experience and Metaphor." *Human Studies* 34, 341–352.

Seung, Sahn. 1999. *Only Don't Know.* Shambhala, Boston, London.

Shear, Jonathan, and Ron Jevning. 2002. "Pure Consciousness: Scientific Exploration of Meditation Techniques." In *The View from Within: First-Person Approaches to the Study of Consciousness,* edited by Francisco Varela and Jonathan Shear, Imprint Academic, Thorverton, UK.

Singleton, Marc. 2010. *Yoga Body: The Origin of Modern Posture Practice.* Oxford University Press, Oxford.

Sparby, Terje. 2019. "Phenomenology and Contemplative Universals: The Meditative Experience of Dhyana, Coalescence, or Access Concentration." *Journal of Consciousness Studies* 26(7–8), 130–156.

Steensland, Brian, David P. King, and Barbara J. Duffy. 2022. "The Discursive and Practical Influence of Spirituality on Civic Engagement." *Journal for Scientific Study and Religion* 61(2), 389–407.

Suzuki, Shunryu. 1995. *Zen Mind, Beginner's Mind.* Weatherhill, New York and Tokyo.

Thich, Nhat Hanh. 1976. *The Miracle of Mindfulness: An Introduction to the Practice of Meditation.* Beacon Press, Boston.

Vicente, Svetlanna J., and Paul T. Stuhr. 2022. "Mindful Yoga: Strategies for Mindfulness and Yoga in Physical Education." *Strategies: A Journal for Physical and Sport Educators* 35(1), 31–44. doi:10.1080/08924562.2021.2000540.

PART 3

Applying Contemplation to Understand Suffering

CHAPTER 5

Empathy! So What?

1 Instead of Introduction. Contemplative Memo

I am constantly writing contemplative notes; it is my way of researching the world through my mind (Konecki 2018; 2022).[1] I assume that the academic mind could be empathetic enough to investigate the world from the first-person perspective (Bentz 1995; Giorgino 2015; Bentz and Giorgino 2016).

For what do we need theoretical, methodological, and abstract elaboration of empathy? Why do we need a justification for thinking about it? Maybe instead of these theoretical contemplations, justifications, and elaborations, we only need empathetic acting? All these endeavors to define everything and categorize the world that we make mean something; it shows how the academic mind works in the modern era. We do not just trust in empathy in the academic world, we do not trust that empathy exists, or do we think that others do not trust and believe it does not exist? Why do we think that empathizing could be helped by theoretical advice on others' feelings and opinions? Maybe it should be less theory and more insight into lived experiences.

Maybe there are other explanations for this consideration of the phenomenon of empathy. There are many definitions; perhaps we need to have clear categories for identifying our activity and feelings. Do we need a scientific or theoretical explanation of what we feel? Am I empathetic, and what am I doing in an empathy-induced action? Or are there other motives behind my behaviors? The art of distrust develops, maybe we still follow Nietzsche's idea of distrust of everything that is officially presented, and especially sociologists follow the debunking motive that supposedly represents the humanistic perspective (Berger 1963).

2 Empathy …

The concept of empathy was translated from the German language, where the term *Einfühlung* was used by psychologists, for the first time by Vischer (1994). It meant taking an imaginary bodily perspective (Ganczarek, Hünefeldt, and

---

1 The chapter is a revised version of the published paper: Konecki, K.T. 2022. "Empathy! So What?" Przegląd Socjologii Jakościowej, 18(4), 194–233.

Olivetti Belardinelli 2018: 141) and, later, was referred to by Lipps (1903; 1906) to explain aesthetic experiences.

Among sociologists, Charles H. Cooley came up with the *concept of sympathy*. This concept is close to the meaning of empathy used in sociology, especially in the symbolic interactionist perspective (Ruiz-Junco 2017).

Empathy involves taking the role of others (Mead 1934) or, using the language of Alfred Schütz (1962), is connected with the reciprocity of perspectives; if it is difficult to achieve this reciprocity, it is difficult to activate empathy. Thus, the breakdown of the basis of the lifeworld (in this case, the reciprocity of perspectives) creates the conditions for the emergence of the Deathworld (Bentz et al. 2018). The lack of empathy here can be both a consequence and a prerequisite for the proliferation of the Deathworld (Bentz and Marlat 2021). Empathy allows us to keep truthful communication base on sharing the norms, and the speakers can examine their experiential background (Bentz and Marlatt 2021: 324–325). Empathy could emerge in such a situation. However, there could be the so-called no-empathy zone (Hochschild 2013), where empathy is absent, like in the territories of war or ethnic conflicts. The media and state propaganda could create such zones (as for the Russian publicity, such a zone was made in Ukraine during the war.)[2]

Suppose I follow Peter Berger (1963) and apply the debunking motif, seeing through the facades of social structure (it is the art of mistrust) what empathy means. In that case, analysts, and theorists analyzing empathy, can see the term in a different light (Shuman 2011). The same principle of historical contextualization should be applied to understanding empathy as a term used by researchers or participants in everyday life in some current historical situation (Endacott and Brooks 2013). It is necessary to see the political location of the empathizing/non-empathizing persons, in what environment they operate, the cultural norms of their social environment, and their social site in the empathizing situation. In such a context, it will be easier for us now to understand the lack of empathy/sympathy for works of Russian artists among many Ukrainian intellectuals (Zabużko 2022) as well as the feeling of empathy for banned Russian artists by some American intellectuals (see Nossel 2022). Empathy is socially-located, even if I reconstruct its essential and universal

2 See: https://foreignpolicy.com/2022/04/26/ukraine-war-russian-orthodox-church-support-patriarch-kirill-homophobia/; https://tribune.com.pk/story/2348088/russia-vows-no-mercy-for-foreign-mercenaries-in-ukraine; https://www.atlanticcouncil.org/blogs/ukrainealert/more-than-three-quarters-of-russians-still-support-putins-ukraine-war/; https://foreignpolicy.com/2022/09/09/putin-russia-ukraine-culture-war-conservative-values/ (all pages retrieved 15.09.22).

qualities, which may seem trans-contextual and unconditional. And I, writing these words, have to deal with such attitudes of people living in *partibus infidelium*, where one empathizes with aggressors causing wars and committing genocide.

However, I'm not a fan of this sociology of suspicion, this "art of distrust," which produces distrust on many levels of human existence, whereby not trusting others and institutions, we ultimately don't even trust ourselves, and we are finally a self-deceiving subject caught up in alien but, after all, *our* discourses and network of institutions. These are situations where an evaluative/critical/misleading attitude precedes knowing another person's voice and, ultimately, oneself. Could we find the golden mean between mistrust, the motive of unmasking, and the trust necessary to create community and social ties? We may try ...

Empathy is connected with knowing. And what we can say about empathy is only knowledge of empathy that exists in the social typifications and a system of relevancies that refers to empathy. This is a *phenomenological view*. According to Schütz, we cannot be empathetic toward other animate organisms, because we do not share the inner view and knowledge of others. We do not have original access to any other consciousness and experience (Barber 2013: 316; see also Barber 2006). Especially with persons far from us and whom we do not know personally, we are not in a familiar situation; we can use mainly typifications. There could be one escape from this dilemma for Schütz by going to sociology, especially the sociology of knowledge that connects the I and the Other. The escape is in the intersubjective knowledge transferred by the language in typifications, cultural language formulas (proverbs and sayings), and, generally, in some systems of integrated experts' knowledge (Schütz 1962). We cannot know what the other feels if we do not have the language testimony in the interaction or some confirmation of it that becomes the social index of the phenomena.

However, my knowledge about the war and the victims of war, while I do not participate in it, is also based on my bodily knowledge (we should turn to genetic phenomenology). I accumulated knowledge about the suffering, pain, fear of losing life, thrill, and sweating in the situation of great anxiety that may become conscious. My body knows that the fear is based on the similarities experienced in the past (Barber 2013: 320–321; see also Merleau-Ponty 2005; Rosan 2014). Based on the similarities of various species and humans, there is a phenomenon of synchronization of feelings among humans and between humans and animals. We could see the synchronization that usually occurs at the bodily level, e.g. when we yawn, laugh, cry, or feel sad (de Waal 2009). Wherever we find the roots of empathy or compassion (in the physiology of the animals or the spirit of humans and human history, evolution, or even in an individual's past), there is proved that they are embodied (Stein 1989), and the acts of empathy are intentional (Jardine and Szanto 2017) and connected with feelings (Svenaeus 2018: 745). The perception of others goes together with the feeling which others could experience at the moment, and it is based on the primordial experience of a living body (Stein 1989: 63; Merleau-Ponty 2005).[3] But the feeling means not only knowledge about feeling, but also experiencing somehow the feelings or emotions:

> But the first important point is that the terms empathy and sympathy suggest that this understanding is not primarily gnostic, cognitive, intellectual, technical – but rather that it is, indeed, pathic: involving the emotions, the body, the poetic, the pathetic, and the pathically inspired. (Van Manen 2014: 268)

And the reaction of empathy is almost immediate and automatic, and we do not have much control over it. We are directly transposed to the position of the subject of empathy, and it goes beyond only imagination (Stein 1989). So, empathy is a unique experience, and intention with the direction to the object of empathy is needed.

We *enter* the bodies of other people, and then their thoughts, emotions, and moves of bodies are like our own (de Waal 2009). The transfer of senses of "animate organisms" can be considered when we analyze how consciousness works:

> Perhaps Husserl emphasized that the transfer of this sense takes place across a wide variety of beings, from humans to dogs to gorillas to fish to worms to accentuate how the smallest similarities evoke the transfer despite much larger differences than those that Schütz points out. (Barber 2013: 321)

Here the sensual empathy can be activated (Svenaeus 2018). Empathy is the essential ability of a human being to access other minds, and it is an intentional experience that any material or social condition cannot determine (Jardine and Szanto 2017). "The feelings we have about other people may not

3 "The other subject is primordial although I do not experience it as primordial. In my nonprimordial experience I feel, as it were, led by a primordial one not experienced by me but still there, manifesting itself in my nonprimordial experience" (Stein 1989: 11).

always be the focus of conscious attention" (Owen 2007: 90). The intention can appear after the first reaction which can be unconscious.

I interpret empathy from the phenomenological point of view inspired by Barber (2013; see also 2017). Suppose we use the contemplative approach and be mindful of our bodies. In that case, we can feel the emotions of others vicariously in our imagination (Jardine and Szanto 2017); it is an appresentation from the self to others, even if the other is not present to us, but the mind imagines as he/she were present (Owen 2007: 79, 84); also, the feelings of other people connected with the war, such as fear, anxiety, rage, or sadness are appresented (see Konecki 2018: 234–235). Seemingly not being there, I never experience it directly. However, my senses are directed by the mind, the memory of the appearance of other bodies when sharing fear and the thoughts about them create the emotions, and the accumulated memory about the death and illness of others brings me closer to the actual situation. I suffer. *Kineasthesia* as a way of knowing works here, although in lieu. There is a mechanism as if I were there and were them. But it is not only the work of my imagination; it is a different mode of experiencing targeted at the Other, not only in my memory and past recollection of feelings concerning the situation. Knowledge of the Other is essential here, but it is not enough to feel empathy. You need to initiate the intention and motivation to go outside your consciousness. According to Husserl (1977a; 1980), the understanding of ourselves is strictly connected with an understanding of others:

1. "In empathy there is the understanding that there is a transposability of perspective.
2. Consequently, it is assumed that we all participate in one world, co-constituting its meanings and objectivities.
3. Mutuality and reciprocity exist with respect to the appresentations of 'co-empathy,' because empathy is a two-way communion, a connection between people.
4. Consequently, there is a single cultural world of shared appresentations of cultural-world senses to objects, at a fundamental level.
5. Through the mutual addition and transposability of senses is constituted the natural attitude. At the natural attitude level, the ordinary ontic level of understanding, each individual person has their own individual perspective and an illusion of privacy and separation from each other and the world. In fact this last point could be called a 'false sense of alienation'. It is false because people are enjoined in an all-embracing mutuality and intermixing that occurs through their common psychophysical Nature" (Owen 2007: 81).

Our "common psychosocial nature" is fundamental to empathy and co-empathy. The crossing of our visions of the world is a necessary condition for the emergence of empathy.

I want to introduce an interpretative understanding of empathy, mainly from the earliest grounds for *symbolic interactionism*. One can find the earliest concepts related to empathy in the work of Charles H. Cooley (1922).

•••

I will do this presentation referring to the war in Ukraine, because I later searched for empathy in the context of war, especially after the mass invasion of Russia on Ukraine on 24.02.2022. The war caused a lot of damage in Ukraine, bringing suffering to civilians, genocide, and the destruction of many cities.

Though my mental and bodily experiments in imagining the war could be very sophisticated and advanced, and create the phantasy of actual war, in the back of my mind I know that I am more or less safe. I am far from the war. Therefore, it should also be critical concerning the context of social actors perceiving the phenomena and feeling empathy (Shuman 2011: 154).

The imagination is important here: "There is nothing more practical than social imagination; to lack, it is to lack everything" (Cooley 1922: 142). Sociologists have forgotten about it and do not treat "the mind with the imagination pictures" as the interesting subject of the study. However, it would be interesting to know why I think I can or cannot imagine other thoughts and feelings in some situations. What is the structure of my knowledge at hand that protects me against the thesis of the existence of empathy? One can only say that some people do not want to be empathetic or are protected by their socialization or other social influences (propaganda) from some empathy. What is the knowledge at hand (Schütz 1962); what are *the emotions at hand* (or the knowledge about possible feelings) that influence my imagination skills?

Sociologists underline the socio-psychological phenomenon of role-taking. So, the cognitive way of going into another body and environment is significant here (Mead 1934; Misheva 2009). Mead gives the cognitive base to empathy; however, it does not mean sharing feelings with others (Ruiz-Junco 2017: 417). The sympathy could appear as the consequence of taking the role of others (Ruiz-Junco 2017) And as the cognitive frame, it could be changed in society and shaped by political decisions and educational activity.

Empathy is a social construction according to Ruiz-Junco (2017: 415). It is a social construction not only at the direct interactional level when it is launched by observation and/or imitation (de Waal 2009). The activity in the interaction and being active in observation is at stake here. Empathy starts in our communicational processes and embodied communication. However, it could also be constructed at the macro level by informational and propaganda policy as well as an educational system that directs us to whom one should feel empathy and to whom not.

Empathy/sympathy[4] concerns the mental operations:

> one has to bear in mind that it denotes the sharing of any mental state that can be communicated, and has not the special implication of pity or other 'tender emotion' that it very commonly carries in ordinary speech. This emotionally colorless usage is, however, perfectly legitimate, and is, I think, more common in classical English literature than any other. (Cooley 1922: 137)

Therefore, sympathy/empathy is mainly *cognitive* and, for Cooley, is socially-grounded. The human being could be morally evaluated by having the skills to feel sympathy for others ("sympathy is a measure of his personality"). Also, *the skills help to have power* ("sympathy is a requisite to social power" – Cooley 1922: 141). So, empathy can also be used for purposes of domination and power. It allows one to diagnose the thoughts and emotions of another person and, therefore, in a sense, predict his/her future actions. It could be helpful in the work situation (instrumental empathy; see Hochschild 1983; Junco-Ruiz 2017: 429). These social and cognitive levels of empathy could be dissociated from some emotions: "I have already suggested that sympathy is not dependent upon any particular emotion, but may, for instance, be hostile as well as friendly ..." (Cooley 1922: 159). One can enter another person's mind, but one can hate the person, and the emotion could be a stimulus to act (Cooley 1922: 160). *Sympathy is not necessarily connected with the feeling of altruism, friendship, and love.* It could be used differently. It is not compassion. As Cooley indicates:

> Sympathy in the sense of compassion is a specific emotion or sentiment, and has nothing necessarily in common with sympathy in the sense of communion. It might be thought, perhaps, that compassion was one form of the sharing of feeling; but this appears not to be the case. The sharing of painful feeling may precede and cause compassion, but is not the same with it (Cooley 1922: 137, Footnote 1).

4 Cooley used the term 'sympathy'; however, it signifies what we mean by empathy today.

However, some sympathy can have a universal meaning when it connects with the love of God (Cooley 1922: 160) or with the whole nature, as is the case in Buddhist teachings (Hanh 1999). One sees a need for values, *including the humanistic coefficient*, not only from the sociological and methodological perspective, but also in the standard educational system of humanistic education based on values (Znaniecki 1988).

The society exists, because we are able to be empathetic and to understand the social order we should in order to feel empathy (at least cognitive empathy) and understand the Other. The effects of empathy we can see in the institutions that organize our society and are organized by the empathetic attitudes:

To come into touch with a friend, a leader, an antagonist, or a book, is an act of sympathy; but it is precisely in the totality of such acts that society consists ... And, turning the matter around, we may look upon every act of sympathy as a particular expression of the history, institutions, and tendencies of the society in which it takes place (Cooley 1922: 167).

Susan Shott's concepts (1979) follow the classical way of thinking about empathy, not only in symbolic interactionism. She also emphasizes imagination and the importance of *taking the role of others*, which could be the base for feeling other people's emotions (Ruiz-Junco 2017: 418). Susan Shott's conception also touches on sharing negative and positive emotions with others. The feelings of the empathizers are not identical to that of the recipients, but the empathizers trie to evoke similar emotions in themselves.

Natalia Ruiz-Junco (2017) proposes her own concept of empathy, also rooted in the symbolic interactionist perspective. However, at the beginning, she also follows Goffman's concept of a frame (Goffman 1974). Individual-experience empathy is based on the cultural frames of experiencing emotions. *The frame consists of three elements: the culturally-defined role of empathizers, the role of the recipients of empathy, and moral claims of empathy* (some kind of beliefs or ideology; see Ruiz-Junco 2017: 421). The sociological vision of empathy indicates the societal and structural determinants (the frame) that define the possibility of the emergence of empathy.

"The frame predetermines an empathizer position by the visual presentation of suffering children, who, as victims of the conflict, fall into the position of model empathy recipients ... rights. In summary, empathy frames have a discursive structure that defines a moral claim for empathy based on shared values and on different positions for empathizers and recipients" (Junco-Ruiz 2017: 421).

The media can be a very influential agent of empathy (Höijer 2004). We have this situation now that the war in Ukraine is going on. Media in the West create a mood of empathy for Ukrainian citizens experiencing genocide and a lot of suffering, including theft of belongings, torture, rape of women, killings of children, and the destruction of houses, hospitals, and schools (see Harding 2022).

Junco-Ruiz introduces to her sociological view of empathy the concept of empathy rules. She follows Hochschild's (2016) idea of the ideological background of empathy. *Empathy is socially-defined* and indicates an empathy-deserving situation (e.g. in a war zone). Secondly, there is the identification of rightful empathizers and proper empathy recipients. Empathy-deserving situations are socially-defined, so her perspective is also sociological and oriented at recognizing and identifying the social conditions of empathy constructions.

3 The Method

We know that there is much information and media coverage of the wars. And one can experience this by observing what is going on in Ukraine: bombing, refugees fleeing to other countries, the fear and cry of civilians, etc. And the massive amount of information could be significant for getting to know about the life of the people in war, but also for evoking empathy. At the same time, it is too much of a burden on our perception and emotional responsiveness. However, one feels pressure that one should respond to: "Global compassion is considered to be morally correct in the striving for cosmopolitan democracy, and the international community condemns 'crimes against humanity'" (Höijer 2017: 19). We know that media-mediated process of experiencing others is a common phenomenon of modern times; we are affected emotionally, and we know that we never meet the persons presented in media (Höijer 2004). Mass media and social media are the phenomena of modernity. However, the sympathy and empathy aroused by the narratives have been known in many cultures since ancient times. *The Odyssey* was told in antiquity, passed down from generation to generation, and aroused various emotions among the hearers.

There are also a lot of critics concerned with our interest in distanced suffering that we want to keep far away from our situation. There could be an experience of empathy deficit in contemporary society (Junco-Ruiz 2017: 414). Also frequent is that our charity is connected with this strategy of maintaining ontological security.[5]

5 "In the critical media debate it is a quite common view that suffering is commodified by the media and the audience become passive spectators of distant death and pain without any moral commitment" (Höijer 2017: 25).

I wanted to check how the pictures of the war evoke empathy. The photos for an experiment were chosen to show the war and refugees' circumstances and to have a punctum (Barthes 1981). It means that it should have something that can disarrange one perception of the world at the moment. It is an element in the photo that attracts one and *makes* thinking and feeling. It also causes some surprise and says something more than one sees. What emotions, thoughts, and body feelings are revealed at the moment of looking at pictures? What reflection appears when some emotions emerge? I thought about the reflection on the meaning of empathy and its presence in modern society, as well as about empathy deficit. I did a contemplative experiment with my students (for contemplative experiments, see Konecki 2018: 233–235, this one is the "empathetic experiment") in order to answer these questions.[6] It is not an experiment on discourse and the context of text-appearing. It is an experiment on experiencing empathy:

> Empathetic experiments are a part of the practice of contemplation. We put ourselves in the role of other, with the full awareness and observing our emotions and bodily feelings. We make an imaginative transfer of our body to the position of the other ... This practice is very useful for social education ... After making the experiment, we should write down what we experienced during it: our thoughts, visual images, bodily feelings and emotions. (Konecki 2018: 234)

The experiments are understood here not scientifically but more as creating the situation to experience emotions and bodily feelings. It is more about uncovering the essential features of the phenomenon in order to understand it than about explaining the reasons for its emergence. Empathetic experiments are the contemplative methods to search for the meaning and the essence of lived experiences (Konecki 2018: 234–235). I *borrow the lived experiences* of the students to understand the meaning of empathy.[5]

I think that contemplation and contemplative or phenomenological studies with students can teach us more about the concepts, theories, and social phenomena one experiences in the lifeworld (Bentz and Shapiro 1998; Bentz and Giorgino 2016; Konecki 2018; 2022; Bentz and Marlatt 2021). It is often not only about understanding, but also transforming ourselves (Rehorick and Bentz 2008). Moreover, as teachers and researchers, we can also learn from

6 The empirical part of the chapter was presented at a workshop on *Empathic Leadership: A Trauma Informed Perspective*, The Fielding Graduate University Summer School, July 12, 2022.

our students. The didactic process is interactive and we cannot assume that, as teachers, we have a better position for knowing (Rehorick and Taylor 1995).

4 Contemplative Experiment

I presented to the participants of the experiment, the students, the photos from the media, newspapers, and some websites which distribute the news from newspapers.[7] I asked the students what they felt in their bodies and minds and what emotions they experienced when they looked at the pictures. The pictures referred to the war in Ukraine between March and April 2022: pictures of destroyed cities, rescued civilians, children in the war, pregnant women fleeing hospital, a farewell of boyfriends and girlfriends, and refugees. I did the experiment in April 2022. Before the whole experiment, we had practiced for a few weeks hatha-yoga and meditation (I am an instructor of hatha yoga), and directly before the experiment, we practiced breathing exercises (*pranayama*) as well as a short meditation.[8] I instructed the students on the exercises, i.e. how to do them and what will happen afterward. Later, before and after seeing each picture, the students breathed deeply three times and tried to concentrate on breathing to clear the mind and the heart (the practice of *pranayama*), and be prepared for seeing and feeling the next visual image.

My inspiration for the experiment comes from my lived experiences of empathy with Ukrainian citizens and refugees. I was moved emotionally by the sufferings of the Ukrainians and their sad stories that I read and watched on TV or the Internet, but also from personal testimonies. I felt fear, anxiety, anger, and even hate for the aggressors at the beginning of the war, and empathy for Ukrainians. I wanted to create the base for identification with the victims of the war in the experiment by using some questions and instructions, and see how it works when the imagination is triggered by photos. Especially for me, it was important, because I had students from different cultures and countries,

7 Two doctoral students assisted me in the class and the experiment – Dagmara Tarasiuk and Aleksandra Płaczek.

8 The students participated in the research: "Experiencing corporeality and gestures in the social world of hatha yoga. Meanings and knowledge transfer in body practice." The research project was supported by the National Science Center in Poland [*Opus*, grant number 2018/29/B/HS6/00513].

The experiment on empathy resulted from the learning process and from reflecting on emotion during hatha-yoga practice. The eruption of the war in Ukraine also had an impact on constructing the experiment.

mostly those far away from the space of war. I wanted to see if their lived experiences share the same themes of empathy.

The students were from the course "Meditation for Managers" (2021/22, summer semester; University of Lodz), which was dedicated mainly to the Erasmus+ mobility program students from many countries, such as Spain, Turkey, Greece, Japan, Portugal, as well as Poland. The active participation in the experiment (writing self-reports on the feelings) was voluntary, 35 students took part in the class (22 women and 8 men), and, finally, I received 14 self-reports describing the emotions, thoughts and body feelings from the experiment. The students were aged 21–26. They gave their informed consent to participate in the investigation which was going on during the classes and to the researchers using their protocols in our research for explicating their lived experiences. The structure of the experiment was as follows:

1. At the beginning of the experiment, I asked the students the question – "What is empathy?" It was necessary as an introduction to further reflection on the sufferings of the war victims.
2. I asked the students about their feelings when they watched the pictures from the Ukrainian war (destroyed buildings, rescued people, rescued children, pregnant women, farewells of girls and boys).
3. Finally, I asked about empathy deficit in the contemporary world, i.e. if it exists, and if yes, why it happens. The question aimed to trigger more reflection on empathy, especially the conditions for empathy to emerge or not.

I took for analysis pictures from Internet media; however, I did not discuss the media discourse on compassion or empathy (see Höijer 2004; 2017). The photos were only the tool for the investigation of empathy. Visual images were important tools for attracting the public's attention to social and human problems.

5 Explication of Results

5.1 *What Is Empathy*

I practiced *pranayama* (Iyengar 1983) with the students, which meant deep breathing at the beginning of the experiment. It was work on the mind (cleaning the mind), releasing tensions, and building energy, and its aim was to prepare for the direct reception of the pictures. Below I quote the attitude of the students toward the practice of breathing:

> Starting the class with breathing exercises made me start to relax and have a greater connection with myself. (woman)

> I was breathing since many of these photographs have significantly impacted me due to the hardness they represent. (man)
>
> As always, we start with breathing, which I appreciate to be able to mentalize that what we are going to do is calm down, think, meditate and concentrate on ourselves. (woman)

The breathing also helped to release the tension because of the difficulty of the situations presented in the pictures:

> I would like to mention that I liked and it helped me a lot the pause we did after each question to take a breath because the questions were related to tough situations (due to the war). I noticed how my body got tense because I imagined myself in that situation and felt a lot of anxiety inside me. (woman)

Generally, in this chapter, I present the students' evocative first-person statements from self-reports. Sometimes, I think it is better not to interpret them but present them as they were written down in order to show the original expressions without any possible bias by the interpretations of the author of this chapter.

After breathing exercises, I asked the students the question and gave an instruction: "What is empathy? Just write down, please, do not refer to the Internet."

The most often expressed description and understanding of empathy was the following: it is connected with *"putting yourself in the place of others"* and understanding the emotions of others (see the quote below). This common-sense definition is similar to that proposed by symbolic interactionists. Therefore, one sees that often the theoretical concepts are constructed above the mundane understanding of terms that are used conventionally (the so-called "construct of the second degree"; see Schütz 1962: 6, 59):

> Then, when the debate began on what empathy is, I began to reflect, and I agree with many of my colleagues on the definition of empathy: it consists of always putting yourself in the place of the other and trying to understand what their emotions and feelings are like so that we can take care of the way we act with these people. After this, and showing some images of the tragedy that Ukraine is experiencing, we were able to put the concept of empathy into practice and try to put ourselves in the shoes of the Ukrainian people and feel what they are feeling. (woman)
>
> What is empathy for each one? For me, empathy is about thinking about others and putting yourself in their situation, communicating

> feelings and thoughts, understanding them, and being able to feel the other person's feelings. (woman)

But understanding the emotion of others could go on together with understanding our own emotions. What is interesting here is that it is also connected with self-identifying with others and their feelings for the moment of empathizing:

> For me, empathy is the feeling of understanding the other person and your own emotions. It is learning multiple perspectives, trying to identify with others and their feelings, problems, dilemmas. (woman)

Some of the students write about empathy as the synchronization of feelings with others. This understanding is close to the ethologists' vision that emphasizes the *synchronization of emotions* among animals (de Waal 2009). However, the answer below underlines the real feelings, not only the presentation of self, as is the case in the Goffmanian vision (1959). What is interesting for the students (see below) is that it also relates to the past, not only to the present.[9] The present is the base to evoke the past to experience empathy with others here and now. For this reason, the historical persons could also be understood by using empathy. This kind of reflection appeared spontaneously in our research:

> Synchronicity of feelings with others, and to have the same emotion at the bottom of heart, not on the surface. It is shared beyond time; we can have empathy towards historical people. (woman)

For what do we need empathy? We can feel it and do nothing. However, empathy was created for some purposes, to make something in social relation, to

9 "Even though history may illuminate our erroneous suppositions about how others, including animals, are like us, the writing of history itself presupposes and extends the fundamental experience of empathy in the present" (see Barber 2013: 320). The protest that we can sometimes observe against the possibility of understanding empathy, as putting ourselves in the situation of others, comes from a hard scientific mind that wants to see only "the hard facts." However, "the hard facts" are also interpreted. Our mind has to treat the facts uniquely, abstracting them from the context: "Strictly speaking, there are no such things as facts, pure and simple. And facts are from the outset facts selected from a universal context by the activities of our mind. They are, therefore, always interpreted facts, either facts looked at as detached from their context by an artificial abstraction or facts considered in their particular setting" (Schütz 1962: 5). However, after abstracting them, we must put them back into the context to keep the understanding in everyday life by experiencing them by mind and body.

generate the 'we' relationship. If the pro-social activity follows the feelings of empathy, we can observe the whole social meaning of it. Some students emphasize that empathy is a *human feeling which precedes helping others*:

> I think it is a very human feeling because through knowing the suffering of another person you can take actions to improve their situation, and you always tend to take care of others. (man)

It is the human emotion that is often *associated with compassion*, which is felt because of suffering; it is the feeling of sympathy for others that is also important for protecting the community life:

> If I had to define empathy from a more personal point of view, I would say it is the natural human reaction to the pain that surrounds us and a way to protect ourselves and help us live in a community. (man)

Interestingly, one of the students said that *empathy is a way of connecting with others*. It is a very sociological interpretation; empathy creates the solidarity between humans, because it connects them. Another sociological meaning in the quotation below is an opinion that empathy is socialized and *can be learned* (see Heyes 2018). This opinion about empathy indicates that it is a *social construct*:

> To me, *empathy is a way of connecting*. Empathy shows or tries to show that you know what someone is experiencing, even if you don't know how they are feeling. Empathy says, 'I want you to know that you are not alone, and I want to understand how you feel.' Also, I think that empathy is not something you are born with; it is something you develop throughout life. (man)

From these quotations above, one can see that the students understand the term 'empathy'. It is, according to them, the ability to "put yourself in the place of others," but also understanding the emotions experienced by others and the synchronization of emotions. The students also wrote about compassion with the suffering ones, and connecting with others.[10]

---

10 One can notice that the common sense of empathy is similar to the phases of empathy constructed by Edith Stein (1989; Svenaeus 2018: 742–743). "Stein takes empathy to be a three-step process in which the experience of the other person (the empathee) (1) emerges to the empathizer as an experience had by the empathee, the empathizer

5.2 *Bombing the City*

I presented to the students the slides with the following descriptions:

> Description of Bombing Kyiv: A multi-story residential building is severely damaged, likely from an explosion. Multiple floors are missing, balconies are destroyed, and windows are shattered. Debris, including metal pieces and rubble, is scattered across the ground. Water fills the gaps in the ruined building, adding to the sense of chaos and destruction. There are no visible signs of life except for a single figure in the distance, hinting at a once-lived life in this place. (https://bit.ly/4h5cdPh)
>
> Description of Rescuing civilians: The central focus is a severely damaged building. It appears to be a residential or commercial building. Windows are shattered, balconies are missing, and parts of the structure have collapsed. Debris, including metal pieces and rubble, is scattered across the ground. Water is pooling in the craters, and depressions are caused by destruction. In the distance, we can see a single person walking through the rubble. This figure is small, and it is about the scale of the destruction. The figure appears to be walking cautiously, perhaps surveying the damage or searching for something. Their body language conveys a sense of caution and unease. (https://politi.co/3C3zORj)
>
> Description of Bombing Kharkiv: The image depicts a scene of devastation and destruction. A large, open area, possibly a square or plaza, is littered with debris. A mangled car lies in the foreground, its hood open and its body twisted. The surrounding buildings show signs of damage, with shattered windows and debris scattered around them. The debris field suggests a recent and violent event, possibly an explosion or attack. The presence of the wrecked car further emphasizes the destructive force at play. (https://bit.ly/4jAbNCn)

---

then (2) follows the experience of the empathee through, in order to (3) return to a more comprehensive understanding of the meaning of the experience had by the empathee" (Svenaeus 2018: 742). After the incentive giving the reason for empathy to emerge (pictures with suffering people, phase 1), there is a phase of following the experience, "putting yourself in the place of others" (emotions appear, phase 2), and, finally, there is understanding the emotions of the suffering people and their reason, and referring to the social values (interpretation of the situation of empathees, phase 3).

After seeing the slides, the students were asked:

1. "Try to feel what the people in Ukraine feel now."
2. "Look how the people are living in Kyiv and Kharkiv."
3. "Try to be there; you are one of the inhabitants of Kyiv or Kharkiv."

Seeing the picture of the bombed city, students felt *fear, anger, helplessness, sadness, and a lack of understanding* (*they often asked: 'Why does it happen?'*). It could be seen further that the fear and anger repeat many times in the descriptions of the war situation. The pictures affect the viewers emotionally; the felt emotions seem strong. The feeling of impotence is evident. The students also refer to their position and feel fear for their families. Therefore, the lived experience that emerges connects the imagining of other people's situation and feelings with own ones. Embodied emotions are also perceived:

> In a situation like that, I think that I will feel fear obviously, but also impotence and anger from the sensation that there's nothing I can do about the imminent destruction of my home. (man)
>
> I feel destroyed on the inside, lost, surprised. I'm trying to find something to cling to help me through this hard time: the grief, the sadness, the injustice. I care for my loved ones, and I am afraid. I wonder if my home is still a safe place. (woman)
>
> I'm sad and terrified; I don't want any of my family and friends to die. I'm confused because I don't understand why this is happening. (woman)

Often, the reactions full of emotions coming at the same time were also *embodied*:

> Helplessness, sadness, anguish, and injustice were some of the feelings I experienced. Seeing the harsh images makes me sad, and chills run through my whole body.

We see here that the body can be tuned to emotional reactions, and we can understand more from my relations to the world:

"The pathically tuned body recognizes itself in its responsiveness to the things of our world and to the others who share our world or break into our world" (Van Manen 2014: 269).

5.3 *Empathy with Children*

After breathing deeply, the students observed the following pictures and wrote their self-reports. The instruction was short: "Write what you feel, please. Body, mind, and emotions." According to their definition of empathy, the students tried to imagine being in the situation of refugees (see Junco-Ruiz 2017: 421).

> Description of Child refugees: It shows a refugee, likely a woman, carrying a child. The woman's face may display a mixture of emotions, such as exhaustion, worry, and perhaps a glimmer of hope. The child might be looking at the camera with curiosity and fear. The image may evoke empathy and compassion for the plight of refugees. (https://x.com/AFPphoto/status/1497874398274936832/photo/1)

The students felt cognitive empathy for children suffering during the war. They could imagine being in the situation. There is the ethical stance that children should not experience such conditions. On the other hand, there are statements about *not understanding* the problem of children. In empathy, there is also some prediction of the future, that the war will *leave a mark on them for life*. Beyond this, children could feel confusion and helplessness:

> You are a child in the war. How do you feel?
>
> It is a situation that no child should go through. It must be very confusing for them; they don't understand the magnitude of the problem, they don't understand why they have to leave home, don't understand why they see fire, don't understand why mom and dad cry or they don't understand why dad is not with them. It's hard because they can't do anything about it. They take it with them. And the most challenging part is knowing that this incident will leave a mark on their personal lives that they will carry with them for the rest of their lives. (man)
>
> This is very difficult for me. I think a child's mind is much more innocent than a teenager's, but I still believe that children should not understand what is happening. To me, they must know something strange is happening, but they do not understand. They are leaving their stuffed animals, beds, movies, and playgrounds, but they don't know why. If I were a Ukrainian child, I would feel confused with a strange feeling and a lot of helplessness to have to leave everything I know. I would feel a sense of being clueless and not understanding what my new situation would bring. Although I don't think they know what is going on. (man)

The difficulty of understanding children's situation is felt together with *the defenselessness of the child, impotence*, and the evaluation of the condition of children from the moral point of view ("heinous act"). The concerns about the children and the future of the child also appear:

> I would feel a sense of bewilderment for not knowing what is happening since the innocence of children means that they do not fully understand why this type of situation occurs. In the same way, I would feel great

> sadness knowing that I am moving away from my family, my friends, and the place where I was born and that I will probably never have many of these things again.
>
> I also think it is tough to put yourself in the shoes of a child since each one can act differently, while in the case of adults, the answer we would give would be much more similar. In the same way, many of these children are defenseless, and there is no one to watch over their safety, and that seems to me to be one of the most heinous acts in this war. (man)
>
> Terrified, very afraid, for the baby above all. And impotence and uselessness when you cannot save him from that situation and see that you are facing a situation that does not depend on you. We can see the desperation and abandonment on the mother's face as she no longer knows what she can do to save the baby. (man)

The self-confidence disappears, and the weakness of the self and concerns about the children and the child's future emerge. The self-identification with the role of the mother appears among women:

> I feel weak without strength, I don't believe in myself, and I don't think I will make it. The war is more than me, I want to give peace to my baby, but there's no peace in our place now. I want the best for him and give it to him, but if I can't, even if this makes me sad, I'll send him wherever he can be in peace. (woman)

There are often mechanisms of "*as if*" used, 'what would happen if I were in such a situation.' The sense of being lost as well as fear commonly *appear by interpreting conditions presented in the pictures*. Self-identification with the child emerges:

> I'm trying to understand why every day looks different; I feel fear, an inexplicable sense of loss. I cling to loved ones (mom, dad). I'm looking for my bed and warmth. (woman)

There are also *difficulties* with understanding/imagining the situation of children during the war. Mainly it happens to children:

> I think that, even if we make an effort to put ourselves in their place, it is very difficult to feel what they are experiencing. (man)

Children usually are empathized more than adults. They belong to the so-called "ideal victims" (Höijer 2017: 26), and it could be seen in media reporting from the wars. The "ideal victim" is a social construction that also depends on the current political and historical situations.[11] The interpretation in the frame of the "ideal victim" could also happen in our experiment.

The relations with parents are also noticed, and the suffering is connected here with the whole group of the family. It could be seen through the prism of own relations with parents, and it helps to imagine what the feeling would be in a real war situation:

> I feel a lot of pain to think that some people kill others, that children have to live through hell to see their mother, father and other family die. (man)

The empathetic reactions were full of emotions of fear, but the fear was also *embodied.* The empathizer could imagine the *feelings of the body such as discomfort, cold, fatigue, stress, and pain,* and, once again, the relations with parents are visible:

> I would be scared; I don't know if I would understand what was happening if I could trust people because I couldn't say who is good or bad. It would be tough for me to have to leave my house. I would be terrified. From the photos I have seen, I suppose I would also be freezing and hungry; it would hurt me to see my parents sad and scared. Sleeping in stations or public transport to be able to leave Ukraine, I would feel awful physically, my neck would hurt, my back, indeed, would be combined with mental fatigue from sleeping poorly, and the stress that each one endures. (woman)

The direct experience of seeing the situation of refugees is engaging empathy here (not only from the pictures); the mother and the children who finally meet (it is the same student as above). The empathy works here in terms of seeing the picture and seeing the actual situation:

> The other day, I went to Warsaw, and the station was full of Ukrainian people, with blankets, food offered by Poles, and children playing with what people gave them; it was a challenging situation to watch. On the return train, when I got off at the station, I saw two small children with

---

11 "And it is not until our present time that male soldiers' systematic rapes of civil women from the enemy side are being condemned. During the Second World War it was more or less accepted that Russian soldiers, for instance, committed massive rapes of German women immediately after the capture of Berlin" (Höijer 2017: 27).

flowers waiting for their mother, and the mother was crying because she was seeing her children. That image gave me a mixture of sensations. This shiver made my hair stand on end to see how hard the feeling must be for the mother and the children. There is also a lot of tenderness in seeing the image of the happy children hugging their mother with the flowers, and a feeling of sorrow in seeing how devastated Russia is leaving Ukraine and the damage they are doing to many families, older people, and young people. (woman)

5.4 *Pregnant Woman*

After seeing the previous pictures and after a deep-breathing exercise, the instruction to students was as below:

> You are a woman giving birth in the bombed hospital; how do you feel? What do you feel in your body and mind? What thoughts are coming to your mind?
>
> Description Pregnant woman:[12] In the picture is the pregnant woman. The image shows four men carrying a woman on a stretcher. The men are dressed in dark clothing and vests, and one is wearing a helmet. In the background is a damaged building with broken windows and a ruined facade. There is a lot of debris on the ground, and the trees are bare, suggesting a winter setting. The atmosphere of the image is dramatic and tense. (https://www.bbc.com/news/world-europe-60734706)

Concerning the empathy for the pregnant woman under the bombing, the students feel *desperation*. The future horizon is taken into account, but it is difficult to predict what will happen, and this causes the feeling of *sadness*:

> Desperation. It's the first feeling that enters my head. It makes me reflect that life is hard, and some people suffer more than others because, in a moment as beautiful as having a child when you should be happier than ever and eager to see what the future holds for your child, you are thinking about whether the war will let Ukraine have a future or not. It's sad. At that exact moment where you can't move from the hospital, and you have to see how they destroy your country while you suffer the pain of the last weeks of pregnancy. (man)

---

12 I have not presented the article's title: "Ukraine war: Pregnant woman and baby die after hospital shelled." Students have seen only the picture.

As I mentioned before, sometimes the students express their problems and *difficulties* with self-identifying with other situations and emotions, especially when the empathy receiver is different in an important aspect of the case presented in the picture:

> Then we saw the infamous image of a woman being evacuated from a hospital when she was pregnant. I don't think I would be able to understand such a pain, so I prefer to respectfully not give an opinion. (man)

A difficulty in understanding the situation appears once again. However, it does not mean that the person is unable to feel empathy. Just the opposite; it is possible to see many proofs of the emotional manifestation (fear, sadness):

> Definitely; the first word I thought of was "fear". I try to put myself in that woman's shoes, and, as I said before, I think it's impossible to feel the same way. The thoughts that come to my mind are of great concern, the uncertainty of not knowing what will happen to your life and that of your baby, and above all, great sadness at seeing that you are bringing a child into the world in the worst of situations. (man)

The student quoted below evidently empathizes with the pregnant woman. She is like her and wants to give birth to her child desperately. *She asks a question – 'Why?'* As the author of this text, I believe her; I *feel* it (my meta-empathy). Below we can read a very evocative statement:

> Why should this happen to my unborn child? It is a life that was finally given to me, and I finally came this far after overcoming a painful period of hyperemesis gravidarum, but ... I want to give birth to her. I want to show this child to my husband and parents. I don't care what happens to me.
>
> Sincerely clinging to God. (woman)

Strong emotions such as *fear, pain, anxiety, and uncertainty* are experienced in lieu. However, they look very authentic to me:

> Unimaginable fear – for myself and the baby. Uncertainty, pain, desire to disappear for the moment. The desire for a safe place and people around. (woman)

> I would feel a sense of fear and dread because the most important thing for me would be the safety of my child above my own, but the fact is that

> I know that I can do nothing to ensure the safety of my baby. It would make me possibly be with the worst feeling of anxiety that I could experience throughout my life. In addition, I would have to be alert at all times since, at any moment, I may have to run out of there in a state that could generate great consequences due to the inhumane conditions that many Ukrainian cities are going through that are no longer suitable for living, or for giving birth or for anything. (man)

The emotions observed during empathizing with the different situations of the war horrors are similar (mainly fear). The fear happens frequently, as well as the feeling of *helplessness*:

> If I were a pregnant woman, I think what would matter most to me would be to be able to give birth safely. If I were in a hospital, I would feel much fear. There is a lot of pressure in my chest because you know that you will give birth to the most important thing in your life and the unconditional love you feel. That's why I think I would feel a lot of desire to survive and, above all, a lot of fear. I would also feel helpless and want to scream because it would seem unfair that my child had to be born in those conditions. (man)

5.5 *Saying Goodbye to Boyfriend*

After *pranayama*, a breathing exercise, the instruction for the students was the following:

1. "You are the girl saying goodbye to your boyfriend."
2. "You're a boy saying goodbye to your girlfriend."
3. "What do you feel? Body, mind, emotions, write it down."

The students gave comprehensive reports concerning the issue of parting with a close person. The reason could be that it is at their age when they start close relationships with partners. They recognize the emotions from the nonverbal signs and gestures (see Cooley 1922); for this reason, they can feel empathy for this situation and people.

> Description of People who are close to each other say goodbye. The image depicts an emotional farewell scene. Soldiers in military uniforms with patches showing the Ukrainian flag embrace their loved ones. In the background, more people are seen in similar situations. The atmosphere is filled with emotion and poignancy, suggesting the difficult parting moments as they head to the front. The uniforms are in muted tones, and the presence of civilians adds contrast to the military context. (https://cepa.org/article/the-compass-of-my-love/)

The questions of despair often happen ('Why does it happen?') together with the intense emotions of sadness, fear of death, and anger, and even the willingness to fight together with the boyfriend:

> I would feel great sadness and injustice. The questions that come to my mind are: why choose us? Why does my boyfriend have to leave me and defend our country? After all, it's not his fault ... Why do young people die because of Putin's cruelty? Why does anyone have to die overnight because of the war? I would be sad, torn, and angry at the same time. I would have thought that we may never meet again. I wish he would stay with me, but I would understand why he has to stand up for it. (woman)

> I feel so sad; I want to stay with him; why is he the one who must endure, and I am the one leaving? Why is he fighting, and I'm not? It's not fear. We are the same age; the only difference is gender. I don't want him to die, he is in danger, and I wouldn't be able to live my life without him; I can't lose him. I wish I could stay and fight, and he could leave and be in peace. He should come with me; this is unfair. I'm so sad my heart is broken. I think the worst because I cannot be optimistic about this situation. (woman)

In the self-observation quoted below, the student (woman) shows the fear and probable *pride* in him fighting for the country, but also a lot of pain connected with parting. Her empathizing is *embodied; she feels the warmth* and does not want to forget this feeling:

> Want to meet again, I may not be able though ... He will fight for our country; I should be proud of him. But it's painful. I want to be with him. Tears come out. But I'm happy to be in love with such a brave person. I also have to live strong as he does. I want him to be safe. This can be the last moment; I don't want to forget this warmth. (woman)

The bodily reactions come together with the fear and concerns about the future of the relations. The perception of the world combine here with the lived bodily feelings (see Van Manen 2003; Merleau-Ponty 2005):

> I would feel despondent because, from what I have studied and know of similar situations in the past, I know that it is difficult to meet a person again after the war. Also, I would feel terrified if that person is a man I know who has to fight in the army. A terrible lump in my throat that

> wouldn't let me breathe. Despite that, when I say goodbye, I would try to be positive so that the last memory of this person with me will be as pleasant as possible. I would try to feel her touch as much as possible; I would listen to her voice so I wouldn't forget her, her smell, the color of her eyes ... (man)

Many emotions appear, such as fear, anxiety, and restlessness, and it can even end in depression. Moreover, the feeling of empathy can be here extended to other people, not only the closest one:

> Fear, feelings of loss. Confusion and a lack of clarity about the future. A desire to turn back or speed up time. Moving away from closeness, from warmth. Hope, love, faith in people. (woman)

> I would feel a horrible sense of fear if I was part of the couple who had to go to war, knowing that I might not be able to see not only my partner but all the people who have been a part of my life or who I'm not even going to get out of there alive. On the other hand, if I were part of the couple who fled the country or was not on the front lines of the war, I would feel anxiety and restlessness that would probably bring me depression. Knowing that it is very probable that I will not return to see the most important person in my life with whom I would like to form a future and that I may not even be able to communicate with her. (man)

There is also a sense of *the self that is split into two parts*:

> I am split in two, one half of my self, or at least best part of me, hopes to see each other again. (woman)

Another student also expresses these feelings of splitting:

> A lot of anger; I would want to cry because a part of you is leaving with him. It's a moment of uncertainty because you don't know if you're going to see him again ... nobody deserves that. Besides, you don't even have the opportunity to be in contact to know how each of the parties is doing, it must be very hard, and you have to be very strong to face such a situation. (woman)

Difficulties of the emotions of parting with a close person are expressed by some of the students, even if students *do not want to imagine the situation*:

> I don't want to imagine how hard it must be to separate you from your partner knowing that there is a possibility of never seeing her again. Again, the feeling of sadness takes over me. (man)

The difference between the standard parting in a peaceful time and parting during the war is emphasized, with the feelings of sadness and uncertainty:

> But here it is different because it is overnight, because of the feeling of knowing that you can meet again but that nothing is certain and you may never see each other again. It's hard and sad. (man)

One of the students described, besides the embodied fear (sleeping difficulties), also the activity that she would take in the situation of parting with her boyfriend (*checking the news and providing support*):

> If I was a girl saying goodbye to the boy? If I had to say goodbye to a person I love and kept thinking he was putting his life in danger, it would be cumbersome on my conscience. I would have a hard time sleeping; I would be worried all day and attentive to the news, I would try to be in contact with that person as much as possible, and I would try to support him at all times and encourage him. (woman)

Often mentioned is *impotence*, not only in this situation, but the helplessness is a significant part of the mode of empathizing with the victims:

> I would feel very sad and afraid to think that I might never see him again, impotence for not being able to do anything to change the situation and not being able to be with him. (man)

5.6 *You Are Refugee*

> Description of Refugees: The image shows a large group of people, many wearing warm clothing like jackets and hats, suggesting cold weather. They are carrying luggage and backpacks, indicating they are traveling. They appear to be outside, near infrastructure resembling a border checkpoint. In the background, there are signs, barriers, and more people and vehicles. The scene suggests a migration or displacement situation. (https://bit.ly/4hgNlDV)

One student wants to escape her thinking and feeling about the suffering (see the quote below). She also shows her worries and fear about her family. She thinks about the historical moment and asks why it happened. Her empathizing is also *embodied*; she has even sensual feelings such as cold and pain, asking why it happened and why the world does not help us. This tone of the narrative is almost like crying:

> What should I do from now on? I can't help; I would like to escape all the suffering ... I don't know what to do from now on, but I have to move my legs to survive tomorrow. I'm worried about my family remaining in Ukraine. Are they safe? Or not alive anymore, no, I don't think anymore. Cold, painful. I'm living in the middle of history. Is it the 21st century? Isn't it a nightmare? Why the world doesn't help us? (woman)

The emotion of *anger* is always present, although the countries receiving the refugees do their best:

> I think you feel weird. You miss your home, you feel like a foreigner looking for a new home, but it will never be your home. The countries that host refugees do their best to make them feel comfortable, but even so, I would feel alone, sad, helpless, and angry because you have been kicked out of your home. (man)

Evocative statements are connected with the *uncertainty about the life* of the refugees:

> Feeling that you have to flee your country to stay alive has to be one of the worst emotions. It's hard to feel this. To think that you have to carry your whole life in a simple travel suitcase. Your house, clothes, memories, and whole life are left behind with the uncertainty of not knowing if you will ever get it back. (woman)

Along with the feeling of sadness, a sense of *gratitude* also appears because of receiving help from others:

> I would feel a great sense of melancholy and sadness since I have left behind my family, my friends, my home, and the country where I grew up and where I have lived all the years of my life, but at the same time, gratitude and a feeling of appreciation due to the great reception that the refugees are receiving in the countries of Europe. Above all, I would feel obligated to return that favor because they are doing it without receiving anything, especially from the families that welcome many refugees. They feed them, give them a mattress to sleep on, a roof to live under ... and all

> this without expecting anything in return. Also, thank all the volunteers and the mobilizations people for what they are doing to stop the war, since knowing that we are not alone gives me more strength to continue fighting. (man)

The gripping reaction is *the sense of pride*. When others help the refugee, self-esteem can go down, and protecting the sense of self is necessary. There is an interesting psychological problem of being grateful and at the same time keeping high self-esteem. The student empathizes with this feeling:

> I feel like it is a new opportunity in life, but at the same time, I think I'm living a life that is not mine because this is not what I'm used to. I feel thankful to the people that are helping me, but at the same time, I don't want them to help me because I don't want them to think that I'm less than them. After all, I'm not. But seeing how they look at me with sad faces makes me feel this way. Am I a less worthy person? (woman)

Despite the emotional empathy when the students try to feel the emotions of the people presented in the pictures or generally the feelings of the refugees, they also recognize the emotions that refugees could handle. There is *the cognitive aspect of recognizing the feelings of other people* from the faces or from the details of the situation that is described (Cooley 1920), shown or presented at the moment:

> I consider myself very empathetic, and I can feel their suffering the most by looking into their eyes. I see emptiness, a feeling that they cannot express; I see it in the Ukrainian families who have moved to Lodz. It's a shame. I imagine it has to be a mixture of feelings such as sadness, anguish, helplessness, discomfort, anger, loneliness, or silence. (man)

The cognitive recognition of emotions among the suffering people can be blocked by own feelings of the potential empathizer. There appears to be anger against journalists taking pictures of the victims. Finally, however, the psychological mechanism of cognitive empathy – 'what I would feel if I were there' – helps to recognize the emotions of others:

- How would you feel if you were a citizen in Kyiv?
- A disappointment and feeling will arise about photographers and journalists who take pictures and don't help. My heart will die. I can't feel anything. I will kill my emotions to protect my heart. But if my

> family, friends, or loved ones get hurt or even die, sadness, anger, and resentment will all come at once. It was a happy place, but now … I might be disappointed to realize the gap between the hometown in my memory and reality. (woman)

5.7 *Deficit of Empathy*

Another question I asked at the end of the experiment was – "What is 'empathy deficit', and what are the reasons for it?" (for the concept of empathy deficit, see Junco-Ruiz 2017).

Some of the students observe the different approaches to different groups concerning empathy. Some indicate that in Poland, the approach to Ukrainian refugees is different to that concerning refugees coming from other parts of the world (e.g. from the Middle East). So, empathy is politically and socially contextualized, and connected with some assumptions of the proper group and individuals that can be receivers of empathy, compassion, and help. Therefore, it can be noticed that empathy deficit is created by *some assumptions and prejudices*. Moreover, we also had "better victims" and others, those not deserving empathy (Höijer 2017: 26). The "better victims" deserve more empathy and attention than "less worthy victims":

> I think the answer to this question [about empathy deficit – K.K.] can be varied concerning the issue or area we are talking about, but focusing on the issue of the war, I think there is a lot of lack of empathy. The reason for this is that right now, we see that countries like Poland are doing everything they can to help the Ukrainians who have been affected by the war by providing enough resources to make them feel at home and at ease. I have noticed that they have not done the same with other countries like Israel or Syria, which have been at war for much longer. This is an example of the lack of empathy because what is happening in Israel or Syria is not as close to us as in Ukraine. Therefore, we do not pay any attention to what is happening there, and we do not put ourselves in their shoes to try to understand their situation and help them in the best way we can. (woman)

The deficit of empathy is also caused by *technology* that is used in everyday life, which creates a lack of direct contact and face-to-face interactions with others:

> I think that the deficit of empathy is experienced today, and I believe that social networks are the critical factor. It is something positive that

> the world is much more globalized. The appearance of new technologies to unite people from different parts of the world has made many things more accessible. Still, at the same time, feelings cannot be shown 100% through a screen, and the world has gotten out of the habit of dealing with people face-to-face and not over the phone. I am just as addicted as all teenagers to social networks, but at the same time, I am fully aware that the value of living in the world outside the screen is much greater, and I think that the goal of all should be to find the balance. (woman)

But there is a different opinion, namely one that technology helps in empathizing; it gives information about other people and makes it easier to empathize:

> but I think that people's empathy is increasing because thanks to new technologies and social networks, we can be continuously updated on what is happening in each part of the world. This helps us be more aware of what is happening; therefore, it is easier to put empathy into practice with other people. (woman)

Some students had a general reflection on the reasons for empathy and the empathy walls (Hochschild 2016; Konecki 2021: 125–126). Something in us can protect us against feelings of empathy; Edith Stein calls it "negative empathy" (Stein 1989: 15). It can be connected with some background experiences that generate a blockage of empathy. Except for technology, *the style of life* in contemporary civilization kills compassion and empathy. The *consumerism*, greediness, making a career, and money are all more important than perceiving the suffering of other human beings:

> I do believe that there is a lack of empathy in contemporary society, both on the part of adults and young people. On the part of young people – because it seems that they are more aware of their mobile phones, of the notifications that reach them, the applications they use, the trends that they are wearing at all times or the clothes they want to buy, and none of these things have the importance compared to what is happening in Ukraine or in many other countries that are also at war, like Syria. It seems that people are putting aside the suffering of many others, and we selfishly focus on ourselves and our well-being, but then when we need help, we are the first ones who, if they do not give it to us, feel betrayed or experience a sense of no one caring. On the other hand, concerning adults, the lack of empathy they have is not so strong, but many of them only think about moving up professionally to earn more money to use

> later for themselves. Ultimately, the more money people have, the more they want. They always use it for their benefit, which is what many adults wish for in life, a high salary and good quality of life, so they don't have worries about their future, but then the concerns of the rest do not seem to matter to them. Likewise, concerning the war in Ukraine, we have seen a significant citizens' mobilization to end this horror. Still, as the days go by, people return to their everyday lives and look the other way when talking about this issue. (man)

Some of the students, while seeing the concentration on the self and selfishness, also mention the *educational problem* connected with the issue of empathy. Empathy is not taught at schools:

> I can feel the empathy deficit in the contemporary world. I think that nowadays almost everybody thinks about themselves and not about others. In the theme of the Ukrainian war and the refugees, I believe Poland is very empathic because people are helping so much. But in my country (Spain), this is not like that. Some people are offended if others give more opportunities to refugees than own citizens because they aren't empathic; they only think they are losing a chance to work; for example, they are not thinking about those people's problems and situations. This is an education-related problem. Also, I see this inside schools; kids should be taught in an empathic environment to understand how differently others think, feel, and act. (woman)

Some students indicated that the lack of empathy could be connected with the *self-defense psychological mechanism*. Too much bad news around could be challenging to bear:

> At last, in conclusion, we have talked about the lack of empathy today. I would say that sometimes I understand it as a self-defense mechanism because we are constantly being informed about bad news worldwide, and it would be impossible not to be depressed if we were always being empathic with those suffering. But still, I think it is time to be strong and help as much as possible and not be afraid of others' pain. (man)

> But if we speak in general, I think there is a huge lack of empathy in the world. I don't know why; maybe our mind blocks anything that hurts us, and by doing this, we don't feel what the other person is feeling, which makes us less empathetic. (man)

And so, this self-defense psychological mechanism is used, but another reason for empathy deficit could be seen in media (Höijer 2004; 2017). If one hears too much bad news from the *media*, one can become indifferent to the real problems of others:

> Speaking more specifically about what the culprit is, in my opinion it is the social networks. I also think that part of the blame lies with the media, for the news has put us in anguish. After bad news do this, we get tired of so many bad things we take that we finally act in a way that is not ours. This is how, in my opinion, we also lose that ability to react empathetically to the pain of others. (man)

One student's meaningful reaction (see below) is that she is lucky not to have experienced such a situation. She indicated how important existential security is in life. She also has a future perspective, but is connected with the hope that the war will finish soon:

> I have also finished the class reflecting on how lucky I am and how lucky that we have a home to live in and family and friends with whom to share life. After seeing these harsh images of Ukrainians, I feel luckier than ever. I hope this tragedy ends soon and all these people get their homes back as soon as possible. (woman)

After the experiment, some of the students are saying that they *should be more reflective* about themselves concerning empathy. Looking deeply into the self could help overcome the deficit of empathy. And it happened after the experiment. I think that the statement below touches on the *didactic goal* that we assumed at the beginning of the empathy experiment:

> I think I am an empathetic person, but it is also true that I often assumed or criticized things that if I were empathizing, I wouldn't criticize. It is effortless not to self-evaluate and say that you are empathetic to feel comfortable with yourself. I believe that I am empathetic frequently but that many other times I lack empathy. (man)

6 Theorizing Empathy

I present some theoretical conclusions now, taking into consideration the results of the research. According to Hochschild (2016: 5), *empathy wall* is "an obstacle to the deep understanding of another person, one that can make us feel indifferent or even hostile to those who hold different beliefs or whose childhood is rooted in different circumstances." The author indicates that the socialization process as the base for empathy is a profoundly sociological perspective (Hochschild 2016). Politicians can also create the empathy wall which is socially-constructed (Konecki 2021: 126–127; see also Stein 1989: 15). Therefore, the attitudes built around the walls can be changed by practicing empathy.

The experiment presented in the chapter shows that it is possible to gain some insight into the situation of sufferers. *The first step is cognitive empathy*, when we can see a particular case from the point of view of another person, the receiver of empathy. Of course, this is an experiment, and you cannot be entirely realistic in this situation (if we are distant from this situation). Still, we try to use various images to activate the memory, enter this situation in our imagination, and see how it might look. This is cognitive empathy. We use it in our "practice of consciousness to project itself beyond itself" (Barber 2013: 317). We have the inherent tendency to transgress ourselves and go beyond our minds and self.

Many self-reports show that you *can experience certain emotions*, even vicariously. The second layer of empathy is the basis for compassion. The cognitive layer (similar to "perception-like empathy"; see Jardine and Szanto 2017) is a prerequisite for the occurrence of the emotional empathy layer, when the imagination begins. It refers to many situations presented in the pictures. Of course, a further step may be the emergence of compassion and the helping phase, which is also a continuation of empathy. The activity can be a kind of the summary of learning about the other person's situation, and feeling their emotions. The students generally show significant level of empathy in the cognitive and emotional layers. This is indicated by the language etiquettes related to naming emotions and describing situations from one's own perspective as well as the Others' points of view (fear, anxiety, agitation, regret, sadness, loss, depression, hope, gratitude, etc.)

The second important element of empathy is the *embodiment of emotions*. The students often feel the emotions in their bodies concerning many situations presented in the pictures. The reaction *of empathy in imagining extreme conditions* seems to be common, if not universal. It could be called *a high level of empathy* (Svenaeus 2018: 744). Therefore, the embodiment also has the second property, namely the embodiment of empathizing feelings. The breathing exercises and the earlier hatha-yoga practice in the project helped the students notice the bodily reactions and also see how the mind works, how the emotions appear, and where they are located. The experiment was a didactic tool for teaching about recognizing the emotions in the body and the role of the body in empathizing. The breathing exercises also show how the physical exercise helps to reduce stress while empathizing with the problematic situations and terror that the victims of war experience.

The third element that can be distinguished in self-reports is the moment of *doubting the possibility of fully empathizing* with the situation of people suffering during the war and of refugees. But that is not a strong theme in the auto-reports. Sometimes students feel confused about empathizing with war victims and war refugees. They do not know what to do in the face of the horrors of war. They also wonder how others will react to such situations. Although empathy is noticeable in all the students participating in this project, it was often said that it is challenging to imagine and impersonate characters whom you should empathize with. This may be understandable as the war situation is an extreme one. But still, you can imagine what can happen to you, being isolated from your loved ones, being under fire from artillery, or hearing and seeing bombs falling nearby. One can make such an experiment and imagine it; of course, one cannot fully imagine it without experiencing the situation directly. But usually, my reaction of empathy is immediate (Jardine and Szanto 2017). Nevertheless, the answer I could not understand would have been answered in terms of running away. From the phenomenological point of view, I can say that the students have a problem in living in two worlds, even imaginatively in one of them (war); there is some discrepancy between their lifeworld and the lifeworld of the Other that is becoming Deathworld (Bentz and Marlatt 2021; Konecki 2022: Chapter 3). These two worlds are challenging to understand at the same time. The taken-for-granted assumptions about the "normal" lifeworld become questioned (Schütz 1962; Schütz and Luckman 1973; Shuman 2011). We should be careful about romanticizing empathy in perceiving victims in extreme situations which we can feel the same as the receiver of empathy (Berger and Harris 2008; Shuman 2011). But what is optimistic about it is the reflection that appears. The short moment of alienation from the so-called "normal" world starts the process of thinking about the fragility of taken-for-granted assumptions about the "normal" lifeworld.

The empathy related to imagining the situation of war victims and refugees is connected with the assumption that there are things that are unimaginable and impossible to understand. It is justified when encountering death, imagining death, and coming across an imminent death threat. But this assumption removes us from the compassionate empathy that can arise if we do not fully embrace it. When we activate our imagination, we do a thought experiment; we will force ourselves emotionally to live a surrogate experience in a particular situation. We do some self-violence in this situation, but emotional feelings are necessary to fully activate empathy and compassion. Merely imagining and cognitively structuring a specific situation is not enough; it is a prelude to genuine empathy in general and compassion for the suffering in particular. We should remember "the basic and widespread tendency of mental life to identify and assimilate" others in their conditions of life (Barber 2013: 317), and we should remember that refusing the possibility of empathy is connected with not seeing "the level beneath thought at which empathy occurs" (Barber 2013: 317).

Suppose we base our approach to morality – empathy on the sociological vision that everything comes from the society that wants to be integrated, and that morality and religion have this function (Durkheim 2008). In that case, we are in the cognitive trap, which cannot aid in explaining why people help each other and empathize with others without concern for social norms that divide people on who is worth empathizing with. *The ontological anxiety and safety problem* is significant here (Giddens 1990), but when it is interpreted from a contemplative perspective, different conclusions arise (Bentz and Giorgino 2016). Sometimes, in order to be empathetic, we need to show our courage against the whole of society and find ourselves in danger of being killed. It happened during the time of the Holocaust when some people from the occupied countries helped Jewish to survive. It was dangerous for life, but it did happen. And we had, on the other hand, the silence of society, indifference to the murders of Jews. It was socially acceptable to be silent when the Holocaust was going on around during the Second World War (Bauman 1989).

Zygmunt Bauman (1989: Chapter 6) opts for a different vision of the human morality. He suggests that there is a presocialized road of moral behavior. And I think that it also refers to empathy and compassion. Similarly, Hannah Arendt (referred to in Bauman 1989) is against such a vision of social responsibility based on social background. The resistance to the socialized norms can be ethical. The difference between good and evil cannot be based only on social forces. If I consider Bauman's solution, it is still social, but the moral responsibility comes down to social relations and is not grounded in the structure of social institutions (Bauman 1989). The context of the activity of the individuals and their connections with others are what determines the moral choices (being with others). Although Bauman was against the social origin of morality and introduces the concept of "*being with others*," the concretization of the idea still directs us to the social meaning of the situation. He tries to go out of this dilemma by referring to Emmanuel Levinas' concept of "being with others": "To Levinas, 'being with others', that most primary and irremovable attribute of human existence, means first and foremost *responsibility*. 'Since the other looks at me, I am responsible for him, without even having taken on responsibilities in his regard.' My responsibility is the one and only form in which the other exists for me; it is the mode of his presence, of his proximity ...

Most emphatically, *my responsibility is unconditional. It does not depend on prior knowledge* of the qualities of its object; it precedes such knowledge. It does not depend on an interested intention stretched towards the object; it precedes such intention" (Bauman 1989: Chapter 7).

So, in this approach, severe doubt is expressed in the cognitive frame of empathy that is socially-based. There is something more profound and primary, although as sociologists, we should be aware of the strength of the social forces influencing our justification system, for our behavior that does not always have rational grounds.

We decide about the human side of our deeds here and now. By acting individually with an empathic intention, we can create collective empathy as an everyday mood that permeates social life. We can empathize with other collectivities, groups, or nations.[13]

7 Conclusions

Do we teach empathy in the modern world? Are we prepared to sympathize with other, suffering people in the face of a significant life's misfortune, ecological trauma and tragedy of war? Probably, we can never be well-prepared for such extreme situations. Already the Stoics tried to prepare for the worst conditions that could affect us soon, using the *praemeditatio malorum* technique (Hadot 1995; Robertson 2010). Did they always manage to stay calm? We do not know this, although written testimonies of philosophers show that it did happen. These could, of course, be didactic measures on their part, demonstrating by their example the effectiveness of this type of meditation, anticipating the worst situations that may happen.

Feeling empathetic is a process; maybe it is given once, but it can be forgotten and not developed. Just as it is essential to maintain motivation in any action, it is also crucial to the act of empathizing, which is not only an experience but also an effort if it is to be sustained over an extended period. *The intention* and attention directed to the receiver of the empathy are both necessary to keep the motivation for compassion and helping others.

---

13 Empathy can also sometimes have adverse effects on the persons that experience it. Strong empathy can lead to actions taken at the expense of the self. Also, the outgroups can be neglected here (Konrath and Grynberg 2016). Moreover, empathy could lead in some occupations, such as social work, to distress (Grant 2014).

Empathy, therefore, should be taught with the help of various types of thought experiments, but also by genuine support for multiple types of suffering subjects; we should have empathy bridges over empathy walls. The consciousness of the body should be included in the process. Hatha yoga and *pranayama*, and meditation, help in this. Then the anxiety and ontological insecurity (Giddens 1990; 1991) can be tamed; maybe they cannot be eliminated, but you can learn to live ethically with them. Individuals always have a choice (Melnikov and Johnson 2021: 136–137). Empathy is given to our existential situation, which is an unconditional first reaction when the ego is suspended or forgotten (Stein 1989; Owen 2007; Barber 2017), but the motivation to cultivate it and keep empathy for helping could be learned and is socially-framed (Höijer 2004; Hochschild 2016; Junco-Ruiz 2017; Rockwell, Ashley, et al. 2019).

I observed similar emotions while empathizing with a situation of war horrors. The fear happens often, as does the feeling of helplessness:

> Learning empathy should be important comparably to learning responsibility for loved ones. Too often, we act neutrally, thinking that 'it doesn't affect us'; this should be changed. There are many ways to do this. I believe that such classes, despite the depressing and troubling mood, were (and are) necessary. I felt nostalgic, I was in a more somber mood than before the class, but I don't regret it because I believe the emotional support we can give others, even if we can't speak, is critical in many respects. (woman)

Our project aimed to develop a reflection on empathy and build the awareness of empathy for the suffering victims in order to overcome the empathy deficit. Was this goal achieved? Empathy is given, but we are not always mindful of it. Above, I provided the citation from a student who said that the experiment was emotionally-tricky. Still, it helped to increase the awareness of empathy and motivation to be empathetic as well as to aid others and maybe contribute to the community of empathetic persons.

Acknowledgments

I want to thank my close collaborators, Dagmara Tarasiuk and Aleksandra Płaczek, for their comments and inspiration. The bright ideas and concepts from Valerie Bentz and her research group are also invaluable.

Bibliography

Barber, Michael. 2006. Alfred Schutz. *Stanford Encyclopedia of Philosophy*. https://plato.stanford.edu/entries/schutz/.

Barber, Michael. 2013. "Alfred Schutz and the Problem of Empathy." In: Embree, L., Nenon, T. (eds) *Husserl's Ideen. Contributions to Phenomenology*, vol. 66. Springer, Dordrecht. https://doi.org/10.1007/978-94-007-5213-9_19.

Barber, Michael. 2017. *Religion and Humor as an Emancipating Provinces of Meaning*. Dordrecht: Springer.

Barthes, Roland. 1981. *Camera lucida. Reflections on Photography*. New York: Hill and Wang.

Bauman, Zygmunt. 1989. *Modernity and Holocaust*. Cambridge: Polity.

Bentz, Valerie. M. 1995. "Husserl, Schutz, 'Paul' and Me: Reflections on Writing Phenomenology." *Human Studies* 18(1), 41–62.

Bentz, Valerie M. and Jeremy Shapiro. 1998. *Mindful Inquiry in Social Research*. London: Sage.

Bentz, Valerie M. and Vincenzo Giorgino. 2016. *Contemplative Social Research. Caring for Self, Being and Lifeworld*. Santa Barbara, CA: Fielding University Press.

Bentz, Valerie M. and James Marlatt (eds.) 2021. *Deathworlds to Lifeworlds. Collaboration with Strangers for Personal and Ecological Transformation*. Berlin/Boston, MA: De Gruyter.

Bentz, Valerie Malhotra, David Rehorick, James Marlatt, Ayumi Nishii, and Carol Estrada. 2018. "Transformative Phenomenology as an Antidote to Technological Deathworlds." *Schutzian Research* 10, 189–220.

Berger, Harris M. 2008. "Phenomenology and the Ethnography of Popular Music: Ethnomusicology at the Juncture of Cultural Studies and Folklore." Pp. 62–75 in *Shadows in the Field: New Perspectives for Fieldwork in Ethno-musicology*, edited by G. Barz and T.J. Cooley, Oxford: Oxford University Press.

Berger, Peter. 1963. *Invitation to Sociology: A Humanistic Perspective*. New York: Doubleday, Garden City.

Cooley, Charles H. 1922. *Human Nature and the Social Order (Revised edition)*. New York: Charles Scribner's Sons.

De Waal, Frans. 2009. *The Age of Empathy: Nature's Lessons for a Kinder Society*. New York: Penguin Random House.

Durkheim, Emile. 2008/1912. *The Elementary Forms of the Religious Life*. New York: Courier Corporation.

Endacott, Jason and Sarah Brooks. 2013. "An Updated Theoretical and Practical Model for Promoting Historical Empathy", *Social Studies Research and Practice*, 8(1), 41–58. https://doi.org/10.1108/SSRP-01-2013-B0003.

Ganczarek, Joanna, Thomas Hünefeldt and Belardinelli Olivetti, M. 2018. From "Einfühlung" to empathy: exploring the relationship between aesthetic and interpersonal experience. *Cogn Process* 19, 141–145. https://doi.org/10.1007/s10339-018-0861-x.

Giddens, Anthony. 1990. *The Consequences of Modernity*. Cambridge: Polity Press.

Giddens, Anthony. 1991. *Modernity and Self Identity: Self and Society in the Late Modern Age*. Cambridge: Polity Press.

Giorgino, Vincenzo. 2015. "Contemplative Methods Meet Social Sciences: Back to Human Experience as It Is." *Journal for the Theory of Social Behaviour*. DOI: 10.1111/jtsb.12078.

Grant, Louise. 2014. Hearts and Minds: Aspects of Empathy and Wellbeing in Social Work Students, *Social Work Education*, 33:3, 338–352, DOI: 10.1080/02615479.2013.805191.

Hadot, Pierre. 1987. *Exercices spirituels et philosophie antique*, 2e édition revue et augmentée, Paris: Etudes Augustiniennes, (English edition: Hadot, P. 1995. *Philosophy as a way of life: spiritual exercises from Socrates to Foucault*. Malden, Mass.: Blackwell).

Harding, Luke. 2022. *Izium: after Russian retreat, horrors of Russian occupation are revealed*. Retrieved September 23, 2022 (https://www.theguardian.com/world/2022/sep/17/izium-russian-occupation-ukraine-horrors-donbas-bucha).

Heyes, Cecilia. 2018. "Empathy is not in our genes." *Neurosci Biobehav Rev*. Dec;95, 499–507. doi: 10.1016/j.neubiorev.2018.11.001. Epub 2018 Nov 3. PMID: 30399356.

Hochschild, Arlie R. 1983. *The Managed Heart. Commercialization of Human Feeling*. Berkeley, CA: University of California Press.

Hochschild, Arlie R. 2013. *So How's the Family? And Other Essays*. Berkeley and Los Angeles, CA: University of California Press.

Hochschild, Arlie R. 2016. *Strangers in their Own Land: Anger and Mourning on the American Right: A Journey to the Heart of Our Political Divide*. New York: The New Press.

Höijer, Birgitta. 2004. "The Discourse of Global Compassion: The Audience and Media Reporting of Human Suffering." *Media, Culture & Society* 26, 513–531.

Höijer, Birgitta. 2017. "The Discourse of Global Compassion and the Media." *Nordicom Review*, 24(2), 19–29. https://doi.org/10.1515/nor-2017-0305.

Husserl, Edmund. 1977. *Cartesian Meditations*. Translated by D. Cairns. The Hague: Nijhoff.

Husserl, Edmund. 1980. *Phenomenology and the Foundations of the Sciences*, translated by T.E. Klein and W.E. Pohl. The Hague: Nijhoff. Original work written in 1912.

Iyengar, B.K.S. 1983. *Light on Pranayama. Pranayama Dipika*. London: Unwin Paperbacks.

Jardine, James and Thomas Szanto. 2017. "Empathy in the Phenomenological Tradition." Pp. 86–97 in *Routledge Handbook of Philosophy of Empathy*, edited by Heidi Maibom. New York: Routledge.

Konecki, Krzysztof T. (2018) *Advances in Contemplative Social Research*, Lodz: Lodz University Press / Krakow: Jagiellonian University Press.

Konecki, Krzysztof T. 2021. "Emotions and Politics: Emotional Work That Allows One to Regain One's Dignity and Survive", Pp. 117–133 in *Studies in Symbolic Interaction* (Vol. 53), edited by N.K. Denzin and S. Chen. Emerald Publishing Limited, Bingley.

Konecki, Krzysztof. 2022. *The Meaning of Contemplation for Social Qualitative Research.* NY, London: Routledge.

Konrath, Sara and Delphine Grynberg. 2016. The positive (and negative) psychology of empathy. In D.F. Watt & J. Panksepp (Eds.), *Psychology and neurobiology of empathy* (pp. 63–107). Nova Biomedical Books.

Lipps Theodor. 1903. „Ästhetik. Psychologie des Schönen und der Kunst." (vol. 1: Grundlegung der Ästhetik). Leopold Voss, Leipzig.

Lipps, Theodor. 1906. „Ästhetik. Psychologie des Schönen und der Kunst." (vol. 2: Die ästhetische Betrachtung und die bildende Kunst). Leopold Voss, Leipzig.

Mead, G.H. 1934. *Mind Self and Society from the Standpoint of a Social Behaviorist* (Edited by Charles W. Morris). Chicago: University of Chicago.

Melnikov, Andrii, and John Johnson. 2021. "Situational Analysis: Existential and Interpretative Perspective". Pp. 135–149 in n *Studies in Symbolic Interaction* (Vol. 53), edited by N.K. Denzin and S. Chen. Emerald Publishing Limited, Bingley.

Merleau-Ponty, Maurice. 2005. *Phenomenology of Perception.* London: Routledge.

Nhat Hanh, Thich. 1999. *The Heart of the Buddha's Teaching.* London: Rider.

Rehorick, David A. and Valerie M. Bentz. 2008. *Transformative Phenomenology. Changing Ourselves, Lifeworlds, and Professional Practice.* Lanham, MD: Lexington Books.

Rehorick, David. A., & Taylor, Gail. 1995. "Thoughtful Incoherence: First Encounters with the Phenomenological-Hermeneutical Domain." *Human Studies*, 18(4), 389–414. http://www.jstor.org/stable/20000253.

Robertson, Donald. 2010. *The Philosophy of Cognitive-Behavioral Therapy: Stoicism as Rational and Cognitive Psychotherapy.* London: Karnac.

Rockwell, Ashley, Chris M. Vidmar, C.M. Penny Harvey, & Leanna Greenwood, L. (2019). Do Sociology Courses Make More Empathetic Students? A Mixed-Methods Study of Empathy Change in Undergraduates. *Teaching Sociology*, 47(4), 284–302. https://www.jstor.org/stable/26978666.

Rosan, Peter. J. 2014. "The varieties of ethical experience: A phenomenology of empathy, sympathy, and compassion." *Phänomenologische Forschungen*, 155–189. http://www.jstor.org/stable/24360726.

Ruiz-Junco, Natalia. 2017. "Advancing the Sociology of Empathy: A Proposal." Symbolic Interaction, 40(3), 414–435.

Schütz, Alfred. 1962. *Collected Papers I, The problem of Social Reality*, eds. Maurice Natanson, The Hague: Martinus Nijhoff.

Schutz, Alfred, and Thomas Luckman. 1973. *The Structures of the Life-World*, trans. Richard M. Zaner and Tristram Engelhardt Jr. Evanston: Northwestern University Press.

Shott, Susan. 1979. "Emotion and Social Life: A Symbolic Interactionist Analysis." *American Journal of Sociology*, 84(6), 1317–1334. http://www.jstor.org/stable/2777894.

Shuman, Amy. 2011. On the Verge: Phenomenology and Empathic Unsettlement. *The Journal of American Folklore*, 124(493), 147–174. https://doi.org/10.5406/jamerfolk.124.493.0147.

Stein, Edith. 1989. *On the Problem of Empathy*. Washington, DC: ICS Publications.

Svenaeus, Fredrik. 2018. "Edith Stein's phenomenology of sensual and emotional empathy." *Phenomenology and the Cognitive Sciences* 17, 741–760. https://doi.org/10.1007/s11097-017-9544-9.

Owen, Ian R. 2007. *On Justifying Psychotherapy. Essays on Phenomenology, Integration and Psychology*. Lincoln, NE, eUniverse.

Van Manen, Max. 2003. Researching Lived Experience: Human Science for an Action Sensitive Pedagogy. London: The Althouse Press.

Van Manen, Max. 2014. *Phenomenology of Practice. Meaning-Giving Methods in Phenomenological Research and Writing*. London and New York: Routledge.

Zabużko, Oksana. 2022. *Planeta. Piołun*. (*Planet. Wormwood*) Warszawa: Wydawnictwo Agora.

Znaniecki, Florian. 1988. *Wstęp do socjologii* (*Introduction to Sociology*). Warszawa: PWN.

CHAPTER 6

A Contemplative Sociologist Looks at War

1 Introduction

In this chapter, I focus on the existential experience of war and the Deathworld from the pathic, first-person perspective of a Ukrainian writer and soldier.[1] First, Artem Chekh described the war that began between Ukraine and Russia in 2014, and then in two further texts he spoke of the war that erupted in 2022. My explication will be inspired by contemplative and phenomenological sociology. I want to show the war through lived experience to avoid reifying the concept. I want to understand the war in Ukraine through my role as a symbolic interactionist and contemplative sociologist inspired by phenomenology and contemplative studies. I concentrate on the experience of the body, space, and time in the context of being in the Deathworld (see Bentz et al. 2018).

Moreover, I present the view of the Other's perception of the war in the context of my self-definition (the looking-glass self) as a supporter of the Ukrainian nation. It will be a first-person perspective on my emotions and views of the war and on communicating with opponents regarding my perceptions of the war. I also present poetry, photos, and collages to enhance understanding of the war.

When examining the existential aspects of war, my approach will be contemplative, drawing inspiration from the framework proposed by Bentz and Giorgino (2016). I define contemplation as follows: "Contemplation is a kind of activity that leads to a certain state of mind, and at the same time, it is a method of obtaining knowledge about some objects at present, and also about getting knowledge itself, here and now, by mindful insight into the perceived (and also imagined) phenomena or objects, and also into the self" (Konecki 2018: 22). I contemplate lived experience as it appears during the war in the soldier's mind and heart, based on the first-person perspective of Artem Chekh (2020, 2022, 2023), who describes everyday life in a war zone and in the Deathworld. He does not focus solely on combat; he recounts the daily routine of the Lifeworld and numerous incidents involving military bureaucracy, soldiers' conversations, food, sleep, and leave, among other things. I see what kind of lived experience shapes the context of enduring the war (Dutta 2021). I also

1 The chapter was first published in *Polish Sociological Review* no 4 (228)2024, https://doi.org/10.26412/psr228.05.

add material interpreting journalists' accounts of the Russian-Ukrainian war and testimonies of Ukrainian psychotherapists.

My exploration will also be guided by the Deathworld concept developed by Valerie Bentz (Bentz et al. 2018; Bentz and Marlatt 2021). The Deathworld is intricately linked to the colonization of the Lifeworld by technocratic systems and technology. In this context, fragmented consciousness fails to comprehend the underlying causes of the proliferation of the Deathworld. This phenomenon is also intertwined with the absence of free choice and the erosion of "we-relationships," giving rise to systems of oppression and domination within this space (Bentz and Marlatt 2021).

In this death space, the destruction of the Lifeworld is evident; where individuals lack freedom, a stable environment is absent (typifications and systems of relevancies are difficult to recreate and apply), life projects are shattered, and we-relations disintegrate (Konecki 2022: 77). Ontological security disappears, while the meaning of space can change (Konecki 2018: 99–102). The space may be either dangerous or safe: "The skies are not safe at home. The skies are used for murder. Enemy military planes, fighter jets, and many missiles are flying in the sky above our country. Then, the sirens start" (Kovalova's narrative in Sneed et al., 2023: 348).

The time horizon changes. The prevalence of "wrong speech" further contributes to the suffering in this field of death. The language is dichotomous and divisive, failing to reflect the unity between humans and nature (Konecki 2022: 78–79). The community excludes strangers, and the use of incorrect language, especially when labeling certain individuals as "strangers," associates them with notions of infection, fatal illness, the spread of diseases, religious enemies, and monsters bringing violence. "Wrong speech can be hidden behind lofty, patriotic, and/or religious slogans, but the specific emotional energy still accompanies them" (Konecki 2022: 87).

In my contemplation of language, I direct my focus toward emotions, bodily sensations, and the embodiment of users' perspectives (see Konecki 2018). I too think, as Narozhna (2022) emphasized, that the impact of war is frequently *disembodied*, not only within scholarly discourse but also in our everyday perception, especially when people are distanced from the deadly realities of a war zone.

Specifically, my contemplative perspective and attention is centered on the viewpoint of an active participant in the war, as elucidated in the first-person narrative of Chekh's book (2020). Chekh was a soldier in the Ukrainian army fighting the Russians. The narrative revolves around the embodied experience of the war (Merleau-Ponty 2005). I analyze the story to dereify war as a concept that is connected with rationalist and materialist perspectives of military strategic studies and discursive and disembodied critical war studies (Narozhna 2022). The military's strategic approach to space is pragmatic and rationalistic; location and territory are fundamental in planning a strategy for fighting (Carter 2010). "Critical war studies" concentrate on the discourse of war as the generative power that shapes the mode of knowing and power relations in society (Barkawi, Brighton 2011).

Both approaches ignore the body and feelings and how the war is experienced situationally by the direct participants living in the Deathworld. I want to add some materials and reflections on this issue from the first-person perspective of direct participants of the war. The concept of the Deathworld is important in my explorations. Furthermore, I explore my own environment and emotions in an attempt to understand an author directly involved in the war and to offer my perspective as an outsider. The above-mentioned authors did not use a first-person approach to analyze war. When I focus on the existential experience of war and the Deathworld in the paper, I look at the pathic dimension of Artem Chekh's writing. My explication is also inspired by existential sociology (Douglas and Johnson 1997; Johnson and Kotarba 2002) and phenomenological sociology (Schütz 1944, 1962). Existential sociology focuses on the emotional dimension of lived experience, which is embodied and situated within a concrete context. The subject feels, suffers, responds to the suffering of others, and decides whether or not to care for them (Douglas and Johnson 1997). Phenomenological sociology introduces the concept of the lifeworld, where we often make use of the typification of others to see them not as unique individuals but as social types. This framework also involves a system of relevance or values to justify our choices, which may not necessarily be empathetic to others (Schütz 1944, 1962).

This pathic dimension helps us dereify war, which is often considered an abstract term, without the deep and personal meaning of the people experiencing it. Dereification involves refraining from conceptualizing human activities as reflections of natural forces, universal dispositions, or expressions of divine will (Moore 1995: 701). This dereifying perspective can be attained by focusing on the concept of "emptiness," engaging in the application of a "non-conceptual mind," or practicing "no-mind" (Moore 1995: 699). In this way, I get to the pathic dimension of the experience (emotional, embodied, and situational in the broad sense). As an individual, I perceive illusions that may be traps for my mind. I do not see and feel the experience and suffering of the Other or my role in this perception: "Anything perceived as existing independently of the perceiver can be dereified by recalling the subjective experiences out of which the object was constituted and by apprehending the reflexive connections of the object to its extent" (Moore 1995: 703, as cited in

Konecki 2018: 40).[2] Derefication does not oppose the critical social science approach, which primarily seeks to uncover the structural and discursive conditions of war. Rather, it serves as an addition, enriching our understanding of war by providing a more holistic perspective – not only from that of an external observer, but also from the first-person experience.

I do not refuse other explanations of the war; I can find and see the global, economic, political, ideological, religious, and discursive circumstances of the war and its causes (Leder 2023: 297–298; Ehrenreich 2011). However, I want to look at it mainly from the perspectives of a direct participant (Artem Chekh) and an external observer (the author of this chapter), who collaborate on a final reading of Chekh's text without seeing and knowing each other. Nevertheless, the broader context, which includes political, economic, and symbolic dimensions, holds equal significance. As Patočka (1996: 120) noted, these explanations have "all approached war from the perspective of peace, day, and life, excluding its dark nocturnal side." However, it is imperative to recognize that war also plays a pivotal role in shaping our daily interactions, emotions, energy, spirit, and character. War often starts in a time of peace. It begins in our heads and hearts, not only in politics and the economy. I learned at school about the atrocities and heroism of war, about just and unjust wars. These wars are with me in peacetime. I feel them; the pathic dimension of past battles is overwhelming and even embodied (see also Dutta, 2021). I have often been the recipient of narratives passed directly from participants in a war.

I understand the term "pathic" after Max Van Manen (2016: 267):

> Knowledge is *pathic* to the extent that the act of practice depends on the sense and sensuality of the body: personal presence, relational perceptiveness, tact for knowing what to say and do in contingent situations, thoughtful routines and practices, and other aspects of knowledge that are in part pre-reflective, and yet thoughtful – full of thought. (see also Merleau-Ponty 2005)

But it could also be argued that such pathic knowledge not only inheres in the body but also in the things of my world, in the situation(s) in which I find myself, and in the very relations that I maintain with others and the things around us. For example, pathic "knowledge" also expresses itself in

2 The chapter was also to dereify the concept of war and empathy. I hope that my approach to the Ukrainian war will counteract the kind of attitude in which the suffering of others who are not connected with us interests us only in so far as we feel lucky not to be there. Photos of war may provoke passive sympathy (Sontag, 1978).

the confidence with which I do things, the way that I "feel" the atmosphere of a place, the manner in which I can "read" someone's face, and so forth. Knowledge inheres in the world already in such a way that it enables my embodied practices. Past experience shapes the everyday life's bodily perception, here and now:

> An encounter with a world-shattering event, like a sudden attack by established acquaintances, strips away the protective casing that comes with our body being at ease with the familiar world around us. The body then begins to relate to everyday objects through the tragic incident. (Dutta 2021: 214; see also 2015)

Sensory knowledge also encompasses the perception of space. I can understand it rationally through categories and types (knowing maps, creating them, setting boundaries, giving names to areas),[3] but also intimately. In that case, space becomes a place for us to pause and momentarily feel safe. The same person can know a place both intimately and conceptually; he/she can articulate concepts but, at the same time, struggle to express what is known through the senses of touch, taste, smell, hearing, and even sight (Yi-Fu Tuan 1987: 17).

It is also important to remember that the pathic dimension fluctuates just as a mood does; for example, it changes in the same way that the mood I have in a building (e.g., a church) changes when I enter it at different times of the day or year. I will be in a different mood in a place such as my home depending on whether I am listening to bomb explosions or pleasant music from a neighbor's window.

•••

My analysis is rooted in the book *Absolute Zero* (Chekh 2020). This work provides a detailed account of the daily experiences of soldiers on the front line during the onset of the war between Russia and Ukraine in 2014. The narrative is crafted through the narrator-soldier's everyday observations of life at the

---

3 The meaning of physical space also changes on the front line: "Thus, as an important contemporary psychologist describes it, in the experience of a front-line artillery gunner, the topographic character of the landscape changes, so that abruptly there is an end to it, and the ruins no longer are what they had been – villages and so on – but they have become what they could be at the given moment – shelters and reference points. Thus, the landscape of life's fundamental meanings was transformed, it acquired an end beyond which there could be nothing further, higher, more desirable" (Patočka 1996: 131).

front and his writings during his free time. It resembles a memoir, unfolding as a continuous record akin to a diary but enriched with mindful, reflective insights into the conditions of war. I also use Chekh's first-person narratives published in the *New York Times* during the second phase of the war, which started in 2022 (Chekh 2022, 2023). Analyzing personal documents is especially useful for studying a subject's pathic dimensions and lived experience. Some documents (e.g., diaries, memoires, letters, and even literary books and poetry) can be treated as empirical materials, where I find expressions of emotions, bodily sensations, and thoughtful interpretations of the Lifeworld (Konecki 2022a, see chapter 4).

Ludwig Wittgenstein wrote a similar narrative during the First World War – a diary with his philosophical contemplations on one side and depiction of a soldier's daily life on the other (Wittgenstein 2022; also referenced in Konecki 2023). Despite the differing political and technological contexts and historical timelines, striking similarities emerge in the lived experience of war: courage, uncertainties, bodily sensations, the fear of death, the defiance of that fear, and the inherent drive to describe, conceptualize, and document ideas. Wittgenstein (2022: 139) candidly acknowledged grappling with depression. Additionally, he frequently referenced his relationships with close friends and family. As a volunteer and an educated individual, he encountered challenges in communicating with his fellow soldiers. Despite these difficulties, he endeavored to maintain coherence in his personality through activities such as reading books, keeping a diary, and engaging in philosophical reflections. Notably, these reflections culminated in one of his significant post-war works, the *Tractatus Logico-Philosophicus*.

War, which permeates the Deathworld, establishes a consistent existential context for human beings, transcending temporal and contextual differences. I aim to approach Chekh's text on war with a contemplative mindset, seeking to sense the pathic mood within it and to describe and explicate it in alignment with the writer's perspective.

2 A Contemplative Explication of a Witness from a Neighboring Country

The war (2022) initially caused – if not panic – increased fear in Poland, and I felt it. The refugees coming to Poland contributed to this fear. Social media, the mass media, and refugees transmitted information about the atrocities the Russians had committed, and also fear and anxiety, sadness, and everyday mourning. How do you respond to this situation? Only by empathizing and helping, collecting donations, and often by accepting refugees into our homes. A majority of Polish people made such choices (Scovil 2023).

A group of scholars, composed of one Ukrainian and six Poles, including myself, provided evidence of these activities in an autoethnographic-collaborative text based on meetings and discussions among us (see Dobosz et al. 2023, as well as the video *The Reverberations of War*, https://www.youtube.com/watch?v=QtGef9cxopA). In that collaborative, autoethnographic paper, anger and the pervasive fear of war took center stage. I grappled with the constant dread of a potential Russian attack on Poland – a fear that weighed heavily on us. Simultaneously, we found ourselves profoundly empathizing with Ukrainian citizens and refugees, who were enduring the harsh realities of the conflict. The emotions of fear, anxiety, and worries about an uncertain future were vividly manifested in the dreams the Polish scholars recounted.

In the face of the aggressor's atrocities and cruelty, we sought solace and understanding through writing. Our reflections took various forms, from memoirs and diaries to contemplative memos; some even evolved into poetry and philosophical musings. Throughout all these texts, there was a pervasive pathic mood, one that allowed us to share in the collective experience.

Andrii Melnikov, a direct participant and victim of the war who was in Ukraine during that tumultuous period, wrote the primary narrative thread of the paper. We endeavored to comprehend his lived experience and to integrate it with our own. Some of us opened our homes to Ukrainian families, providing them with shelter and support. As a group of seven scholars, we each contributed in different ways to assisting Ukrainian refugees and citizens still in Ukraine. Our engagement was active and heartfelt. I also recall the invaluable assistance we received from our American friends, expertly coordinated by Professor Joseph Kotarba from Texas State University San Marcos.

Making a summary of the text (Dobosz et al. 2023) is a demanding task, as it is an emotional, contemplative, and deeply personal piece of work written in a pathic and vocative style that mirrors our collective thought process. I urge you to read the paper, which has been published, and to watch the performance film that delves deeper into the core of the text. (Dobosz et al. 2023; see also the video, *Reverberations of War* (https://www.youtube.com/watch?v=QtGef9cxopA).[4] Below is a continuation of how I dealt with war in a neighboring country.

•••

4 My strategy for coping with the war and the associated emotions was writing. I also authored a text on empathy in the context of the war in Ukraine (Konecki, 2022).

After some time, you get used to war in a neighboring country. It does not touch you directly. We do not see now the death, the killing, the kidnapping of children, and the destroyed houses. We do not have Russians controlling our streets (yet). And we don't see the Russians attacking our family members. Thus, we can go about our business and relax. As time goes by, we read less and less about the war, have no contact with refugees, and do not hear about these horrors; after all, we have no chance to influence events. Great-power politics is going on somewhere, and we are just little pawns in the games of the superpowers. Why bother?

On the other hand, when I watch my colleagues isolate themselves from information and look after themselves, I feel guilty: a war is going on! Every time I look at them, I imagine that at any moment, a plane could fly over and bomb my city. We could be killed. This is what I think when I think of Ukrainians in all the cities on the other side of the border. They live in permanent fear and danger. And here we are going to schools and restaurants, going on vacation, and enjoying life (see also Dobosz et al. 2023: 8). My existential situation is entirely different from that of soldiers on the front line and citizens in Ukrainian cities. I feel bad and guilty.

Ukrainian soldiers live in a completely different existential situation. Being on the front line for many months or years, they could be angry, feel rage, their bodies could be injured, they might doubt what they are doing there, and ask many existential questions.[5]

•••

How do I see it? Below will be my personal, though external, interpretation and explication of a description of war by a Ukrainian participant, Artem Chekh (2022), a soldier and writer. His book Absolute Zero is about the war in 2014, based on his diary, and my empirical materials contains also two articles concerning the second phase of the war, which started in 2022. Actually, the war we see in Ukraine started in 2014, although many Western observers forget the fact.

Chekh was an active participant in the war, and he described the daily life and lived experience of a soldier – his everyday activities and thoughts, doubts, and emotions while on the front line; his thinking about death and the suddenness of death was an everyday reality. He often thought *about death*, fear of death, isolation, hopelessness, and apathy.

---

5 Many soldiers do not want to fight and kill the enemy; many studies have demonstrated this fact (Grossman 1996).

> I think about my probable life and my probable death. Will it be sudden? Will it be here, in this damp bunker? Or maybe I'll live for many more years and die somewhere in a pastoral landscape raising sheep and cattle? And the whole village will come to the funeral of the old man who rejected city life and moved close to the knotweed and duckweed … Am I sleeping? Or maybe I'm just in a stupor. Absence and weightlessness. (Chekh 2020, chapter Absolute Zero, paragraphs 6–8)

This is the soldier's state of mind and heart during the war. Being constantly on the alert because of the danger of being killed also forms part of the battle experience on the front line. This leads to permanent fatigue, indifference, and bodily diseases, as well as chaos and disorganization in the cognitive perspective and values. Trauma appears. The death of others becomes a matter of indifference. It is difficult to enjoy everyday things; there is a longing for routine, but it is also difficult to accept it when it occurs. Meeting a loved one becomes difficult, and thoughts revolve around battle sites and colleagues on the front lines.

Staying longer in the zone, where the proximity of the enemy is even palpable, leads to a reevaluation of one's entire life. The emerging numbness and routine can lead to deeper reflection on one's past. Absolute zero is a turning point where one redefines one's biography, values, and identities. It is the point of liberation from unnecessary, redundant things in the face of the struggle for life and the experience of the threat of death. It is, as it were, a wartime *epoché*, which cleanses our minds of socially imposed assumptions about life and death.

> It is probably the best time to evaluate how you've lived your life so far. It's also that the possibility that death – your death – will occur rids you of all the baggage of the accepted norms you've so far stupidly ignored. I myself created this comfortable ignorance about everything I believe. This is what absolute zero really is. The boundary across from which lies madness and delusion. Beyond it there's only the end of thoughts, feelings, wishes. It's full immersion in yourself, freedom from wants and worldly needs. This is a total transformation into a different person, one I would've never been capable of becoming under any other circumstances. (Chekh 2020; chapter *Absolute Zero*, paragraph 2)[6]

6 Patočka (1996: 125) underscores the transformative nature of war, drawing upon the reflections of Ernst Junger and Pierre Teilhard de Chardin: "Both Junger and Teilhard emphasize the upheaval by the front line, which is not an immediate trauma but a fundamental

Below, I present quotes from the book and explicate them from my point of view as an outsider. I also consider Chekh's reflections and the experiences he described in two articles published in *The New York Times*. Soldiers frequently question the purpose of the war, harboring fears that its conclusion is elusive, and the perception of time undergoes a shift. If somebody spends five days in a trench waiting for death, the time perspective is completely disturbed; only the present is important – the time associated with the will to survive:

> That's what happened, and I accept it. But did I really want to fight? Do hundreds of thousands of Ukrainians really want to risk their lives, to be separated from their families in flooded trenches or dry steppes? Did I really want to die at the end of the world, from which not everyone returns? Probably every Ukrainian soldier asks these questions that don't have answers. In Bakhmut, where I served in May, they were inescapable. The unit I commanded was given the task of building a combat position on the outskirts of the city, but everything was changing very quickly. The Russians captured the rest of the city and most of the Ukrainian units left. Suddenly we found ourselves in a trap – there was no one to cover us. Seeking protection, I lay down in a tiny trench. I spent five days in that tomb waiting for death, sometimes urinating in a plastic bottle and, for fun, counting the calories I consumed and the amount of water I drank (Day 1: 560 calories, 350 milliliters of water. Day 2: 780 calories, 550 milliliters of water. And so on.). For 115 hours, I lay in this four-foot-deep hole and looked up at the clear sky, wincing at the explosions next to me. All around was pure hell. (Chekh 2023)

The question of defending the country and participating in battles is existential. Being in the field and fighting does not mean that a person is fully embedded in this position. There are still questions. But at the same time the threat

transformation of human existence: war in the form of the front line marks humans forever." A human being on the frontline can feel a specific sense of freedom: "The front-line experience, however, is an absolute one. Here, as Teilhard shows, the participants are assaulted by an absolute freedom, freedom from all the interests of peace, of life, of the day" (Patočka 1996: 129–130). One can then forget about the ideological, cultural or national motives for war. Similar feelings are shared by war victims who are not soldiers; below is a statement by Ukrainian psychologist Marta Kovalova: "War became such a painful way of cleansing [ourselves] from false values. Understanding that you will not take anything with you into eternity changes the angle of vision. What was in the shadows becomes visible. It becomes the center of everything. You can see the essence of human existence and the value of meaningful life with much greater clarity" (Kovalova's narrative in Sneed et al., 2023: 351).

and fear are there, and the battle is going on around one. This is an existential situation, with a Deathworld, but still with questions behind it that unfortunately do not have any answer.[7]

In the quote above, there is a defense of the body and fear expressed by flinching which is maybe not fully conscious; only the body feels it (see Meacham, 2007). And the space of the trench, a tiny, lived space, has a condensed lived time that helps the person survive. The soldier is in isolation for many days and suffering from it. The body must eat and drink; how many days? When the body is alive, the soldier is alive. The lived body expresses suffering and the will to survive (Narozhna 2022; Dutta 2021). It is fed so that it will stay alive, at least for some time, here and now. Only the present time is felt. The coda of this passage, "All around was pure hell," expresses the chaos, suffering, and hopelessness associated with all the ongoing battles in the war. However, when the body is alive, the soldier is alive. The space of the trench turned out to be a "place" (see Yi-Fu Tuan 1997) protecting the body (and relatively safe), and the "space" outside the trench turned out to be "pure hell."

The Deathworld appears to have zones. The trench zone is also a *deadly space*, but to a lesser extent than the open space outside the trench.[8] In the Deathworld, space becomes nuanced, although the shadow of death continually advances with each soldier. Sometimes, open space can be a realm of the Lifeworld for soldiers (for example, when they can escape from the trap of a trench or bunker). The lived body is connected with the lived space and coexist together.

---

7 A Ukrainian journalist writes about survival and about a future horizon (see also Dutta, 2021: 208–209), which is almost broken in the context of survival. The future is almost not important because it was already broken in the past: "The old life is slowly drifting away. The man at the front thinks about survival and then has remorse: What is it all for if there is no family? If there is no one to come back to? Divorces and separations are a scourge and a frequent cause of suicide among soldiers" (Kolesnychenko, 2024: (https://wiadomosci.wp.pl/ludzie-sie-koncza-6981373556255232a, retrieved 8.01.2023).

8 Open space can be a death space. The Ukrainian soldier treats his activities in the war as work: "Dawn. Fine snow dusted the yellowed grass. Three Russian soldiers creep toward Ukrainian positions. 'Antifryz,' the pilot of the "Foxtrot" aerial reconnaissance group, presses a button on the joystick. The drone drops a grenade. The two survivors cover themselves with the wounded man. This one is still moving. 'Antifryz' considers the morning a success. He pulls a long chain of grenade pins from his pocket. 'A garland for the Christmas tree.' Except that the mood is far from festive." (Kolesnychenko, 2024: https://wiadomosci.wp.pl/ludzie-sie-koncza-6981373556255232a, retrieved 8.01.2023).

The narrator contemplates family and incomplete tasks in the realm of life (see the quotation below);[9] the time horizon momentarily shifts, and the significance of the future takes center stage. The Deathworld is around and coming personally to the narrator, but he is still in the practical Lifeworld in his imagination. He contemplates death. The experience of time, here and now, changes his assumptions about accepting death. The direct threat changes his attitudes (I think that mine would change, too):

> I was lying at the bottom of my grave thinking that even though I had accepted my death long ago, I was still not prepared for this death right now. My wife doesn't know how to pay utility bills; I didn't leave her my email and internet banking passwords; and there are parcels in the mail that I didn't have time to tell her about. (Chekh 2023)

His contemplation continues. Positive emotions appear, and love for those closest to him. His mind is divided, with one part saying, "I want to survive," while the other says, "I will be killed." The mindful imagination works very hard, fantasizing about possible death. The emotional mix and emotional flux are speedy, changing, and chaotic:

> At the same time, I thought about what I would do if I survived. There is such a possibility – to survive. Well, then, I would write a message. I would say, "My love, I survived." But it was difficult to think about a happy ending. I preferred dreaming about my death, when, soaked to the bone by the rain, after falling asleep for an hour under the artillery fire, I would be killed by a Russian mine. (Chekh 2023)

There is *fear of death*, isolation, suffering, questions: "Why? For what?" Here is the answer from a first-person perspective:

---

9 A Ukrainian journalist described this situation empathically in her report. Thinking about family can be contrasted with the difficult living conditions at the front. The embodiment of memory of family is presented in the quote below. Family is associated with warmth; the front line with the smell of damp earth, squeaking mice, the explosion of projectiles, and bodily fatigue (Kolesnychenko, 2024). Family is also important for those who are not on the front line: "God, I don't want to die now. I want to live. I love my loved ones so much. I want them to do well. We still have so much to do together" (Kovalova's narrative in Sneed et al., 2023: 348).

> How could I not pick up a weapon here? For those who lived for many decades in the cozy arms of democracy and freedom, who don't know the fear of captivity and torture, it is difficult to understand why such peaceful people – who from time immemorial grew wheat, mined iron and coal, and grazed cattle on boundless meadows – are defending every meter of their country with such fury. But I know the answer. This is our wonderful land. And it must be free. (Chekh 2023)

Justifications are given, but they are strongly linked to values. We need motives for our activities, especially when faced with extreme choices and situations that result from participation in combat. The narrator wants to explain the Ukrainians' determination to defend their motherland, which cannot always be understood in the West. Love for the country (the "wonderful land") and "freedom" are values for which the author may fight. Patriotic feelings are expressed mainly by people away from the frontline. There should be a space and time for contemplation. This kind of contemplation takes place in the pathic mode:

> At the same time, something else is beginning to emerge, something very genuine. Pride that I am Ukrainian. A feeling of love for the Ukrainian language. Interest in the history of Ukraine and its culture. It feels like something familiar, full of light and warmth. This realization gives me hope, and along with this warmth, there also grows hatred and intolerance for everything Russian – everything, with no exception. (Kateryna Tomova's narrative in Sneed et al. 2023: 355)

3 My Contemplative Coda

I must take a break from these explications. *I feel guilty* when I read articles on the war and Chekh's book, *Absolute Zero*. I live in a safe apartment; I have a fridge full of food and a comfortable life. I can look at the stars, and I don't have to look for incoming bombers (although I feel they will come here) or drones. I can admire the full moon and the stars in the September sky. My lived space is completely different from Chekh's. But at the same time, I think about those soldiers lying in the trenches, in mud and dirt, scared but angry. The idea of defending the homeland is somewhere in the back of my consciousness, but here and now, there is fear of death, tense nerves, and all my senses are aware of the surroundings and want to defend my body (see Näser-Lather 2018). After all, that is what senses were made for. Animal existence is very real; after all, mine is identical, only covered with a thin layer of culture still untouched by threat and war. I watch the moon getting bigger and brighter; what a relief that it's not an approaching ball of fire – a rocket that can reach me. I breathe deeply.

When I looked at a picture of a Ukrainian soldier kneeling in a trench full of mud and water, looking up, I thought: Why does this happen? Why the hell must people suffer this way in the twenty-first century? I was angry; I was angry at that. People are still evil-doers (https://www.nytimes.com/2023/08/10/opinion/ukraine-war-bakhmut.html). I understand the sociological explanations of how ideologies, politics, the economy, nationalisms, and colonial mentalities can create wars full of suffering (Ehrenreich 2011). Still, I think that behind these explanations is just the pure, biological joy of killing strangers and taking their territory. We are still brute creatures and use culture to justify aggression. This belief is valid for me; it is what I feel at this moment of writing. This does not mean we should stop explaining the cultural and socio-economic reasons for the war. They are still important. But at the same time, I should be aware of how thin the cultural coat is that covers my brutal skeleton.[10]

3.1 *Contemplative Explication Continued ...*

The Deathworld dominates soldiers' minds. Their emotions are seen on their faces. Traumatic experience gives the soldiers a different view of the Lifeworld and motivation to live. The bulletproof vest becomes the cover of their bodies, which, like their minds, are always on the alert. Their eyes show emptiness. Trauma is the backdrop of the soldiers' everyday life; fear and hopelessness never leave them. It is even better to die, as one soldier said:

> Recently, one of the companies in our battalion returned from a mission in eastern Ukraine. When we saw our comrades a month earlier, they had

---

10 Concerning this topic, I wrote the following poem, "About Culture in One Sentence," to address the problem:

> I search for culture, especially in places,
> that bear names related to culture,
> cultural, with culture,
> and I don't find it there,
> it seems to have vanished,
> driven away, crushed by the name,
> which pushed it,
> into an ideal reality,
> to leave empty letters down here,
> envy, aggression, hatred,
> and that's why it's a good feeling.

> been smiling and cheerful. Now they don't even talk to one another, never take off their bulletproof vests, and don't smile at all. Their eyes are empty and dark like dry wells. These fighters lost a third of their comrades, and one of them said that he would rather be dead, because now he is afraid to live. (Chekh 2022)

What is going on in the mind and heart of a soldier? Fear of death, a permanent consciousness of mortality. It's a good time for contemplation. Feeling the end is palatable; death is next to him; it is a neighbor and follower. However, the willingness to live is extreme, and words have motivational power; the time to die has not yet come. "In the 10 months I spent on the front line near Popasna, in the Luhansk region, I thought often about death. I could feel its quiet steps and calm breathing next to me. But something told me no, not this time" (Chekh 2022).[11]

Accepting death is a point of *transforming the self* (see also Chekh 2022). The anxiety vanishes, and bravery comes. Is this the experience of brave, unstoppable soldiers? Is war a situation for self-development? Such people become this way because they experience the trauma of war and adapt to it in this way. The negative pathic dimension of the perception of war (fear and anxiety, mental rejection of the situation) changes and becomes more balanced. The narrator already inhabits the Deathworld – "my death, as an almost accomplished fact":

> But I have accepted the possibility of my death, as an almost accomplished fact. Crossing this Rubicon has calmed me down, made me braver, stronger, more balanced. It must be thus for those who consciously tread the path of war. (Chekh 2022)[12]

---

11 During the First World War, another soldier, a volunteer, grappled with the conflicting emotions of fearing death and longing to live, contemplating both sentiments: "Yesterday, I was fired at. I fell apart! I was afraid of death! I now have such a strong wish to live! And it is hard to renounce life once one is fond of it. That is precisely what sin is, an unreasonable life, a wrong view of life. From time to time, I become an animal" (Wittgenstein 2022: 185).

12 Similar thoughts came to Wittgenstein during the war on the front line. The acceptance of death also means accepting life: "I may die in an hour; I may die in two hours. I may die in a month or only in few years; I can't know and I can't do anything either for or against it. That's how life is. How then must I live so as to be prepared for that moment? One must live for the good and the beautiful until life ends of its own accord" (Wittgenstein 2022: 59).

I find a similar awareness of death in a poem by Maksym Kryvcov. Writing poetry can also be a way of dealing with the trauma of war. Kryvcov was a soldier on the front line:

> My head rolls from thicket to thicket
> as it rolls across a field
> or a ball
> my hands detached
> will grow violets in the spring
> my legs
> will be torn by dogs and cats
> my blood
> will dye the world in a new Pantone red
> human blood
> my bones
> will drag the earth
> and form a skeleton
> my shotgun
> will rust
> poor guy
> my change and equipment
> will be handed over to the new recruits
> so that spring will come sooner
> to finally
> bloom with violets
>
> (https://lubimyczytac.pl/jeszcze-wczoraj-czytal-swoje-wiersze-ukrainski-poeta-maksym-krywcow-zginal-na-froncie; KTK translation; retrieved 3.02.2024)

The Deathworld is spreading, and this war liquidates even people's names; the identities of the dead vanish like their bodies and existence. The anonymous bodies indicate the "catastrophic" character of the war, which takes lives daily. We see closed coffins that are real, but that also symbolize the cruelty and sadness of the war and hopelessness:

> This is another kind of war, and the losses are, without exaggeration, catastrophic. We no longer know the names of all the dead: There are dozens of them every day. Ukrainians constantly mourn those lost; there are rows of closed coffins in the central squares of relatively calm cities across the country. Closed coffins are the terrible reality of this cruel, bloody, and seemingly endless war. (Chekh 2022)

The senses are an important part of the lived body in experiencing the war. I become immersed in the experience of death and mourning by capturing the essence of the scent of death.[13] Soldiers also have to heighten their awareness of their surroundings by perceiving with all their senses (Näser-Lather 2018; Sookermany 2011). *The sense of smell* plays a crucial part in wartime narratives among civilians, too; it transforms into a tool for bearing witness to death:

> There was a mass grave that held 300 people, and I was standing at its edge. The chalky body bags were piled up in the pit, exposed. One moment before, I was a different person, someone who never knew how wind smelled after it passed over the dead on a pleasant summer afternoon. In mid-June, those corpses were far from a complete count of the civilians killed by shelling in the area around the industrial city of Lysychansk over the previous two months. They were only "the ones who did not have anyone to bury them in a garden or a backyard," a soldier said casually. He lit a cigarette while we looked at the grave. The smoke obscured the smell. (Yermak 2022)

The sense of hearing works differently in wartime, anticipating danger and possible death. It can be one of the causes of trauma when exposure to the loud noise of rockets or bombs increases hypervigilance and stress levels (see Näser-Lather 2018):

> It felt different in the west, away from the front. In the Donbas, almost every sudden odd noise was exactly what you suspected it to be: something lethal flying nearby, seeking out the living. (Yermak 2022)

Bodily sensations bear witness to the trauma of war:

> unsuspecting people – children among them – blasted apart or burned alive inside malls and medical centers in broad daylight. It left tight knots in our stomachs, but they hadn't transformed yet into something almost

---

13 According to a Ukrainian journalist, the smell is overwhelming: "He is in his mid-40s, with a long beard and prominent belly. Every day, he delivers the bodies of those killed in Avdiyivka to the morgue in nearby Pokrovsk. The stench of decomposition is musty here. Over two years of war, it has eaten into the walls of the morgue and the surrounding blocks of flats. It floats for hundreds of meters, making it impossible to catch one's breath" (Kolesnychenko 2024: https://wiadomosci.wp.pl/ludzie-sie-koncza-6981373556255232a, retrieved 8.01.2023).

> genetic, a terror that would be passed on to their offspring by the survivors of this war. (Yermak, NYT, 08.08.2022)[14]

After encountering the harsh realities of war through the senses, individuals often find themselves contemplating general concepts, a phenomenon illustrated in the narrative above, where the author reflects on the transmission of trauma through generations.

The soldier also contemplates death. Death, in his thoughts, could take various forms, including a dignified death (a general, abstract term in this context, tinged with pathos) or a "normal" end, if I can use such a term to describe this process. Dying during war is entirely different, often in nightmare-like circumstances. The fight is not only for life but also for the commonness of death.

Dying in barbaric conditions is reminiscent of medieval times for the narrator:

> To quote Kurt Vonnegut, even if wars didn't keep coming like glaciers, there would still be plain old death. But encounters with death could be very different. We want to believe that we and our loved ones, the modern people of the twenty-first century, no longer have to die from medieval barbaric torture, epidemics, or detention in concentration camps. That's part of what we're fighting for: the right not only to a dignified life but also to a dignified death. (Chekh 2022)[15]

At some point in time, *silence appears* in the Deathworld. Soldiers do not want to talk; the silence is a choice; it can be a sign of solitude[16] but also proof of understanding. There is no need to communicate with words; everything is

---

14 But it is possible that the terror will last in future memories and will be passed to the next generations (Dutta, 2021:211). A similar opinion was expressed by Ukrainian psychotherapist Zoryana Koshulynska: "That and many other experiences brought me to the most painful realization – that these children will always be children of war. I, as a psychologist, as a psychotherapist – understand this very well" (see in Sneed et al., 2023: 358).

15 Dignified death can also be connected with the dignified treatment of dead bodies. It often happens during war that bodies are desecrated, and parts, such as skulls, may be treated as trophies of war (Harrison 2012).

16 Loneliness is a widespread feeling among soldiers; they interact with animals to feel some intimacy. Touching the animals is important, such as a cat in the bunker: "Loneliness afflicts everyone. Eduard reaches out to pick up the black and white male cat, still curled up, sleeping on his bunk a moment ago. He cuddles it and scratches it behind the ear" (Kolesnycheno 2024: https://wiadomosci.wp.pl/ludzie-sie-koncza-6981373556255232a, retrieved 8.01.2023). Individuals cope with the trauma (coping self); living with animals helps (Myers and Sweeney 2004).

understood. The traumatic situation is the background for understanding the gestures and silence of the night. The body mainly communicates, and understanding comes without words, spontaneously, pre-reflectively. Meaning is conveyed without the use of words:[17]

> I stop socializing. More than that, I stop talking. Oh, maybe accidentally I exchange some words: "Hi, what are you up to?" "Sure, oh, okay" ... We hardly ever even speak to each other in our bunker. Everyone keeps to themselves. Some watch a movie; I write. Or I also watch. And then write some more. And then go to my post ... It seemed like that would be the place to talk, but we are silent, as if we are afraid of disturbing the cold, quiet night. As if we aren't friends. As if we just met. (Chekh 2020, chapter "Silence," paragraph one)

> Seven months on the front – that's when you understand everything, but you have no desire to speak, when speaking isn't necessary, but you understand everything. (Chekh 2020: chapter "A Lifetime and Little More," paragraph nine)

Silence pertains to a collective comprehension of the existential implications of what has transpired – an unspoken acknowledgment of the underlying realities of past and present actions, the conduct of war, which no longer necessitates an explicit explanation. The initial understanding of another person begins with a visceral awareness of their presence in physical proximity. I sense them more profoundly than I comprehend them in my immediate space. Verbal communication seems superfluous; familiarity arises from shared physical existence in a shared place over time. As soldiers spend considerable time together, a more profound connection evolves, allowing for the exchange of intimate details. Silence and quietness emerge when the "we-relationship" has developed. In this situation, there is camaraderie among soldiers:

17 "The person on the frontline is gradually overcome by an overwhelming sense of meaningfulness which would be hard to put into words." (Patočka, 1996: 126) Moreover, the body serves as a communicator of emotional states, including depression, as illustrated by Wittgenstein (2022: 139): "Situation unchanged! –. No work. Depression. The pressure on the chest –.––." The war becomes embodied here, and the *pathic* dimension is easily observed. The wartime routine entailed intellectual endeavors for Wittgenstein, not solely combat, a rarity in his military service while writing the diary we know and can read.

> For a parting gift, Vlad gets us a bottle of wine. I accompany him to headquarters. We embrace, we cry. He drives away and I go back to the outpost with a bottle of dry red wine and half a kilo of wieners. That evening Sanya and I sit by the fire and talk a lot. We get drunk from the wine, as if it was vodka. Having had our fill of the wieners, we sit poking at the coals with skewers and think about everything that has happened in the last fourteen months. Later, already in our bunker, lying in our sleeping bags, we spend a long time sharing secrets and revelations. It seemed that if we didn't do it now, we never would. (Chekh 2020, chapter "The Last Night," paragraph two)

Silence also emerges in certain situations where not only is there no need to speak to understand, but it is also the only possible response to the trauma that has occurred. Death and burial can be such a situation. It is the ultimate silence, a concluding silence for some soldiers, marking the end of the nightmares of war. Silence then becomes a witness to death and mourning:

> There was no thud of artillery or shriek from a missile, just the quiet hum of a funeral procession. (Yermak, 2022)

4 Communicating with Opponents regarding my Perceptions of the War

With the interpretations and descriptions of lived experiences and understandings mentioned above, I engage in conversations with individuals from countries far removed from the conflict. I often struggle to comprehend when they attempt to normalize the situation or analyze the war from technical, economic, or political perspectives. My perspective on this war is shaped predominantly by the firsthand experiences of those involved. However, I am not a direct participant; I apply the principle of empathy, and strive, if only in my imagination, to place myself in the victims' shoes (see chapter 5; Ruiz 2017). I know this is entirely impossible, but I make the effort, nonetheless.

What do I feel when I do this? I experience profound fear, anger directed at the aggressors, and even a sense of hatred, though these emotions are not aligned with my usual values. Over nearly two years of war, there is also a growing sense of indifference. While these emotions are not identical to those experienced by the actual participants and victims of the war, they share similarities, albeit in a hypothetical context.

When I hear expressions of sympathy for Russians, Russian artists, and athletes who cannot perform or compete in the West, I am overwhelmed with anger and frustration due to the lack of empathy and understanding for the victims and the war's context. The question of who constitutes the aggressor and who the victim becomes particularly relevant. While it is true that Russian recruits, often deceived and sent to the frontlines, are victims of this conflict, they are being used as tools by the aggressor, whose intentions include seizing neighboring land, causing harm to countless families, looting resources like grain and coal, and demolishing family homes. This question of "who is the victim and who is the aggressor" often marks the endpoint of such conversations and discussions. I frequently argue as follows: "Would you have agreed to Leni Riefenstahl's visiting the United States during the Second World War to promote her films? Would other prominent German artists and scholars who supported Hitler have been welcomed to perform in free nations? Could Martin Heidegger have given lectures at Harvard during the Second World War? The situation is analogous; it's a wartime scenario. The Russians' behavior in Ukraine resembles that of the Nazis during the Second World War and their occupations. How would you respond to this question?"

5 Conclusions

Concluding becomes a formidable task when confronted with the harrowing accounts of war atrocities and the profound suffering endured by war's victims and soldiers on the front line. "The front line is absurdity par excellence. What we had only suspected here becomes reality: all that humans hold most precious is ruthlessly torn to shreds. The only meaning is that of a proof that the world capable of producing something like this must disappear …" (Patočka 1996:126). The world may vanish, but does the experience of war and the front line shift attitudes toward it? Patočka is not overly optimistic: "How can the 'front-line experience' acquire the form which would make it a factor of history? Why is it not becoming that? Because in the form described so powerfully by Teilhard and Junger, it is the experience of all individuals projected individually each to their summit, from which they cannot but retreat back to everydayness, where they will inevitably be seized again by war in the form of Force's plan for peace" (Patočka 1996: 134). There is not much solidarity with those buffeted by the war; maintaining awareness of the common and traumatic experiences on both sides of the front line could create a more meaningful historical factor. To accomplish this, I adhere to a pathic understanding of war and its dereification. In this way, we can also adopt critical positions on the war as sociologists. In the future, a more holistic perspective from both sides of the front line will be essential.[18] Nonetheless, it's important to acknowledge that the distance achieved through contemplation could potentially result in indifference, and this represents an ethical decision.

I have tried to dereify the concept of war. I have presented how the war is embodied as a pathic experience, full of fears, trauma, and horrors, and how it is embodied by experiencing space and time in the overwhelming Deathworld. War is not only a matter of fighting, as is commonly assumed in critical discourse studies or strategic military approaches (see the critics of these approaches in Narozhna 2022). War also creates the tactics of survival and endurance (Dutta, 2021). The war is a Deathworld, which keeps soldiers and civilians alive for a time but with the threat of death. The Deathworld changes the meaning of space and time; the lived body predominantly experiences the war and cognizes it directly. Time is condensed in the present; sometimes, the horizon changes to memories of family and those who are closest; there are also projections about the future that connect individuals with their nearest and dearest. However, the present trauma of war generally shatters the future horizon.

The Deathworld has been proven to have zones. The trench zone is also a deadly space, but to a lesser extent than the open space beyond the trench. In the Deathworld, space nuances itself, although the shadow of death always

---

18 What follows is the narrative of Russian soldiers: "Then I heard (the Ukrainians) approaching us; I started shouting 'We surrender.' Then they threw a grenade at us," he says. "I felt it cut my hand. They asked me who I am, and I said that I am Russian and that I surrender. I started to get up, and a second grenade arrived. I managed to crawl halfway out of the trench in a second," he tells CNN. The Russian soldier behind him was killed by the grenade and Sergei felt a cut through his leg.

A Ukrainian soldier later explained that it's difficult to hear what the Russian soldiers are saying during gunfights. (https://edition.cnn.com/2023/07/06/europe/captured-russian-soldiers-ukraine-intl-cmd/index.html, 06.07.2023; retrieved 15.09.2023). The horror of war is experienced on both sides of the front line:

"Unlike the rest, he is a contract soldier, not a convict. He says he served the time he signed up for last year in Kherson. After he got back home, he says the military prosecutor threatened him with prison for desertion if he did not go back to the battlefield. The young father says his previous military experience did not prepare him for what both sides call the 'meat grinder' in Bakhmut. 'It was very different from what I saw on TV. A parallel reality. I felt fear, pain, and disappointment in my commanders,' he says … Sergei believes his injuries will keep him away from future deployments and out of prison once he is exchanged with Ukrainian prisoners of war. Slava and Anton are not so sure. Russia toughened up its penalties for voluntary surrender last September, imposing up to 10 years in prison" (https://edition.cnn.com/2023/07/06/europe/captured-russian-soldiers-ukraine-intl-cmd/index.html, 06.07.2023; retrieved 15.09.2023).

advances with every soldier. In above explications, I may uncover pathic war experiences, touching on topics like the fear of death, acceptance of mortality, the silence of war, a departure from established worldviews, attempts to preserve the body, the scent of death, the definition of one's place, the desire to live, and more. By dereifying the concept of space as a territory of war (in a geographic and strategic military sense; Carter and David 2010), I can reveal its pathic and embodied significance, emphasizing the lived space. The text has also highlighted the contemplative role of the perceiver, the reader, who depicts the war to himself in a pathic manner. It has underscored that dereification necessitates a subject to interpret the lived experiences of others, by actively participating, even imaginatively, in their Lifeworld.

Rather than attempting a definitive conclusion, let us delve deeper into the emotional resonance of the war, reexamining its impact with empathy and pathos, to dereify it further. Expressing these sentiments in prose proves to be a challenging endeavor.

To summarize my exploration, I would like to conclude this paper with photos and collages (see: https://www.youtube.com/watch?v=p6vTbtSu13M), and three poems that I wrote during pivotal moments of the war. They center on the lily-of-the-valley flower, which symbolizes the transient nature of innocence and beauty, but also renewal and new beginnings. Through poetry, I aim to preserve the empathetic understanding that defines my perspective and experience of war as an outsider observing this traumatic phenomenon. Finally, I believe that despite everything, some hope can be derived from the symbolism of lilies of the valley.

I don't write haiku about death (May 2022)

It's spring.
I do not see flowers in Bucha
or Mariupol in the pictures.
I can't see, they can't see,
but some flowers are still there?!
I go to the balcony.
It is a dark May night.
Lilies of the valley.

The lilies of the valley remember (May 2023)

The lilies of the valley are in bloom again.
They remember,

the war has been going on for over a year now,
nothing changes,
or instead, it is changing,
there is more cruelty,
lies,
torture and rape,
broken homes
and crying children and mothers.
Fathers are in short supply.
The lilies of the valley want to live,
more and more of them bloom on the balcony,
More and more bombs, gunshots,
the terrifying sounds of falling rockets.
The lilies of the valley pay no heed to these hardships,
they only want water and my gaze,
to keep them beautiful.

Lily of the Valley and Kharkov (May 2024)

This year I did not write a poem
About lilies of the valley in bloom
I wrote about lilies of the valley dying
About the killed
Forgotten
Frightened
Having no hope
Not yet murdered
Those waiting
For the next spring
Without a fearful look upward
Brave to the east
And forgiving to the west
Silence
Fullness of love
And empathy
In the moon setting
Over the withered
Flowers of Hope
Of mothers crying
Without a day of mourning

Bibliography

Barkawi, Tarak, and Shane Brighton. 2011. "Powers of War: Fighting, Knowledge and Critique." *International Political Sociology* 5(2), 126–43.

Bentz, Valerie Malhotra, David Rehorick, James Marlatt, Ayumi Nishii, and Carol Estrada. 2018. "Transformative Phenomenology as an Antidote to Technological Deathworlds." *Schutzian Research* 10, 189–220.

Bentz, Valery M. and Vincenzo Giorgino. 2016. *Contemplative Social Research: Caring for Self, Being, and Lifeworld. Santa Barbara*, CA: Fielding Institute Press.

Blumer, Herbert. 1969. *Symbolic Interactionism: Perspective and Method.* Berkeley: University of California Press.

Carter, David. 2010. "The Strategy of Territorial Conflict." *American Journal of Political Science*. 54(4), 969–987.

Chekh, Artem, 2020. *Absolut zero*. Glagoslav Publications, electronic version.

Chekh, Artem, 2022. "I'm a Ukrainian Soldier, and I've Accepted My Death." New York Times, Aug. 10, 2022. https://www.nytimes.com/2022/08/30/opinion/ukraine-soldier-war.html?action=click&module=RelatedLinks&pgtype=Article (retrieved 10.08.2023).

Chekh, Artem, 2023. "I Spent Five Days in a Trench Waiting for Death. It Was Pure Hell." New York Times, 10. Aug.10,2023. https://www.nytimes.com/2023/08/10/opinion/ukraine-war-bakhmut.html?smid=nytcore-ios-share&referringSource=article Share (retrieved 20.08.2023).

Dobosz, Kala and Anna Kacperczyk, Marcin Kafar, Krzysztof T. Konecki, Hanna Kroczak, Andrii Melnikov, Colette Szczepaniak, and Oskar Szwabowski. 2023. "The Reverberations of War: Ukrainian and Polish Academics Write a Collective Autoethnography of Experiencing War in Ukraine" *Cultural Studies ↔ Critical Methodologies*, online first, https://doi.org/10.1177/15327086231178013.

Douglas, Jack D. and John M. Johnson. 1977. *Existential Sociology*. Cambridge: Cambridge University Press.

Dutta, Anwesha. 2021. "A Phenomenological Exploration into Lived Experiences of Violence in Northeast India, South Asia." *Journal of South Asian Studies*, 44(2), 201–217, DOI: 10.1080/00856401.2021.1852489.

Ehrenreich, Barbara. 2011. *Źródła i historia naszej namiętności do wojny*. (*Blood Rites: Origins and history of the passions of war*). Grupa Wydawnicza Relacja.

Grossman, Dave.1996. *On killing: the psychological cost of learning to kill in war and society*. Boston: Little, Brown.

Harrison, Simon. 2012. *Dark Throphies. Hunting and the Enemy Body in Modern War.* New York, Oxford: Berghahn Books.

Illouz, Eva. 2010. *Uczucia w dobie kapitalizmu*, (*Cold Intimacies: The Making of Emotional Capitalism*). Warszawa Oficyna Naukowa.

Kinetz, Erika. 2023. "'Never saw such hell': Russian soldiers in Ukraine call home." AP (https://apnews.com/article/russia-ukraine-war-intercepts2b14732d88b3f58d4a9d0b2b562bdb28, retrieved 14.12.2023).

Kolesnychenko, Tatiana. 2024. "Ludzie się kończą." (https://wiadomosci.wp.pl/ludzie-sie-koncza-6981373556255232a, retrieved 8.01.2023).

Konecki, Krzysztof T. 2022. "Empathy! So What?" *Przegląd Socjologii Jakościowej*, t. 18(4), 194–233.

Konecki, Krzysztof T. 2022a. *The Meaning of Contemplation for Social Qualitative Research. Applications and Examples*. London, NY: Routledge.

Konecki, Krzysztof T. 2023. "Wittgenstein and Bauman: Creative Minds in the Lifeworld." *Symbolic Interaction*, First published: 16 February 2023, https://doi.org/10.1002/symb.635.

Kotarba, Joseph A. and John M. Johnson (eds.). 2002. *Postmodern Existential Sociology*, Walnut Creek: Altamira Press.

Leder, Andrzej. 2023. *Ekonomia to stan umysłu. Ćwiczenie z semantyki języków ekonomicznych*. Warszawa: Wydawnictwo Krytyki Politycznej.

McScorley, Kevin. ed. 2013. War and the Body: Militarization, Practice and Experience. New York: Routledge.

Merleau-Ponty, Maurice. 2005. *Phenomenology of Perception*. London, New York: Taylor and Francis.

Meacham, Darian. 2007. "The Body at the Front: Corporeity and Community in Jan Patočka Heretical Essays in the Philosophy of History." *Studia Phaenomenologica*, 7, 353–256, Bucharest: Humanitas.

Moore, Robert. 1995. Dereification in Zen Buddhism. *The Sociological Quarterly* 36(4), 699–723.

Myers, J.E., & Sweeney, T.J. 2004. "The indivisible self: An evidence-based model of wellness." *Journal of Individual Psychology*, 60(3), 234–245.

Narozhna Tanya. 2022. "The lived body, everyday and generative powers of war: toward an embodied ontology of war as experience." *International Theory*. 14(2), 210–232. doi:10.1017/S1752971921000129.

Patočka, Jan. 1996. *Heretical Essays in the Philosophy of History*. Chicago: Open Court.

Ruiz-Junco, Natalia. 2017. "Advancing the Sociology of Empathy: A Proposal." *Symbolic Interaction* 40(3), 414–435.

Schütz, Alfred. 1944. "The Stranger: An Essay in Social Psychology." *American Journal of Sociology* 49(6), 499–507.

Schütz, Alfred. 1962. *The Problem of Social Reality*. The Hague: Martinus Nijhoff.

Scovil, Jonathan. 2023 August. "Polacy o Ukraińcach." CBOS, (https://www.cbos.pl/PL/publikacje/fokusy/pliki/2023/fk_005_2023.pdf, retrieved 1.10.2023).

Sneed, Candace R. and Marta Kovalova, Kateryna Tomova, Zoryana Koshulynska, and Ivan Shuflat. 2023. "Of Social Construction, Gemeinschaftsgefühl, and Courage:

One Day in the Lives of Ukrainian Psychologists During the War." *The Journal of Individual Psychology*, 79(4), 344–366.

Sontag, Susan. 1978. *On Photography*, London: Penguin Books.

Sookermany, Anders. 2011. "The Embodied Soldier: Towards a New Epistemological Foundation of Soldiering Skills in the (Post)Modernized Norwegian Armed Forces." Armed Forces and Society 37(3), 469–93.

Van Manen, Max. 2016. *Phenomenology of Practice. Meaning Giving Methods in Phenomenological Research and Writing*. Abingdon, New York: Routledge.

Wittgenstein, Ludwig. 2022. *Private Notebooks 1914–1916*. Translated and edited by Marjorie Perloff, London, New York: Liveright.

Yermak, Natalia. 2022. "In My Homeland, the Smell of Death on a Summer Afternoon." New York Times. 8.08.2022 https://www.nytimes.com/2022/08/08/world/europe/ukraine-war-funeral-death.html.

Yi-Fu Tuan. 1987. *Przestrzeń i miejsce*. (*The Space and Place, The Perspective of Experience*) Warszawa: PIW.

Conclusions

Contemplation requires awareness of both the mind and the body. We must engage with the body to capture the moment of being and understand our living situation. The body connects the self with the material world, making it an integral part of our being. What is outside becomes inside. The oppositions created by the mind vanish, allowing us to feel the wholeness of the human experience in the world. By pausing the mind for a moment, we can connect with both the world and the self. Consciousness allows us to affirm what we experience in the here and now. Even memories appear as factual events, but they occur within consciousness, and through awareness, we recognize them as memories.

Contemplation can be the seed for the emergence of fear and existential anxiety, often tied to the fear of death and the lack of meaning in life. However, at the same time, we can understand that fear and anxiety are inherent elements of the lifeworld. They are created by the mind and body, appearing and fading away. The experience of life unfolds from moment to moment. Life is a momentary awareness of perceptions and feelings. We can reflect on the past and the future as qualities that are changeable and do not exist in the present. We can also experience epiphanies and feelings of forgiveness towards others.

Existential anxiety disappears and lingers simultaneously; it is either felt or exists in the background, waiting to fully emerge in a specific context generated by our mental activity, similar to other feelings such as empathy or compassion. These feelings are always present but come to the forefront in particular situations, prompted by our impulse to experience them.

Entering a contemplative mood is not easy. We live in an accelerated world where technology, work systems, and a competitive lifestyle exert pressure on our minds and bodies, urging us to live and work faster and to compare ourselves with others. It is difficult to pause and contemplate the meaning of life, we experience often burnout effect and depression (Rosa 2020; Han 2015), our responsibility in making choices, how we live, and our thoughts about death. We often escape from contemplating death by accelerating our activities, and we tend to blame external forces for the problems in our lives, including our inability to stop and reflect. Acceleration can also manifest during meditation, where a torrent of thoughts about working life often appears and is difficult to halt.

We are immersed in the capitalist market of goods and ideas. The so-called therapeutic narrative has been increasingly gaining prominence in contemporary media and everyday life. Understanding oneself and one's suffering is a vital component of personal development. Self-improvement and individual growth are tied to overcoming psychological challenges and death and identity-related struggles. Achieving emotional well-being has become a key goal (Illouz 2007).

This type of discourse, which involves sharing personal stories in the media or published autobiographies to demonstrate the possibility of overcoming suffering, is becoming more widespread. It permeates literature, journalism, cinema, other art forms, and even the therapeutic business sector (Illouz 2010: 81). The recreational industry also aligns with this trend – practices such as yoga and various relaxation activities are increasingly imbued with therapeutic or quasi-therapeutic qualities (Konecki 2015; Konecki, Płaczek, Tarasiuk 2024). Mental and emotional health has been commodified.

A new and significant cultural competence, which can be described as emotional competence, has also emerged. Psychologists like Daniel Goleman (1995) refer to it as emotional intelligence. This involves recognizing, controlling, and appropriately managing emotions, enabling harmonious social interactions, and maintaining good mental health. However, this creates a challenge for contemplative researchers: it is not always clear whether our emotional responses are authentic, arises from within, or are internalized through the corporate rhetoric of emotional competence, characteristic of liberal emotional capitalism.

Identifying and articulating emotions has become a core element of psychotherapeutic and emotional discourse. Emotional competence now functions as a form of capital (Illouz 2010: 93) that can be transformed into social and economic capital. In this way, what is private becomes a commodity that can be marketed and distributed economically and become public.

In this context, there is a risk that contemplative practices and research may be absorbed into this discourse, driven by the logic of capitalism. However, I believe this danger can be avoided through deep contemplation and critical reflection on qualitative methods (Denzin 2017; Hadley 2017; Grant and Young 2022; Grant 2023). Examining the origins of our emotions and the language we use to describe them is essential. Do our feelings genuinely stem from within us, or are they shaped by therapeutic or corporate discourses, products marketed within the psychotherapeutic industry, or self-help guides available in supermarkets? It is possible that our emotional barriers are embedded in our bodies, which serve as reservoirs of inherited trauma and injustice (Laing 2021).

It requires careful contemplation of mind, emotions, and body.

Understanding how the mind works can help us grasp the meaning of many feelings and emotions. We can experience how empathy functions and emerges rather than just understanding it intellectually. Empathy does not stem from a rational analysis of the situation of the empathy recipient; it is a direct reaction to the suffering of others, grounded in our bodily feelings and reactions. Observing the mind lets us see how social assumptions and prejudices later filter this reaction. We often interpret empathy through the lens of socialized perceptions and categorizations of others based on national, racial, or social class distinctions that divide society into different groups.

Contemplation of empathy can deepen our understanding of the emotional aspects of our perception of the world. We can recognize empathy deficits and realize that, although naturally developed in human beings (and not only in human beings), empathy skills can be improved. While some victims are perceived as more deserving of empathy ("better victims") and others as less deserving ("less worthy victims"), we can experience and acknowledge that a community of shared feelings exists everywhere, not just within our group, nation, or social class. There is something profound in our being and our attitude toward the Other. Understanding shared suffering and the compassionate and empathetic response to that suffering connects living beings. To truly grasp this, we must continually contemplate these feelings. Social research can unearth the feelings that rational thinking often suppresses, which are essential to preserving our humanity and our natural connection with wildlife and the material environment. Rhizomatic thinking is essential here to grasp the multiplicity of connections, the heterogeneity of relationships, the absence of hierarchy, the lack of linear structure, and the complexity of scale (local versus global; Pyyhtinen, 2016; Schultz 2023; Latour and Schultz 2022). However, such an approach to understanding reality is insufficient to transform it from the perspective of the human subject. Existential and pathic contemplation are equally necessary (see Van Manen 2016).

Is it possible to understand others through contemplation of war? One of the most profound questions is whether we can truly comprehend and feel extreme situations we have not personally experienced. We may choose to remain indifferent, believing that we cannot understand the trauma of war, domestic violence, or unexpected and unjustified aggression. However, if we suspend this assumption, we can attempt to empathize through imaginative experimentation and by drawing on our own past bodily experiences. This imaginative experimentation is the foundation of compassion.

Contemplating our assumptions connected with interpreting big politics and minor ones on the organizational level could be helpful. Currently, we observe growing tensions stemming from a lack of trust and increasing suspicion toward state institutions, market forces, and significant supranational organizations. We tend to associate these entities with espionage, deceit, and conspiracies directed against us, our social groups, or our nations. While espionage is often linked to the activities of the Russian state, revelations about counterintelligence efforts also bring other players to light. This creates an image of the world as a web of large-scale conspiracies and espionage.

In such a climate, conspiratorial interpretations of social activities and historical events thrive. To counter this, critical contemplation is essential. This involves examining our thoughts and emotions' structural and personal contexts within our specific existential situations. Such reflection allows us to gain perspective and better understand the political, relational, and subjective processes shaping the contemporary world.

It is not only the actions of individual state agents that generate informational, political, and economic chaos in Western countries and globally. The chaos also resides within our conceptual frameworks – rooted in incomplete awareness of the relationships and emotions shaping our perceptions of other social groups and cultures.

And now, a few words about scientists and critical science. As sociologists, we often discuss the consequences of global warming and the brutality of the contemporary economic system. Humanity faces the threat of a large-scale ecological catastrophe and possibly the final stage of the Anthropocene. Yet, empty rhetoric about the collapse of society, morality, and responsibility toward nature – calls to protect it to preserve humanity – will not lead to our species' immortality. Such performative speeches are often the domain of politicians, but this tendency toward empty critique and oratory also extends to scientists.

This attachment to criticism, devoid of substance or vision, represents a superficial loyalty. Scientists, too, are not always faithful to the process of truth (see Alain Badiou 2001). They often remain stuck at the level of critique – pointing out ecological and systemic failures – without offering visionary alternatives or intuitions for the future. This lack of forward-thinking also applies to scientists who support so-called "just wars" in the fields of politics, international law, and human rights. But what will happen after the war is not predictable for them.

Are they genuinely well-informed? (Schütz 1946). Some might believe so. However, their knowledge often lacks roots in a profound reflection on the interplay between structural conditions and the existential realities of their lives and those of the groups or institutions they critically examine. Knowledge, even when critically analyzed, is insufficient on its own to inspire meaningful action. It must be complemented by an awareness of bodily sensations and an understanding of emotions such as empathy and compassion. Only when thoughts are harmonized with feelings and physical perceptions of living and non-living surroundings can knowledge become a genuine force for action.

Although we do not yet know the exact direction that changes in our thinking and actions should take, faith and radical hope are indispensable in the face of uncertainty and ignorance. These accompany the authors of such reflections but should also accompany us if we are to survive. We find ourselves at the edge of an epistemological leap into the abyss – we are immobilized by a culture that is becoming increasingly outdated (see Lear 2006). We do not yet possess the concepts that could save us, but rescue remains impossible without faith in their eventual emergence.

We do not yet know whether our existing concepts can effectively deconstruct the phenomena of Artificial Intelligence (AI). AI is not merely a tool or plaything; it is transforming paradigms of knowledge, education, technological development, and even the conduct of war. While we often assume that new concepts will emerge naturally over time, relying on this process may be too slow, as social sciences typically analyze and interpret what has already occurred.

We must move beyond exclusively analytical and critical frameworks, opening ourselves to alternative modes of understanding. These include contemplation, intuition, and utopian visions as conveyed through art and other narrative forms. Integrating such approaches with scientific inquiry can foster a more holistic vision of change and the future of both humanity and the Earth.

An inner transformation is essential, and it must begin with contemplation – existential and emotional but also theoretical, always grounded in a realistic understanding of reality. Suppose we mythologize current concepts and ideas, such as democracy, freedom, or justice. In that case, we risk turning away from the reality of our times, in which the advancing ecological catastrophe is becoming an undeniable fact. Fear resides deeply within our bodies, urging us to reflect on its presence. Envisioning a life – and a world – free from that fear could open the door to transformative change (Laing 2021).

The Enlightenment-era belief in technological progress, in the conviction that it can protect and save us, may prove unreliable. It is an idea rooted in a different world than the one we live in now. Humanity will not survive by looking only backward and standing on the shoulders of the giants of progress and social science on the shoulders of theoretical giants of the past. There must arise a deeply felt fear, authentic apprehension, and hope, as well as a readiness to bracket the conceptual and ethical frameworks in which we have believed until now.

We must ask: Is there anything beyond the current status quo that justifies fighting wars in the name of justice for territories and states? What about the broader suffering that wars inevitably cause? Can this suffering indeed be justified under the banner of human rights? Even when defenders of justice and human rights achieve victory, the suffering of individuals persists long after the war ends. Whose rights are we ultimately defending – the ordinary person's rights or the interests of big capital driven by an insatiable desire for profit?

We must cultivate compassion toward other humans, groups, nations, and nature to change the disappearing world before our eyes and halt this process. Contemplating the workings of our minds and the cultural background that shapes our assumptions is indispensable. So, why not try? It is an individual and existential choice and a responsibility to save life and the Earth. If we do not do it now, I know what will happen. There will be nobody to contemplate what happened in the past.

Bibliography

Badiou, Alain. 2001. *Ethics. An Essay on Understanding of Evil.* London, New York: Verso.

Denzin, Norman K. 2017. "Critical Qualitative Inquiry." *Qualitative Inquiry*, 23(1), 8–16. https://doi.org/10.1177/1077800416681864.

Goleman, Daniel. 1995. *Emotional Intelligence.* New York: Bantham.

Grant, Alec. 2023. *Writing Philosophical Autoethnography.* New York: Routledge. https://doi.org/10.4324/9781032229126.

Grant, Alec, and Susan Young. 2022. "Troubling Tolichism in Several Voices: Resisting Epistemic Violence in Creative Analytical and Critical Autoethnographic Practice." *Journal of Autoethnography* 3, no. 1, 103–117. https://doi.org/10.1525/joae.2022.3.1.103.

Grant, Alec. 2023. *Writing Philosophical Autoethnography.* New York: Routledge. https://doi.org/10.4324/9781032229126.

Hadley, Gregory. 2017. *Grounded Theory in Applied Linguistics Research: A Practical Guide.* New York: Routledge.

Han, Byung-Chul. 2015. *Burnout society.* Stanford: Stanford University Press.

Illouz, Eva. 2010. *Uczucia w dobie kapitalizmu*, (*Cold Intimacies: The Making of Emotional Capitalism*). Warszawa Oficyna Naukowa.

Konecki, Krzysztof T. 2015. *Is the Body the Temple of the Soul? Modern Yoga Practice as a Psychosocial Phenomenon.* Kraków: Jagiellonian University Press.

Konecki, Krzysztof T., Aleksandra Płaczek, Dagmara Tarasiuk. 2024. *Experiencing The Body in Yoga Practice. Meanings and knowledge transfer.* New York: Routledge.

Laing, Olivia. 2021. *Everybody. A Book about Freedom.* London: Canongate Books.

Latour, Bruno and Nikolaj Schultz (2022) *On the Emergence of an Ecological Class. A memo.* Cambridge: Polity Press.

Lear, Johnatan. 2006. *Radical Hope. Ethics in the Face of Cultural Devastation.* Cambridge: Harvard University Press.

Rosa, Hartmut. 2020. *Przyspieszenie, wyobcowanie, rezonans. Projekt krytycznej teorii późnonowoczesnej czasowości.* (*Beschleunigung und Entfremdung. Entwurf einer *kritischen Theorie spätmoderner Zeitlichkeit* – translation from German to Polish by Jakub Duraj, Jacek Kołtun) Gdańsk: Europejskie Centrum Solidarności.

Schultz, Nikolaj. 2023. *Land Sickness*. Cambridge: Polity Press.

Schütz, Alfred. 1946. "The Well-Informed Citizen, an Essay on the Social Distribution of Knowledge," *Social Research*, Vol. 13, 1946, pp. 463–472.

Van Manen, Max. 2016. *Phenomenology of Practice. Meaning Giving Methods in Phenomenological Research and Writing*. Abingdon, New York: Routledge.

Subject Index

www.ingramcontent.com/pod-product-compliance
Lightning Source LLC
LaVergne TN
LVHW010544160826
845677LV00013B/2993

* 9 7 9 8 8 8 8 9 0 9 3 4 8 *